Housing Market Renewal and Social Class

Housing market renewal is one of the most controversial urban policy programmes of recent years. *Housing Market Renewal and Social Class* critically examines the rationale for housing market renewal: to develop 'high-value' housing markets in place of the so-called 'failing markets' of low-cost housing. Whose interests are served by such a programme and who loses out?

Drawing on empirical evidence from Liverpool, the author argues that housing market renewal plays to the interests of the housing industry and the middle classes in viewing the market for houses as a field of social and economic 'opportunities', in stark contrast to a working class who are more concerned with the practicalities of 'dwelling'. Against this background of these differing attitudes to the housing market, *Housing Market Renewal and Social Class* explores the difficult question of whether institutions are now using the housing market renewal programme to make profits at the expense of ordinary working-class people. Reflecting on how this situation has come about, the book critically examines the purpose of current housing market renewal policies, and suggests directions for interested social scientists wishing to understand the implications of the programme.

Housing Market Renewal and Social Class provides a unique phenomenological understanding of the relationship between social class and the market for houses, and will be compelling reading for anybody concerned with the situation of working-class people living in UK cities.

Chris Allen is Professor of Sociology at Manchester Metropolitan University, UK.

Housing, Planning and Design Series

Editors: Nick Gallent and Mark Tewdwr-Jones,
UCL Bartlett School of Planning

This series of books explores the interface between housing policy and practice, and spatial planning, including the role of planning in supporting housing policies in the countryside, the pivotal role that planning plays in raising housing supply, affordability and quality, and the link between planning/housing policies and broader areas of concern including homelessness, the use of private dwellings, regeneration, market renewal and environmental impact. The series positions housing and planning debates within the broader built environment agenda, engaging in a critical analysis of different issues at a time when many planning systems are being modernised and prepared for the challenges facing twenty-first century society.

Housing Market Renewal and Social Class
Chris Allen

Decent Homes for All
Nick Gallent and Mark Tewdwr-Jones

Planning and Housing in the Rapidly Urbanising World
Paul Jenkins, Harry Smith and Ya Ping Wang

International Perspectives on Rural Homelessness
Edited by Paul Cloke and Paul Milbourne

Housing in the European Countryside
Rural pressure and policy in Western Europe
Edited by Nick Gallent, Mark Shucksmith and Mark Tewdwr-Jones

Private Dwelling
Contemplating the use of housing
Peter King

Housing Development
Andrew Golland and Ron Blake

Forthcoming:

Rural Housing Policy
Tim Brown and Nicola Yates

Including Neighbourhoods in Europe
Edited by Nicky Morrison, Judith Allen and Arild Holt-Jensen

Sustainability in New Housing Development
Alina Congreve

Housing Market Renewal and Social Class

Chris Allen

Routledge
Taylor & Francis Group

LONDON AND NEW YORK

First published 2008
by Routledge
2 Park Square, Milton Park, Abingdon, Oxon OX14 4RN

Simultaneously published in the USA and Canada
by Routledge
270 Madison Avenue, New York, NY 10016, USA

Routledge is an imprint of the Taylor & Francis Group, an informa business

© 2008 Chris Allen

Typeset in Galliard by Prepress Projects, Perth, UK

Printed and bound in Great Britain by TJ International Limited, Padstow, Cornwall

British Library Cataloguing in Publication Data
A catalogue record for this book is available from the British Library

Library of Congress Cataloging in Publication Data
Allen, Chris, 1969–
    Housing market renewal and social class/Chris Allen.
        p. cm. – (Housing, planning and design series)
    Includes bibliographical references and index.
    ISBN-13: 978-0-415-41560-6 (hardback: alk. paper)
    ISBN-13: 978-0-415-41561-3 (pbk.: alk. paper)
    ISBN-13: 978-0-203-93274-2 (ebook)

    1. Home ownership – Social aspects. 2. Social classes. I. Title.
    HD7287.8.A44 2008
    363.5'83–dc22
    2007028590

ISBN10: 0-415-41560-8 (hbk)
ISBN10: 0-415-41561-6 (pbk)
ISBN10: 0-203-93274-9 (ebk)

ISBN13: 978-0-415-41560-6 (hbk)
ISBN13: 978-0-415-41561-3 (pbk)
ISBN13: 978-0-203-93274-2 (ebk)

For Kate, Fraser and Charlie

In memory of my grandparents: Arthur and Mary Kenny and William and Hilda Allen, who were all from Liverpool

Criticism consists in uncovering [hegemonic] thought and trying to change it: showing that things are not as obvious as people believe, making it so that what is taken for granted is no longer taken for granted. To do criticism is to make harder those acts which are now too easy. Understood in these terms, criticism (and radical criticism) is utterly indispensable for any transformation . . . . To say to oneself from the start 'What is the reform that I will be able to make?' – That's not a goal for the intellectual to pursue, I think. His role, since he works precisely in the sphere of thought, is to see how far the liberation of thought can go toward making these transformations urgent enough for people to want to carry them out, and sufficiently difficult to carry out for them to be deeply inscribed into reality. It is a matter of making conflicts more visible, of making them more essential than mere clashes of interest or mere institutional blockages.

(Foucault 1994: 456–7)

Contents

Acknowledgements

My motivation to write this book was provided by people who live in the housing market renewal (HMR) area of Liverpool, who are currently involved in a struggle to overturn the compulsory purchase orders that have been issued on their homes. Their decency, honesty, friendliness and sense of humanity during my time there was heartwarming, as was their attachment to a place that urban elites wrote off a long time ago. I felt compelled to write this critical account of HMR because people like this deserve to have their side of the story told. They have so far been deprived of the ability to tell their side by urban elites who have denied them access to legal aid and therefore to legal representation at public enquiries into the compulsory purchase of their homes. They have also been denied the opportunity to tell their side of the housing market renewal story by social researchers who have, at worst, ignored them and, at best, arrogantly and patronisingly dismissed resident opposition to housing market renewal as a minority of lone voices. Although these residents deserve so much better, power is ruthless in the way it denies those who deserve more. I hope the residents of the HMR area in Liverpool, as well as residents that I have met in HMR areas elsewhere in the North West, feel that this book counterbalances a literature that, at present, is critically vacuous.

Writing this book was a paradoxical experience. On the one hand, writing the book was emotionally difficult because it was written at a time when I was exposed to the brute injustices of housing market renewal through involvement in public enquiries to oppose compulsory purchase orders. On the other hand, this sense of injustice provided me with the drive and desire to write, which made the actual process of clarifying my ideas and typing text into the computer a relatively easy task. That said, I am grateful to Kate, Fraser and Charlie for making me laugh and smile so much in everyday life. Their love and humour provides the necessary counterbalance to the more serious aspects of life, such as writing about the injuries and injustices suffered by the people described in this book. I am especially grateful to my partner, Kate, who has always encouraged and supported me in projects such as this. She understood the importance of this book even if she doesn't always agree with my views.

Some colleagues have been immensely important to the production of this book too. Rionach Casey was the researcher on the ESRC project that produced the first set of interview data for the book. She undertook most of these interviews so it is not an exaggeration to say that this book could not have happened without her efforts, which produced excellent interview material. I also owe a huge debt of gratitude to several colleagues whose generosity towards me has been touching. Gary Bridge, Paul Watt and Stuart Cameron read the manuscript for this book word by word and each provided me with an excellent set of comments that have enabled me to improve the final product. Thanks also to Paul for providing me with a copy of his PhD thesis, which is an exemplary study of housing and class and an invaluable reading experience. For these colleagues to devote so much time and effort to help me put this book together is heartwarming indeed. Thank you so much. I should also mention Lee Crooks, a PhD student at Sheffield University whom I met through participation in public enquiries. His integrity and dedication to supporting people threatened with compulsory purchase orders has been inspiring. Finally, readers of this book will be able to keep up with the debate on housing market renewal by following the links on my website, which is: http://www.sociology. mmu.ac.uk/profile.php?id=527.

Chris Allen
July 2007

Introduction

This book examines the constitution, and violation, of social class forms of 'being' towards the market for houses. Conventional understandings of the constitution of social class point to the importance of positionality within the occupational structure. For example, classificatory schemes such as the Registrar General's Social Classes (RGSC), which has five social class categories, and the Socio-Economic Group (SEG) system, preferred by sociologists, divide the occupational structure into seventeen different groups. The basic point here is that particular forms of work (e.g. 'blue collar', manual, unskilled work) are associated with the working class, whereas a large pool of 'blue collar' workers is taken to be indicative of the numerical strength of the working class. The corollary of this is the suggestion that high levels of mobility within the occupational structure can be taken to indicate an absence of class division or, at least, an absence of divisions that cannot be transcended. Chapter 1 discusses the claims of social scientists that point to evidence of high levels of occupational mobility out of working-class forms of work, which, apparently, suggests that 'class is dead'. Although an image of sociologists (of all people) proclaiming 'the death of class' might invite incredulity and disbelief among some readers, they will be reassured that Chapter 1 also discusses the counterclaims of social scientists who argue that levels of occupational mobility are not what they seem and that, therefore, the class society is alive and kicking. Indeed some of these social scientists are scathing of those who have proclaimed the 'death of class'. For example, Beverley Skeggs argues that the recent sociological preoccupation with post-class issues such as individualisation and self-identity (see especially Giddens 1991; Beck 1992, 2000) is a consequence of the way in which

> academic agenda setters can be seen to embody . . . a middle class habitus . . . . A retreat from class is just the expression of the class interests of a group of relatively powerfully placed professional intelligentsia . . . . The knowledge class's own interests are actually based upon representing their own position, their perspective, their own cultural politics openly and without embarrassment . . . . This exposes Beck's and Giddens' arguments as a particular kind of intellectual manoeuvre, a celebration of the cosmopolitan intellectual ethic that can only be realised by a small minority of people.
>
> (Skeggs 2004: 54)

Skeggs's argument bears all the hallmarks of Bourdieusian influence. What she is saying is that academics whose lifestyles are constituted at a distance from economic necessity, and with reference to cultural politics of identity, exhibit endogenous reflexivity *within* the context of the individualised lifestyles that they are engaged in constructing, yet fail, completely, to exhibit referential reflexivity *upon* the ontological status of those lifestyles. This absence of referential reflexivity is what has led the middle-class intelligentsia to assume that its devotion to lifestyle is characteristic of the late modern subject per se when, in fact, it is particular to the social and economic circumstances in which such a devotion to lifestyle can be reflexively practised. Put another way, referential reflexivity upon the social and economic circumstances in which 'lifestyles' are produced shows how people who occupy quite different social positions are simply unable to devote themselves to lifestyle issues to anything like the same extent if, indeed, at all (Charlesworth 2000). I am referring here to working-class people although, clearly, this point applies beyond the boundaries of the working class.

This brings us back to the idea of social class and, in particular, how this persistent source of social division can be understood. This is the focus of Chapter 2, which examines the theorisation of class with specific reference to how class processes manifest themselves in housing provision and consumption. Now we have already seen that class has conventionally been conceptualised as an employment category that is best understood by situating occupational position within the context of the social relations of production. This is evident in Marxist accounts of social class, which point to how the forces of production (or 'logic of capital accumulation'), which are based on relations of exploitation, produce class inequalities. For these writers, then, class divisions are an *outcome* of the logic of capital accumulation – given the exploitative nature of the relationships that drive it – rather than an *agent* of economic change. Put another way, the working class is a 'bearer' of social and economic change rather than a cause (agent) of change. To this extent class action lacks explanatory power when we seek to explain social and economic change. This can be seen in the forms of analysis produced by Scientific Marxists. For example, Scientific Marxists have shown how the overriding imperative of capital accumulation in capitalist societies has meant that the state is seldom able to follow, or respond to, working-class demands for change. Insofar as the state does follow social programmes that are in the interests of working-class people this is seen to be a temporary measure, for example to negate the threat of unrest in fragile social circumstances. Such measures are subsequently retracted when 'normality' is restored. Chapter 2 shows that this is the explanation that the Marxist Michael Harloe provides for the expansion and retrenchment of social housing in Britain.

These explanations are unconvincing when we are confronted with the type of analysis that Kemeny presents, as discussed in Chapter 2 below. Following in the tradition of Cultural Marxism, Kemeny argues that capitalist societies do not follow an underlying 'logic' – which means, of course, that neither do housing markets. For Kemeny, then, class action does matter. This is evident in the way he discusses the differential impact that labour movements have had on housing provision in different countries, which he puts down to the effectiveness of their political strategies. He demonstrates this by way of comparative research in Britain and Sweden. The Swedish labour movement did not simply seek 'concessions' that were subsequently 'taken away' when normality was restored. The Swedish labour movement followed a Gramscian political strategy and therefore constructed an ideological hegemony based on collectivist principles. Chapter 2 explains how this ensured the survival of cost-rental housing, even when it threatened profit-making by private landlords in 'normal' circumstances. For Kemeny, then, the essence of the effective class strategy lies in the nature of the political strategy adopted by labour movements in different countries. Labour movements that construct an ideological hegemony, as opposed to seeking concessions, can exert a fundamental impact on the way in which housing markets operate. Swedish housing markets have operated according to collectivist principles for decades, even when economic circumstances have been 'normal' (and thus conducive to profit-making rather than welfare) and the need to placate the working class has receded. According to this form of analysis, then, class action explains a lot about the divergent social and economic trajectories that different societies follow.

This is valuable, of course, but it assumes that a shared class consciousness exists and that shared consciousness would manifest itself in views about housing issues that divide along class lines. Yet Weberians, for whom class lacks ontological validity, have shown that no such 'objective interests' exist and that, insofar as they might, they certainly do not inscribe themselves into the consciousness of people from the same class background. This means that labour movement theories might explain why housing markets operate in distinctive ways in different societies, but this can only be put down to labour movement influence and not necessarily class consciousness.[1] Indeed Weberians have undertaken empirical studies that demonstrate a lack of collective class consciousness and, even, the lack of distinctive class rationalities in relation to key housing issues such as home ownership, social renting and so on. There is nothing about being working class, then, that means that working-class people will *think* about housing issues in distinctive ways. For example, working-class people are no less likely to support home ownership policies than middle-class people.

This leaves us in something of a pickle. On the one hand, we can convincingly argue that class matters. Yet we have difficulty in showing how it matters, particularly in a housing market context. So, how do social classes leave a distinctive mark on the housing market; alternatively, how do housing market processes mark us out as belonging to a particular class? If we move from a concern with the politics of class (labour movement theory, theories of class consciousness) and embrace new sociologies of class formation, which focus on the significance of consumption to processes of class formation, then we have a new way of elaborating the relationship between housing and class. New sociologies of class formation are based on the notion that class is no longer simply a productive category; that is to say, class cannot be 'read off' a position within the employment structure, class cannot be understood as 'effects' of the logic of capitalist production, and class cannot be understood with reference to the institutions that represent the collective or common interest of the labour movement. On the contrary they focus on how social class is constituted in consumption practices that are distinctive to people from particular social class backgrounds. The explanatory power of this argument is exemplified by the gentrification literature.

Conventional middle-class households that are high in economic capital, but that possess modest levels of cultural capital, exhibit a preference for semi-detached housing with gardens in indistinctive suburban sites. In other words, middle-class positions that have been achieved in the employment field are *symbolised* to others via the mobilisation of economic wealth in the housing market as well as other fields of consumption. The new middle class that is rich in cultural capital, but which possesses only modest levels of economic capital, has no way of imposing itself in social space other than through the mobilisation of cultural capital. Their consumption practices do not *symbolise* wealth and therefore class position, since this element of the middle class has only limited stocks of economic capital. On the contrary this group *achieves* its middle-class status by engaging in 'correct' consumption practices. That is to say, a devotion to consumption is an ontological necessity for this element of the middle class, which can only impose itself in social space via engaging in 'correct' consumption. The gentrification literature demonstrates this argument most convincingly. This fragment of the 'new' middle class has been shown to mobilise its cultural capital (cultural power) to renovate and revalorise cheap and run-down Edwardian and Victorian housing in inner-urban areas. In doing so they have created a new 'gentrification aesthetic', which has resulted in those areas becoming more desirable, which, in turn, has enabled them to extract economic profits from the market for houses. In a nutshell, then, the new middle class achieves its class position by accumulating, storing and deploying cultural capital in the market for houses as well as other fields of consumption.

New sociologies of class formation and gentrification literatures have succeeded where other attempts at theorising class have been found wanting. In a context where collective class action is almost absent in Britain, especially relating to housing market issues, and where it has been difficult to identify a class consciousness or rationality towards housing issues, a focus on how people from different social classes consume houses on a very practical level (buying, selling, living in them etc.) provides a way in to understanding processes of class formation in the housing field. We are simply left with three problems, which this book devotes itself to resolving. First, the gentrification literature provides us with some excellent insights into how middle-class formation takes place within the context of the market for houses. However, it says little or nothing about working-class formation in the market for houses. Working-class people are largely represented as 'displaced' by the gentrification activity of middle-class households. Notwithstanding one or two honourable exceptions (Watt 2001; Dench *et al.* 2006) there is an absence of literature on working-class forms of being in the market for houses in the new sociology of class literature. This is a serious omission and one that this book seeks to rectify by providing such an analysis. Further, it is a serious omission that is common to contemporary work in class analysis more generally, which has tended to focus on those who consume and, indeed, who have a devotion to consumption, that is the 'new' middle classes.

This brings me to the second issue. Generally speaking, the new sociology of class formation and gentrification literatures employ a conceptual approach to class analysis that is (largely) derived from Bourdieu. However, it draws from Bourdieu in very specific ways. Middle-class analysis has been undertaken with reference to the resources ('capitals', 'assets') that middle-class households accumulate, store and deploy in various fields of consumption. These are economic, cultural, social, symbolic and other forms of capitals and assets that, as we saw above, are possessed in different combinations by different fragments of the middle class and therefore result in different consumption preferences with all the consequences that this has for middle-class formation and fragmentation. Now a 'resource epistemology' might be appropriate to middle-class analysis and, indeed, writers such as Savage and colleagues have used such ideas to provide brilliant analyses of middle-class formation and fragmentation. However, resource epistemology is less than appropriate to an analysis of working-class formation because a defining characteristic of working-class people is, of course, their poverty of resources such as economic and cultural capital. Indeed Bourdieu (1984) has argued himself that class is not simply constituted on the possession of resources but, rather, is an existential category. That is to say, Bourdieu argues that class should be understood as a form of existence or, as Heidegger would put it, a specific form of being-in-the-world. In this book I will be suggesting that a defining characteristic of working-class existence is proximity to economic necessity, with all that this entails. I will therefore be arguing that working-classness needs to be understood as a form of existence in the world (proximity to necessity etc.) that shapes working-class subjectivities (being) and, therefore, the manner in which working-class people grasp the world around them, which, of course, will be specific to people that share their form of existence.

This leads me to provide a very different form of working-class analysis from recent accounts provided in the sociology literature. Since the class analysis literature has been based on resource epistemology (capitals, assets etc.), working-class formation has been constituted in resource relational terms. For Skeggs (1997, 2004), then, working-class people seek to appropriate the consumption practices of the middle class (as they see them), yet, with impoverished levels of economic and cultural capital, their attempts to appropriate middle-class consumption practices always and inevitably fail. Now, although such contributions to the class literature provide us with invaluable insights into the constitution of the contemporary working class, we must also recognise that they have limits. Specifically, they constitute the working class in relational terms, for example as 'failed consumers'. But the economy of working-class consumption practices cannot be constituted (and therefore understood) simply in relation to middle-class consumption practices. We need to understand the *internal* economy of working-class consumption; in our case, within the market for houses. That is to say, we need to understand how working-class consumption practices (relating to housing and so on) are constituted on a form of existence ('being') that results in ways of grasping the world that are specific to the urgent necessities that govern such existence and condition such 'being'. This means that the economy of working-class consumption is constituted on a form of being that primarily and primordially relates to the necessities of its own practical existence (proximity to economic necessity etc.) *before* even being able to constitute that existence in relation to other (middle-class) forms of being. The purpose of Chapters 3, 4 and 5 is to examine what it means to 'be' working class in such existential terms as well as, specifically, what it means to 'be' working class in the market for houses. The implications of this are that working-class forms of being in the market for houses need to be considered on their own terms and not simply as they are constituted in relation to other groups (Haylett 2003).

Chapters 3, 4 and 5 show that middle-class people, whose class position is constituted on the 'success' of their consumption practices, view the market for houses as a space of positions and, it follows, engage in struggles for position within that social space. We have already seen that these middle-class groups mobilise various forms of resource in order to decipher the 'correct' position for them to take and then to secure it. To this end, the market for houses is constituted as a symbolic economy. Working-class people, on the other hand, do not view the market for houses as symbolic economy that consists of a space of positions. As a form of 'being' that is formed in close proximity to economic necessity, and thus oriented to the imminent necessities that govern working-class life and being, the economy of working-class housing consumption is a *practical* one. That is to say, working-class people, who are faced with an economic world that urgently demands to be dealt with on a very practical day-to-day level ('you just try to get by from day to day. I can't see beyond tomorrow'), relate to houses in a practical and matter-of-fact way and are therefore basically unable to perceive houses as anything other than dwelling space, that is, a place to live. So although urban elites problematise their neighbourhoods as areas of 'urban decline' (that is, suffering relative unpopularity within the space of positions in the metropolitan market for houses), working-class people simply do not view their urban situation in the same 'positional' way at all. Indeed they resent the imposition of positional labels such as 'unpopular neighbourhoods' as well as the imposition of regeneration programmes that such labels are used to justify. By taking these points on board we now have a way of understanding the conceptually violent nature of housing market renewal (HMR), which is a particular type of regeneration programme that is driven by a logic that views the market for houses as a space of positions.

This brings me to the third problematic that this book seeks to address. The gentrification literature has largely focused on the manner in which the middle-class habitus constitutes the symbolic economy of houses as a space of positions, for example by creating a gentrification aesthetic, a suburban ideal or whatever. It says much less about how the field of housing consumption is constituted by other actors, notably institutions that regulate and govern activity in the market for houses. Insofar as such institutions appear in the gentrification literature, they do so *at a late stage* to exploit the 'rent gap' that has emerged in urban spaces that have been valorised by social groups such as the new middle class. Yet institutions such as housing developers, regeneration agencies and estate agents do not simply 'follow' the flow of market activity as if it had a life of its own that was independent of the actions of these institutions, even if these institutions do present their activities in these largely inconsequential terms (Smith *et al.* 2006). On the contrary, these institutions constitute the field of housing in fundamental ways. My argument in Part III of the book is that these institutions not only constitute the market for houses as a space of positions but, further, use regeneration programmes to impose this dominant view of the market for houses on 'declining' urban areas that are said to have become 'disconnected' from the space of positions. It is easy to understand why these institutions would want to reposition such areas within the space of positions in the market for houses. This generates market activity, which, in turn, generates economic profits for these institutions. HMR is never presented in these terms, of course. On the contrary the regeneration problematic is presented in a technocratic language that speaks of the need to 'fix' housing markets that are 'failing', thereby obscuring the nature of the economic 'interests' and involvements that such institutions have in the market for houses as well as the power they have to structure such markets in ways that are consonant with the nature of their interest in them.

But such profiteering takes place at the expense of an urban working class that, quite simply, does not relate to its houses or neighbourhoods as positions in the space of positions and that therefore opposes regeneration programmes that seek to reposition them in the space of positions. There are numerous reasons for this, which I discuss in Parts II and III of the book. Suffice it to say, for the time being, that demolishing low-cost working-class houses in order to build 'high-value' (that is, high-price) 'products' that middle-class people will (allegedly) buy cuts working-class people adrift from these brave new housing markets. Of course regeneration agencies claim that they 'help' working-class people adjust to these markets by providing a minimal percentage of 'affordable' houses and special 'loan' products to help them to purchase. But what they do not understand is that the repositioning of their houses within the space of positions in the market for houses violates a whole way of working-class 'being' towards houses (a place to dwell rather than position within the space of positions). This exemplifies the manner in which housing market renewal has been used by the dominant to secure domination over the dominated. And all in the pursuit of economic profits.

This brings me to my final point, before getting on with the book. The working class is a complex and fragmented entity. Some elements of the working class have 'enjoyed' social mobility and, as a consequence, positioned themselves within the space of positions in the market for houses (Watt 2006). This is evident in the work of Wynne (1998), whose new middle class is partly constituted from working-class people that have 'made good' through promotion at work. Such movement is undeniable when we examine patterns of residential movement in contemporary cities that have seen some working-class people move out of the inner city. But my book is concerned with elements of the working class that have stayed in the inner city: an inner-urban working class. The lives of these working-class people are conducted at such close proximity to necessity and insecurity that they have no way of relating to consumption other than in practical terms, that is, in terms of necessities. This is why I refer to a practical economy of working-class consumption. Further, with dispositions that are oriented to necessity (and little more), these people reproduce the conditions of their own precarious existence. For example, being unable to engage with education other than in terms of the instrumental necessities that it imposes on working-class people to secure a position in the labour market ('You've just got to get your English and Maths') means that working-class people are complicit in the reproduction of their own basic and insecure existence in the labour market.[2] This proscribes the possibility that working-class people will ever be able to grasp the world other than in terms of its basic essentials, that is, the practical business of 'getting by'. Thus I recognise that many writers have written about the aspirations (and concomitant 'failed consumption') of the working class and that such aspirations were also present in my sample. Chapter 4 discusses how they idealised suburbia too! But an aspiration for recognition only really provides us with an insight into what working-class people *ideally* want to be. It does not provide us with an adequate insight into the mundane nature of the everyday lives of my working-class respondents, which were endlessly devoted to the practical accomplishment of survival. These practical necessities, above all else, are what govern working-class lives. I feel that this is important because, let us not forget, the defining characteristic of the working class in conventional as well as contemporary terms is its *social and economic immobility* as well as its insecurity in the brutally efficient labour market of modern Britain.

Empirical origins of the book

The material that has been drawn upon to develop the argument in this book emerged from two research studies. The first, funded by the Economic and Social Research Council (Award Number RES-000-22-0827), was a case study of housing market behaviour in the Kensington district of Liverpool, which was undergoing a major HMR programme at the time. Data collection took place in two stages. First, 16 interviews were undertaken with 'stakeholders' (such as senior city council officers, directors of regeneration, housing developers, estate agents etc.). The purpose of these interviews was to understand how key institutions intervened in the market for houses in Kensington in order to shape it. Second, a series of two interviews was undertaken with 34 households living in Kensington, resulting in a total of 68 interviews. The first interview was biographical and examined the social, economic and cultural histories of households. Second interviews examined how these households related to the market for houses in Kensington and elsewhere. All stakeholder and household interviews were fully transcribed and subsequently analysed. My critical interpretation of these interview transcripts enabled me to identify empirical themes within the transcripts as well as empirical consistency across the transcripts for each of the identified themes. These critical interpretations were informed by ideas drawn from phenomenology, notably the corpus of work produced by Bourdieu, Heidegger and Merleau-Ponty, which I discuss in relation to my data from Chapter 3 onwards.

The core arguments in this book are a product of my critical interpretation of 50 of these interviews, which were undertaken with 25 households containing 30 working-class respondents (see Appendices I and II). These respondents were identified as working class using a triangulated method. First, respondents were initially identified as working class with reference to occupational criteria that have conventionally been used to locate people into social class categories (see Appendix II). Second, analysis of interview transcripts enabled me to identify commonalities in the way working-class people described their social and economic existence that distinguished them from middle-class respondents. Although the sample of working-class respondents includes three that were educated to degree level, these people were all from working-class backgrounds. Consistent with this, they had studied at post-1992 universities (Reay 2001a; Reay *et al.* 2001) and remained in working-class or low-status service occupations (Savage 2000; see Appendix II). The analysis of interview transcripts also showed that these three people displayed attitudes towards housing consumption that were consistent with those of other working-class people and significantly different from those exhibited by middle-class respondents. Interviews with the remaining nine households have not been included in the book because the respondents were middle-class gentrifiers, middle-class students, wealthy international students or asylum seekers.

The second study consisted of my participant observation of a public enquiry into the compulsory purchase of houses in Kensington and other inner-urban areas of Liverpool. Participant observation involved my presenting written evidence to the enquiry, as a witness, as well as making observations of its proceedings. This involved observation of council officers and other institutional interests presenting the case for housing market renewal, as well as listening to residents opposing the formal rationale for housing market renewal. This was followed by an in-depth analysis of several types of document. First it involved analysis of the opening and closing submissions to the public enquiry, made by the legal team representing Liverpool City Council. It also involved analysis of 'proofs of evidence' provided by the six key witnesses that were acting for Liverpool City Council at the public enquiry, and the 'proofs of evidence' provided by 16 objectors whose homes were subject to compulsory purchase orders. Finally, it involved analysis of some of the key 'core documents' that were submitted to the public enquiry by Liverpool City Council. This included neighbourhood renewal strategy documents, housing strategy documents, development plans, strategic investment framework documents, housing investment framework documents, Liverpool City Council discussion papers, housing market renewal prospectuses and research and intelligence reports. Analysis of each of these empirical sources from the public enquiry was undertaken in cognisance of the analytical exercise that had taken place following the completion of the first study. This exercise produced empirical material that either buttressed the analysis undertaken during the first study, or resulted in my need to introduce nuances into theoretical arguments I was developing as a result of my analysis of the first study. Overall, then, this book is a product of my analysis of the empirical themes that emerged from a wide range of material, which included the testimonies of a total of 46 working-class people, as well as my critical interpretation of how my analysis of these materials sits in relation to the official justifications that are given (by academics as well as policy makers) for housing market renewal.

Part I
Invitation to class analysis

Chapter 1
The death and resurrection of class in sociology

Introduction

> The class system is dead.
>
> (Prince Edward)

Proclamations of the death of the class system lack shock value when articulated by a member of the royal family. They can simply be dismissed as ignorant and arrogant mutterings of those who occupy social positions that lack any connection whatsoever with the everyday 'reality' of most 'ordinary' people's lives. Unfortunately those who opine about the death of the class system are not simply confined to the fine and well-bred specimens that constitute the aristocracy. A belief in the irrelevance of class is now so pervasive within the social sciences that issues of deprivation are treated with an indifference, or even disdain, that issues from an arrogance born of security (Charlesworth 2000). Contemporary sociology has become embroiled in 'new' concerns ('individualisation', 'identity', 'difference', 'risk', 'mobilities' etc.) that reflect the lifestyle preoccupations of its middle-class intelligentsia, whose social position is parasitic on a discriminatory higher education system that reproduces the conditions of their class privilege (Bourdieu and Passeron 1977; Reay 2001a; Reay *et al.* 2001) and that, to add insult to injury, they then use to proclaim the 'death of class' (Charlesworth 2000; Skeggs 2004). As the sociological agenda has shifted towards these 'post-material' concerns of 'lifestyle politics' (Giddens 1991) studies of working-class existence have sunk to the bottom of the hierarchy of intellectual subjects (Charlesworth 2000). The decline in the symbolic profits to be gained from scholarship on working-class existence has thus resulted in a recent dearth of publishing in this area (Charlesworth 2000), certainly when compared with the volume of scholarship on issues such as 'risk', 'identity' and 'difference'.

This chapter commences by examining the validity of the scholarly claim that 'the class system is dead'. This claim is based on empirical evidence of increasing standards of living and increasing levels of social mobility, which, it is suggested, undermines the idea that class barriers are impenetrable. The 'death of class' thesis is also based on empirical evidence that people no longer invoke social class labels as identifiers. The second part of the chapter examines critiques of the 'end of class' thesis. Critics of the 'end of class' thesis have presented more nuanced sets of empirical evidence that demonstrate a continuing lack of social mobility. They also argue that working-class people no longer invoke class labels to identify themselves because the stigma historically attached to those labels cause too much pain. The absence of 'class talk', in other words, is indicative of the endurance of class divisions that have never been more painful or relevant to working-class people.

The 'end of class'?

The 'logic of industrialism' and 'end of ideology'

The 'end of class' thesis has a rich history that stretches back to the sociology of Emile Durkheim, who argued that the modern state has tended towards a maximal (rather than minimum) role designed

> to provide for [individual] self-realization. This was not something which could occur . . . when the operations of the state were kept to a minimum. The self-realization of the individual could only take place in and through his or her membership of a society in which the state guaranteed and advanced the rights embodied in moral individualism.
>
> (Giddens 1987: 105)

Durkheim's notion, that the state represents a positive force for change in modern societies, has had a key influence on welfare state theory, where it found its most visible expression in the 'logic of industrialism' thesis that emerged in the 1960s (Donnison 1967; Donnison and Ungerson 1982) and that continues to influence contemporary welfare state theory (Emms 1990; Power 1993). One of the most famous exponents of the 'logic of industrialism' thesis is David Donnison (1967), who identified societies at three different stages of industrial development in the 1960s. He associated the first stage with countries such as Spain, Greece, Turkey and Portugal that (like Britain in the nineteenth century) were in the throes of a transition to industrial society and experiencing high levels of urbanisation. A second group of countries, which included Britain, were said to be at an intermediate stage of industrial development and so a 'residual' form of social housing had emerged that was designed to cater for particular needs, such as those of slum dwellers. The final group of countries, which included Sweden and West Germany, were at a more mature stage of industrial development that had enabled governments to assume responsibility for developing a 'comprehensive' form of public housing, albeit not necessarily provided directly by the state.

For Donnison, the 'logic of industrialism' operates as follows. At 'less developed' stages of economic development, government priorities are directed towards industrial growth and so intervention in the housing market tends to be passive and 'haphazard'. This exacerbates social inequalities and, it follows, encourages social class divisions to develop around working-class resentment of a government that supports industry whilst doing little to address social inequalities. However, as societies attain an 'advanced' level of industrial development, governments become 'resource rich' and are able to broaden their 'interventionist' horizons and, furthermore, have an incentive to do so. Since 'housing makes a fundamental contribution to economic development' (Donnison and Ungerson 1982: 78), for example by promoting a healthy and productive workforce, 'resource rich' governments tend to invest their new-found wealth in 'housing programmes'. The logic of economic development thus pushes *all* governments towards a 'comprehensive' form of social housing provision. Donnison articulated this particular point by making a distinction between 'leader' and 'laggard' societies (Donnison 1967; Wilensky 1975; Gould 1993), with the implication being that the laggards would eventually *have* to follow the leaders largely because the 'logic' of economic development dictated that this was what they would have to do. This historical point engenders an 'end of ideology' because class politics loses its relevance as class divisions and tensions recede (Bell 1960; Lipset 1963; Marshall 1967; see also Giddens 1994 for a more contemporary argument that politics has moved 'beyond left and right'). This end to ideological struggle between the left and right is, apparently, nowhere more evident than in the way 'advanced' welfare societies become more concerned with social cohesion rather than representing the interests of particular (dominant) social groups.

> Governments which pursue [comprehensive] aims far enough find they are applying, in the sphere of housing, a new conception of the state. They are no longer regulating, supplementing or restraining the operations of the market. They have assumed responsibility for shaping the kind of world their people are to live in, and hence for mobilizing the resources and creating the conditions required for that purpose.
>
> (Donnison and Ungerson 1982: 81)

Social mobility and demise of class barriers

Although the welfare sociology of Donnison is based on the apparently outdated perspective of functionalism, its claim about the 'end of class' is current in contemporary sociology. A key sociological literature here is that on 'social mobility', which has sought to 'test' whether or not the idea of 'meritocracy' (i.e. that one can 'progress' through hard work, ability and strength of personality), which tends to elicit widespread support in surveys of attitudes to social mobility (especially Glass 1954), is valid. Glass's respondents emphasised how individuals could 'help themselves' to 'get on' by displaying the right attitude. Only a minority of working-class respondents thought that 'contacts' (16 per cent) and money (12 per cent) affected the prospect of social mobility. Glass's respondents therefore believed in the justice and legitimacy of the 'reward system'. More recent evidence from the British Social Attitudes (BSA) survey suggests that little has changed, with hard work and education continuing to feature as the most common sources of social mobility. Although respondents to the 1987 BSA survey did not deny the value of social advantage to social mobility, they also did not stress it as a factor (Savage 2000).

Social scientists such as John Goldthorpe have subjected these widely held ideas about social mobility to empirical testing. Goldthorpe's analytical approach (which is known as the 'Nuffield paradigm' or 'class structural approach') is to establish the extent of mobility within the class structure, that is, the proportion and flow of individuals from one social class to another. This focus on 'class aggregates' means he is interested not simply in the extent to which British society is 'open', but also in the process of social class formation, that is, the changing composition of social classes as a result of social mobility. His studies have uncovered high levels of social mobility within British society and therefore a dynamic rather than static picture of class formation (Erikson and Goldthorpe 1992). For example, his study with Erikson (1992) found that two-thirds of sons were in a different social class from their fathers. For Goldthorpe, then, social mobility constitutes the norm rather than an exception, whereas there is little evidence of the inheritance of social positions.

The levels of mobility identified by Goldthorpe have not simply been found within the occupational structure, with people from working-class backgrounds progressing into 'middle-class' occupations. Sociologists such as Wynne (1998) have identified similar levels of social mobility within the housing market, with middle-class suburbs now increasingly populated by people from the 'new middle class', that is, people in middle-class occupations but from working-class origins. Others have argued that the level of social mobility is evident not only in the extent of this 'new middle class' flight to the suburbs but also in its consequences. These consequences are identified as the alleged 'decline' of traditional working-class neighbourhoods in inner-urban areas of cities such as Manchester and Salford (Nevin *et al.* 1999). What better indicator of the level of social mobility in Britain than the apparent decline of inner-urban working-class neighbourhoods and concomitant growth of suburbia?

Nevertheless, sociologists such as Goldthorpe have not simply been concerned with understanding the process of class formation and the changing 'class structure'. Goldthorpe regarded this as the 'starting point' of 'class analysis' rather than a basis for drawing solid conclusions about social class formation and fragmentation (Crompton 1998). For Goldthorpe, the other key task for class analysts is to establish the extent to which members of social classes coalesce around their (new and changing) position within the class structure. The key question here is whether the social classes, which Goldthorpe claims are in a constant process of formation and fragmentation, possess a 'demographic identity' that is associated with continuity of membership and individual members' occupation of particular sets of positions over time (Goldthorpe 1983: 467). According to this logic, social immobility is likely to be associated with strong and cohesive class identities whereas social mobility is likely to disrupt such cohesion and therefore the ability of social groups to construct and maintain a coherent class identity. So what do we know about class identities in this changing context of increasing social mobility?

Recent work has shown that people now seldom identify themselves with a particular social class category ('working class', 'middle class' etc.). Thus Savage (2000) suggests that the current tendency is to present oneself as part of the 'mainstream' of 'ordinary' people, which means that class is much less relevant than social surveys might initially indicate. A classic example of this can be found in Devine's (1992) study of affluent manual workers in Luton. Devine found that most respondents defined their social position with reference to terms (such as 'ordinary working people') that she claimed to be reflections of a mainstream consciousness and thus indicative of the abandonment of discursive distinctions between working- and middle-class. This corresponds with Savage *et al.*'s own work, which found that two-thirds of their sample identified themselves with a social class category but that this identification was usually ambivalent, defensive and hesitant, e.g. identification with a class category was often prefaced by terms such as 'I suppose . . .' or 'I'm probably . . .' (Savage *et al.* 2000). Savage *et al.* (2000) suggest that a key reason for this was that significant numbers of their respondents had never thought deeply about their *personal* identification with class before (hence the hesitancy contained in 'I suppose I'm . . .'). It seems, then, that increasing levels of social mobility (which have seen many households abandon working-class socio-economic positions for employment in the service sector and homes in suburbia) have existentially disrupted most individuals' sense of their social class positioning. That is to say, class no longer appears to be an important aspect of self-identity or to evoke the strong sense of group or collective allegiance that scholars writing in the 1950s and 1960s claim to have found in working-class communities (Young and Willmott 1957). For Savage (2000: 40), then:

Admittedly class is a widely understood term, and people do use the term to make sense of some aspects of British society. However, Britain is not a deeply class conscious society, where class is seen as embodying membership of collective groups. Although people can identify themselves as members of classes, this identification seems contextual and of limited significance, rather than being a major source of their identity and group belonging. Furthermore people's social attitudes and views are too ambivalent to be seen as part of a consistent class-related world view. Finally, people's own class location shapes only some of their views and even then in highly mediated and complex ways.

Widespread ambivalence towards the issue of 'class' in late modern societies has led a number of sociologists to claim that 'class as a concept is ceasing to do any useful work for sociology' (Pahl 1989: 710), that it is 'an increasingly redundant issue' (Holton and Turner 1989: 194) and that it is 'dying' (Clark and Lipset 1991); and even to agree with Prince Edward that class is 'dead' (Pakulski and Walters 1996) and therefore to issue a 'farewell to the working class' (Gorz 1982). A key theme in contemporary sociology and social and political science more generally, then, is the claim that class has lost its relevance either per se or, at the very least, vis-à-vis other identifiers of difference (Savage 2000; Eley and Nield 2000). This has led to a dramatic shift in the contemporary sociological agenda, in which concerns about class have been replaced in the mainstream 'sociological imagination' by 'new' concerns with 'individualisation', 'identity', 'difference', 'risk' and so on (Skeggs 2004). A key figure here is Anthony Giddens (1991), whose claim that an individualised concern with 'lifestyle politics' has superseded the 'emancipatory politics' of class has had a fundamental influence on the content of the contemporary sociological agenda. For Giddens (1994), then, politics has moved 'beyond left and right' to embrace new identifiers of 'difference' such as gender and ethnicity (Harrison with Davis 2002) and sexuality (Binnie 2004). Ulrich Beck has made similar claims about the declining relevance of class politics, albeit from a different perspective. For Beck (1992), the issues of key import in contemporary societies (e.g. globalisation, environmental risk etc.) affect everybody and cannot therefore be addressed within a class politics framework. This results in the emergence of a global politics of 'we' rather than a class politics of 'us versus them'. More recently, Beck (2000) has documented the (apparent) emergence of a 'globalization of biography' that, he claims, stems from increasing levels of geographical mobility and, furthermore, is cementing the importance of the new global politics of 'we'.

The position of class analysis within sociology has therefore shifted from its 'core' position within the sociological mainstream of the 1950s and 1960s to one in which it is now seen and practised as a sub-field of sociology (Savage 2000). That is to say, class is increasingly a matter for sociologists who are centrally concerned with class rather than a matter for all sociologists, who are free to ignore it with impunity. Those who have retained an interest in class analysis, and who have kept it alive as a sub-field of sociology, fall into two camps. First, the line that writers such as Thrift and Williams (1987) and Bradley (1996) take is that more complex forms of stratification are now occurring based around factors such as race, religion, ethnicity, gender and sexuality *as well as* class. Class does not determine experience, consciousness and action, then, but neither is it irrelevant. Second, other writers have completely rejected the 'new' concerns of sociology in favour of the continuance of a research programme in 'class analysis' that seeks to understand class relations within a changing social, economic and political context (Goldthorpe and Lockwood 1968, 1969; Eley and Nield 2000).

A welcome back to class

Empirical evidence of the class society

First, it is instructive to note that movement of working-class people into service sector occupations does not necessarily constitute 'social mobility'. For Braverman (1974), this is because the capitalist mode of production tends towards the deskilling of labour, which affects *all* workers and means that the apparent upgrading of the labour force, from manual to white collar, is more apparent than real (see also Wright and Singlemann 1982; Esping-Andersen 1993). Braverman (1974) refers to this as 'labour process theory'. These theoretical arguments aside, the empirical evidence that points to increasing levels of social mobility is less than convincing anyway. Although Goldthorpe identified increasing levels of *absolute* social mobility for example, he argued that analyses of *relative* rates of social mobility (which are based on a comparison of the relative life chances that members of one social class have when contrasted with members of other social classes) indicate that the sons of members of privileged social classes have better life chances than those of the working class. Furthermore he argued that these advantages have remained fairly constant over time, indicating, for him, the enduring importance of class, which has consistently been at the centre of his analysis of social mobility.

Further, albeit qualified, support for these claims has been provided by Savage and colleagues. Drawing on vast amounts of empirical data, Savage *et al.* (1992: 134) found that some middle-class groups (the service class) have higher levels of self-recruitment than others and that working-class mobility into the middle class is more restricted in some places than others. Specifically, middle-class households with 'cultural capital' (e.g. higher education qualifications) were found to be better able to transmit their privileges than those working in management or administration work, who did not possess the same levels of cultural capital. Put simply, cultural assets such as educational competence can be transmitted within the family more easily than can a position within an organisation. This is borne out by empirical data, which shows greater levels of inter-class mobility into management positions (which require service to the organisation rather than education) than into the professions (where entry is based on credentialism), which are more self-recruiting. Thus Savage *et al.* (1992: 138) are able to present empirical data that shows that over half of industrial managers have working-class fathers compared with only 43 per cent of senior administrators and 39 per cent of professional employees. Put differently, over one-third of professionals' children move directly into professional work whereas only 19 per cent of managers' children become managers (Savage *et al.* 1992: 148). Such claims have been substantiated by Wright (1997), who also found that it has been easier to progress into a middle-class position based on authority (i.e. management) than into a middle-class position that requires skills (i.e. a profession).

> The crucial point is that while the sons of professionals appear to be able to follow their fathers' footsteps into professional employment with reasonable regularity, managers' sons are less likely to follow their fathers into managerial work. Their fathers' organizational assets have to be traded in, as it were, for educational credentials if they are to remain part of the middle classes. This reveals once again the specific insecurity of the managerial middle classes.
>
> (Savage *et al.* 1992: 139)

The most likely way that managers can secure their children's middle-class status, then, is by investing their higher levels of economic capital (e.g. high income levels) in the education of their children. That said, Savage *et al.* (1992) point to a solidification of class divisions, which, they argue, are being maintained by middle-class parents who are investing (different combinations of economic and cultural) resources in the field of education in order to defend their children's class position. To make this argument they cite evidence from Halsey *et al.* (1980), which shows that that the children of managers are very successful at gaining qualifications and that, crucially, what matters is the type of school attended rather than the parents' educational history. This means that managerial positions with large incomes that can be invested in a 'good school' are, after all, crucially important in enabling the transmission of privilege within middle-class families, which means that class effects are being mediated through the educational attainment system (Savage 2000: 90). Savage and Edgerton (1998) have conducted an equally interesting piece of work showing that there are powerful class differences between the fates of high-ability middle-class and working-class children: the ratio of high to low ability is 87:13 for sons of professionals whereas it is 32:68 for those of unskilled workers. Savage (2000) claims that this may reflect the social biases built into ability tests (see Bourdieu and Passeron 1977 for a full exposition of the argument about education and class reproduction and an explanation of why this could be the case). Thus, although educational attainment, hard work and ability are all important to social mobility, class processes are embedded in these virtues, which are therefore *not* indicative of a meritocratic system (Savage 2000: 95). When the other social advantages of middle-class children are taken into account (e.g. knowing the correct way to talk and present oneself in the market for middle-class occupations) it is not surprising that a mere 7 per cent of high-ability sons of large business owners and managers end up in manual occupations at age 33 compared with 38 per cent of high-ability sons of unskilled manual workers who end up in the same place. Conversely over half of the 'low-ability' sons of professional fathers join the middle class compared with 10 per cent of low-ability sons of unskilled manual workers (Savage 2000).

The notion that increasing numbers of working-class people are socially mobile is untenable not only within the occupational structure but also within the context of the housing market. For some scholars, then, the picture of a mobile working class moving to the suburban housing estates and forming a 'new middle class' (cf. Wynne 1998) is a very partial one. Moreover, although Donnison (1967) claims that 'comprehensive' social housing provision contributed to social cohesion, Morris and Winn (1990) argue, on the contrary, that its expansion actually institutionalised class divisions. This argument goes as follows: as the availability of private rented housing declined from its peak in 1914 (when it constituted 90 per cent of the total housing stock), skilled manual workers, intermediate and junior non-manual workers and professionals, employers and managers tended to move into owner occupation whereas semi-skilled and unskilled manual workers and economically inactive households tended to locate in public rented housing (Morris and Winn 1990; Watt 2001).[1] The manner in which social class has conventionally mapped onto tenure is significant because the management and administration of council housing has been implicated in the reproduction of class divisions. Reference to Pahl's (1975) work on 'urban managerialism' provides an understanding of how this has happened within council housing.

Pahl (1975) argues that the power to control access to scarce urban resources resides with a range of key occupational and professional groups 'such as housing managers, estate agents, local government officers, property developers, representatives of building societies and insurance companies . . . and so on' (Pahl 1975: 206). For Pahl, then, we need to study urban managers to 'know not only the rates of access to scarce resources and facilities for given populations but also the determinants of the moral and political values of those who control these rates' (Pahl 1975: 207–8). Anne Power (1987) and Henderson and Karn (1984, 1987) have shown how this happens in the allocation of council housing, specifically in the allocation practices of housing officers, who have been shown to place 'respectable' households on 'good estates' in order to preserve them as desirable areas. The same researchers have shown how the same housing officers tend to channel poorer households to the worst housing. Housing allocation processes are therefore deeply infused with considerations about 'class' and have worked to make many council renters feel 'second class'.

Privileged council tenants have not been immune from the malign influence of these discriminatory housing processes. Although council tenants who have exercised the 'right to buy' their homes are those who were originally allocated to the better parts of the council housing stock, this has not been an uncomplicated process of 'gain' resulting in their elevation within the class hierarchy. Many working-class households have been 'forced' to exercise their 'right to buy' as a result of rent rises within public housing. Moreover many of these households became victims of repossession in the late 1980s and early 1990s (Morris and Winn 1990; Forrest and Murie 1994; Ford and Burrows 1999) or have been unable to afford to repair and maintain their properties, which have consequently lost value (Karn *et al.* 1985). The notion that owner occupation is a potential source of wealth accumulation, and that expansion of owner occupation reduces class divisions, is therefore spurious (Hamnet 1999). Although dwellings accounted for one-third of total net wealth in Britain in 1989 (Morris and Winn 1990), the uneven spatial distribution of house price inflation has meant that the expansion of owner occupation creates oligarchic (rather than democratic) outcomes, with those who are economically privileged in one generation being able to pass this privilege onto their children. For Forrest and Murie (1980), then, the expansion of owner occupation places more emphasis on housing as a source of wealth, yet uneven levels of wealth accumulation and inheritance exacerbate social divisions within owner occupation and between owner occupiers and renters:

> At a time when free market processes are likely to become more dominant in the determination of life chances generally, the accumulation of wealth through property ownership may be a crucial element in perpetuating and creating inequalities.
>
> (Forrest and Murie 1980)

The notion that increasing levels of social mobility (within the occupational structure and housing system) have resulted in the demise of the relevance of class is not, therefore, straightforward. Some of the scholars cited above have produced continued evidence of occupational immobility within most sections of the working class[2] whereas others have questioned whether the elevation of working-class people into service occupations fundamentally challenges the class structure anyway – even suggesting that it strengthens it (Braverman 1974; Eley and Nield 2000). Housing allocation processes have been shown to be consistently drenched in 'class' and therefore implicated in the production of class divisions (e.g. the 'respectable' and 'undeserving' working class; Watt 2006). Housing policy, on the other hand, has forced too many working-class households into owner occupation who were not 'ready' for it, which has resulted in high levels of repossession. This is symptomatic of a more fundamental problem of inequality, which has resulted from the increasing policy emphasis on housing as a market 'commodity'. This policy emphasis has exacerbated wealth inequalities between middle-class people who can afford to buy houses in high-value markets and those who are condemned to purchase ex-council houses, whose value does not usually grow to anything like the same extent as those in the aforementioned high-value markets.[3] The important thing to note here, then, is that class divisions have been politically (as well as economically) produced. They are a consequence of policy decisions that have been made in relation to housing tenure rather than simply a consequence of economic processes over which the political class have had little control (Kemeny 1995). This is what makes the idea that 'class is dead', simply because working-class people *say* that they do not employ it to construct a sense of their own social positioning and self-identity, so extraordinary.

Skeggs (1997, 2004) has something pertinent to say about this. For her, it is precisely *because* the institutional processes to which working-class people have been historically subjected – such as those found in housing – are so 'classed' in a negative sense that class is denied. To make her argument, Skeggs (1997) cites studies that highlight a political normalisation of middle-class culture (e.g. Hill 1986) as well as studies by Kuhn (1988) and Nead (1988) that chart a history in which the British working class has been continually demonised, pathologised and held responsible for its own social problems: 'The negativity associated with the working class is ubiquitous' (Skeggs 1997: 76). These historical studies demonstrate the hegemonic power of the dominant classes to stigmatise and thereby undermine working-class identities (Skeggs 1997; Reay 1998; Lawler 2005a). Skeggs (1997) argues that this historical denigration of the working class was further exacerbated by the politics of Thatcherism, which created a series of new inequalities and social divisions. This resulted in the emergence of a 'residual' or 'socially excluded' 'non-working class' or 'underclass', which has exacerbated the 'spoiled identity' of the working class. This comes through strongly in the way Skeggs's (1997) working-class female college students talked about 'the working class' as people that are 'poor, they have nothing'; 'the ones who you see hanging around the dole. They're dead scruffy and they haven't got a job'; 'rough . . . common as muck'; 'the ones who batter their kids'. The notion that the working class is now associated with this so-called 'underclass' was informing the construction of new distinctions and divisions within the working class. This was exemplified in the way her respondents were now reluctant to take on working-class identities given their negative connotations. The prime concern of her sample of working-class women was to establish their 'respectability' and thereby distance themselves from those stigmatised by the dominant culture. This corresponds with the work of Fraser (1989), who also found that working-class women were reluctant to speak about their class identity, which they found to be an embarrassing category to identify with (see also Sayer 2002). It also resonates with work in the USA by Sennet and Cobb (1971, 1993), who noted the sense of failure that a 'working-class' identity instilled in ordinary working people (see also Sayer 2005).

That said, working-class identities were not irrelevant to these women because they refused to identify with them. On the contrary, Skeggs argues that notions of class were central to her respondents' subjectivities and that this was present in their efforts *not* to be recognised as 'working class' given the spoiled nature of working-class identity, which, she argues, is now a label that is used to stigmatise people as dirty, dangerous and without value. This discursive strategy (which is based on a refusal of recognition rather than a claim for the right to be recognised) does not constitute a denial of social class positioning, then. On the contrary, it constitutes a denial of the *representations* of their social class positioning. So in every judgment of themselves a measurement was made against others. The designated 'other' was based on representations and imaginings of the respectable, normalised and judgmental middle class and was constructed as the standard against which they measured themselves (see also Sayer 2005). The classifying of themselves therefore relied on the classificatory systems of others in what Fraser (1995) refers to as a shift from the 'politics of redistribution' to a new 'politics of recognition'.[4] A key element of class politics therefore concerns the struggles for distinction and recognition that take place on a discursive level between social groups (Skeggs 1997, 2004). The logic of discursive struggles is to create and maintain inter- and intra-class distinctions that, at times, become obfuscated, as we have already seen, i.e. when working-class identities become polluted by non-working-class identities, thereby resulting in a denial of class that, in fact, is evidence of the enduring relevance of class. Indeed, this is what makes the idea that 'class is dead' so extraordinary to sociologists who remain committed to the programme of class analysis.

Conclusion

The 'death of class' thesis is predicated on the existence of high levels of social mobility and/or social cohesion. Apparent empirical evidence of high levels of movement between social classes, especially from working-class to middle-class occupations, justifies claims that class is no longer a stable or even valid social category. This view has been buttressed by a contemporary sociological agenda that is constituted on issues that affect the middle-class intelligentsia who formulate them as issues and whose misrecognition of the particularity of their experience, as privileged, has led them to pronounce on the universal pertinence of these issues. Yet they are, in fact, particular issues whose relevance is peculiar to those groups that articulate them as issues. This means, of course, that members of social groups that do not share the privileged position of the middle-class intelligentsia also fail to share their interests and concerns.

The working class is not dead and neither, for that matter, is the class system. Continuing evidence of high levels of social immobility and class discrimination suggest that the class system and the working class are alive and well. Moreover, conceptualisations of the working class, as well as the institutional and social mechanisms that constitute it as such, suggest that there is a need to treat the working class, and the class system that positions it, very seriously indeed. The key purpose of the next chapter is to examine conceptualisations of class and the class system in modern social theory. Another purpose is to examine how these conceptualisations of class and the class system have been used in urban sociological studies of class formation in the market for houses.

Chapter 2
Theorising social class

Introduction

Despite recent pronouncements about the death of class, Chapter 1 has shown that class divisions and identities are alive and well. What we have witnessed in the last few decades has been not the death of class, then, but rather the passing of one type of class society with another materialising to take its place (Eley and Nield 2000). Fraser (1995) has argued that this 'new' class society is based on a politics of recognition as well as the politics of material inequality. This sociological resurrection of class having been noted, the purpose of this chapter is to provide a review of the various ways in which sociologists have theorised social class as well as its relevance to understanding housing provision and consumption.

My initial attention is on conventional Marxist and Weberian theories of class, which have largely focused on the occupational structure. Some of this ground was covered, empirically, in Chapter 1, which examined how increasing levels of occupational mobility have been used as indicators of the death (or endurance) of social class. This chapter moves on to examine 'new' theories of class formation that emphasise how class divisions are created and maintained via consumption practices. A consequence of this attention to consumption practices has been a skewed focus on those who consume. Thus the literature primarily addresses middle-class consumption practices but has much less to say about working-class consumption. The consequences of this are most apparent in urban sociology, in which there is now a rich literature on the gentrification of inner-urban neighbourhoods by middle-class households. Insofar as working-class households appear in these literatures, they do so as victims of 'displacement' caused by middle-class gentrification activity. This analysis sets the scene for Part II of the book, which seeks to develop an understanding of how working-class people relate to the market for houses, with a view to understanding how this economy of working-class housing consumption is implicated in the production and maintenance of class divisions.

Marxist theories of class and stratification

A key problem with Marx is that class can be found literally everywhere in his work yet he does not provide a precise or consistent theory of class that could be invoked as a Marxist definition of class (Crompton 1998). What is clear, however, is that Marx argued that class relationships were embedded in the production system, that is, within patterns of ownership and control of the means of production, distribution and exchange. This has led to assumptions that Marx employed a two-class model of capitalist societies. Yet *The Eighteenth Brumaire of Louis Bonaparte* (Marx 1954) almost slips into a Weberian definition of class (see below) given its references to a number of different classes occupying different 'market situations'. For example, it identifies a landed aristocracy, financiers, an industrial bourgeoisie, the middle class, a petty bourgeoisie, the industrial proletariat, a lumpenproletariat and a peasantry! Another key issue in Marx(ism) concerns the historical role of these ill-defined classes. Although a fundamental Marxist position is the acceptance that capitalism is a society divided by class, perhaps strangely, not all Marxists have chosen to focus their analyses of capitalism on class. Marxists choose either capitalism or class as their focus, that is, they seek *either* to develop an insight into the systemic properties and logic of capitalism *or* to highlight the class driven nature of social and economic change (Savage 2000). Marxists who focus on the systemic properties of capitalism follow what is sometimes referred to as a 'logic of accumulation' approach to analysis, in which either class does not figure or its historical importance to the process of capitalist development is minimised. Marxists who focus on the role of class follow what are sometimes referred to as 'humanist' or 'cultural' approaches, in which class and class consciousness play a prominent historical role. The emphasis here is on the collective agency of social classes.

Marxism and the 'logic of capital accumulation'

A good example of Marxist scholarship that seeks to understand capitalism rather than class is the 'regulation school'. The regulation school has been primarily concerned with what it regards as the epistemological necessity to understand the different means through which capitalism is regulated at the societal level as well as the conditions that secure or threaten capitalist reproduction. It has shown little theoretical interest in class, which it appears to regard as an epistemological luxury. For the regulation school, then, contemporary change in capitalist societies is not a class driven process, which means that analyses of class are not necessary. Put another way, the class basis of capitalist society is taken for granted.

Scientific Marxism is similarly based on the notion that capitalism operates according to objective laws of development that emerge out of the productive forces of accumulation and exploitation. This means that the class struggle has no significant or independent power to shape historical developments. That is to say, social classes are claimed to have little independent force and are therefore regarded as 'effects' rather than 'agents' of structural change, which means that they are of little analytical importance compared with macro processes (Aglietta 1987; Harvey 1989; Jessop 1990). In other words, social classes are regarded as 'bearers' (and therefore products rather than agents) of social and economic change (Cohen 1978). The epistemology of class, as far as Scientific Marxists see it, can therefore be reduced to these objective laws of social and economic development. This is particularly apparent in the work of Scientific Marxists who have provided 'new' class maps of capitalism that interpret the rise and expansion of the white collar middle class in the context of the changing nature of capitalist production (e.g. Abercrombie and Urry 1983; Braverman 1974).

Insofar as Scientific Marxists have assigned epistemological importance to the collective agency of class, this has been in response to the need to explain welfare developments (such as the emergence of a comprehensive system of public housing) that occurred, despite being contrary to the logic of capital accumulation and despite the initial resistance of the capitalist state. The notion that Marxists needed to provide an explanation for these events (which had initially left them with a lot of explaining to do) resulted in considerable amounts of meta-theoretical development especially in the late 1960s and 1970s (e.g. Althusser 1969; Poulantzas 1973, 1975; and in an urban studies context, Lojkine 1976; Castells 1977, 1983; Dickens *et al.* 1985). The essence of the Althusserian–Poulantzian approach was that state officials (whatever their background) were able to achieve positions of power within the state apparatus only if they were steeped in the norms, values and beliefs of the ruling class. This means that the state is 'relatively autonomous' of the bourgeoisie but *tends* to act in its interests, not least because the interests of the state and capital are inseparable given the dependence of the former on capital accumulation to continue functioning. However, even though the actions of the capitalist state are determined by the needs of capital accumulation, its 'relative autonomy' means that it is able to act periodically in the interests of the working class, particularly during periods of 'crisis'. Moreover, Poulantzas argued that this appearance of autonomy (i.e. a separation between 'political power' and 'economic power') also served ideological purposes because it coerced the working class into believing in the merits of democratic capitalism. Althusser and Poulantzas provide the epistemological scope for class conflict to initiate social change, then, but the historical significance of such change is seen to be limited 'in the final analysis'.

Although classes can be 'agents' as well as 'bearers' of social and economic relations, capitalist relations are ultimately determinant 'in the last instance' (Althusser 1969; also Poulantzas 1975).[1] This is evident in the work of the urban Marxist Michael Harloe.

Harloe and his colleague Michael Ball (Ball and Harloe 1992) argue that their 'provision thesis' is based on a 'recognition that there are combinations of social agents involved in housing provision that relate to each other in empirically observable ways' and therefore recognises that the 'world is dynamic and posits institutional (in its broadest sense) change as a key empirical question' (Ball and Harloe 1992: 3). The provision thesis therefore allows for the possibility that the structures of housing provision can undergo a process of change and also the possibility that this can be brought about through class conflict, i.e. because the state acts in ways that are relatively autonomous of the interests of capital (Harloe 1995). Nevertheless Harloe has sympathies with the Scientific Marxism of Althusser and Poulantzas, which are evident in the starting point of his analysis of the 'structures of housing provision': following the First World War, 'many of the new state organs of economic direction were staffed by representatives of large-scale industry' (Harloe 1995: 77). The threat posed by Fordist-organised *working-class* movements after the First World War resulted in the *capitalist* state undertaking a series of defensive manoeuvres (i.e. concessions) so the provision of social rented housing was 'reluctantly accepted and remained severely limited by the interests of private capital' (Harloe 1995: 76) as, of course, we might expect. He supports this claim by quoting a junior minister referring to the rationale behind the social housing reforms of 1919: 'the money we are going to spend on housing is an insurance against Bolshevism and revolution' (Harloe, 1995: 107), resulting in mass programmes of social rented housing that were

> not a simple response to housing needs but a response to *strategically important* housing needs, in brief the needs of those sections of the population – the skilled, organized working class and part of the middle class – whose continuing dissatisfaction posed the greatest threat to the re-establishment of the capitalist social order.

These social housing programmes were subsequently 'scaled back' when the 'Bolshevik threat' had been averted and 'normality' restored. For Harloe, then, the intervention of the capitalist state is all part of a seditious strategy of 'incorporation', which is to ensure that the working class is 'controlled, disciplined and integrated into the social and economic order' (Harloe 1995: 62; also Merret 1979). Indeed, the incorporation of 'strategically important' elements of the working class has the additional benefit of splitting, and therefore weakening, the working-class movement (see Harloe 1995: 63–4). Thus the strategic actions of the capitalist state *ultimately* change very little 'in the final analysis'. This becomes apparent when we examine his sub-thesis. This is that there are generally two forms of public housing, 'mass' and 'residual'. 'Mass' systems of public housing for a wide range of social groups only emerge in 'abnormal' situations, such as the two post-war periods, 'when varying combinations of social, economic and political circumstances limit the scope for private provision *and* when this limitation is of strategic significance for certain aspects of the maintenance and development of the capitalist social and economic system' (Harloe 1995). For Harloe, then, the decommodification of housing is only possible in 'exceptional circumstances'. On the other hand, 'residual' systems of public housing – and the commodification of housing – are seen as 'the normal form of provision in normal times' (Harloe 1995: 7). These normal circumstances can be seen to have quickly re-emerged in the late 1920s and 1930s (following the post-WWI expansion) and in the 1970s (following the post-WWII expansion) when public housing programmes were cut back again. The reason for this, of course, is because the state is only ever 'semi-autonomous' of capital. In summary, then, the working class is able to act as an agent of social change only in exceptional circumstances. It is relatively powerless to effect change in 'normal circumstances'. Thus members of the working class are ultimately 'bearers' rather than 'agents' of social change, that is, they are the (temporary) beneficiaries of concessions such as council housing rather than the cause of the emergence of a comprehensive system of council housing, which, given its temporality, loses its historical significance.

Cultural Marxism

For Cultural Marxists, class plays an important historical role and is not, therefore, a passive container that can only be conceptualised as the 'bearer' of social relations and not constitutive of them. The conceptual starting point for Cultural Marxists is with the Marxian notion that social classes are historical actors that emerge as collective agents because common forms of 'being' determine a common form of 'consciousness'. This concern with how classes exhibit shared meanings and values, and thus develop as collective actors that shape historical developments, underpins the claim that 'men make their own history but not in the circumstances of their choosing'. The Cultural Marxist tradition therefore emphasises two things: first, the ever-present potential of collective agency and, second, the manner in which class action engenders social change.

One of the most prominent Cultural Marxists is probably E. P. Thompson. A key stimulus for Thompson's Cultural Marxism was his opposition to the

American functionalism of scholars such as Neil Smelster (1962; see Savage 2000: 28) who argued that industrialisation had brought about a *mechanical* modernisation of social relations. This meant that Smelster did not recognise (or, at least, acknowledge) the role that historical actors had played in bringing about social and economic changes in industrial societies. On the contrary, the whole point of Thompson's key work *The Making of the English Working Class* (1968 [1963]) was to emphasise that the 'working class had been present at its own making' and that the cultural idioms and values of the working class had played a crucial role in defining the course of British history and, in particular, the democratic freedoms enjoyed in Britain. Thus Thompson saw class 'as something which in fact happens' (Thompson 1968: 9):

> When we speak of a class we are thinking of a very loosely defined body of people who share the same categories of interests, social experiences, traditions and value systems, who have a disposition to behave as a class, to define themselves in their own actions and in relation to other groups of people in class ways.
>
> (Thompson 1968: 85)

For Thompson, then, class cannot be discussed independently of class consciousness:

> Class experience is largely determined by the productive relations into which men are born – or enter involuntarily. Class consciousness is the way in which these experiences are handled in cultural terms: embodied in traditions, value systems, ideas and institutional forms.
>
> (Thompson 1968: 10)

Although Thompson has been criticised for being excessively cultural, that is, for shifting attention *away* from economic structures, it should be stated (in his defence) that he emphasises how it is *productive relations* that determine class experience, which, in turn, results in the emergence of the collective consciousness that provides the basis for collective action.[2] A practitioner of this neo-Marxian cultural approach in housing studies is Jim Kemeny (1992, 1995), who has developed a Gramscian version of 'labour movement theory' to explain how labour movements can fundamentally influence the nature of housing provision. For Kemeny, the type of Scientific Marxism practised by Harloe is unacceptable because, by presenting the relationship between housing and class as a function of underlying logics of capitalism, it is unable to explain how different societies develop fundamentally different systems of housing provision. To demonstrate that there is nothing *temporary* about forms of housing provision that emerge out of class struggles, Kemeny develops a theory of ideology, which he defines as

> being not secondary or derivative of social formations [e.g. the 'logic' of industrialism or capitalism] but central to the way in which social institutions are constituted, sustained and changed. It is ideology that provides the motivation for action and which channels that action into the creation and perpetuation of social forms in its own image . . . . Ideology is not merely a reflection of major social formations but is interactive and plays an important – even decisive – role in determining the kind of society which develops.
>
> (Kemeny 1992: 85)

Kemeny uses this to suggest that political ideologies (conservative, social democratic etc.) are constitutive of housing markets, which are not, therefore, simply driven by underlying 'logics' of capitalism. He powerfully demonstrates this in his next step, when he develops a neo-Gramscian theory of labour movement housing strategy. Drawing on the *Prison Notebooks* (Gramsci 1971), Kemeny (1992) argues that the essence of the *enduringly* effective labour movement strategy is to construct an ideological hegemony, or leadership, so that political dominance of state institutions by labour movements (e.g. as a result of electoral success) becomes enduring over time, thus providing the 'social conditions in which it is possible to change . . . social structure so that it reflects the ideals embodied in the ideology':

> Political dominance is a means of reinforcing and entrenching a dominant ideology in social structure by using the state to form basic laws and to encourage forms of institution that are consonant with the dominant ideology and to disadvantage those which are not . . . . A really powerful dominant ideology . . . is so deeply entrenched socially and so ingrained in public modes of discourse that the political agenda remains 'hidden': implicit and taken-for-granted, with most political parties accepting it without question and with dissent limited to marginal issues or restricted to marginal groups.
>
> (Kemeny 1992: 96, 97–8)

Kemeny therefore distinguishes between political dominance of state institutions (which constitutes a 'shallow' form of dominance) and ideological hegemony (which constitutes a 'deep' and entrenched form of dominance). Political dominance of state institutions is 'shallow' because, for example, 'collectivist' principles might provide the guiding principles for housing policy changes but these housing policy changes are likely to be reversed when political power is lost. This is what makes collectivism potentially unstable and, therefore, susceptible to changes in political or market conditions. Ideological hegemony is a 'deep' form of dominance because it implies moral leadership; in this case, of the labour movement. Members of civil society will turn to those with moral leadership (the labour movement or its representatives) to provide answers to questions posed by changes in market conditions, rather than seeking a change of political leadership at the ballot box. This allows labour movements that are invested with moral leadership to embed 'collectivist' principles into the functioning of housing markets, which ensures, then, that housing provision is driven by political and moral considerations rather than underlying logics of the capitalist market. And, by doing so, this buttresses the ideological dominance of the labour movement. This is nowhere more apparent than when all of the main political parties subscribe to the basic principles of hegemony, and therefore do not seek to make fundamental changes (that is, based on matters of principle) to housing policy on arrival in office. This ensures that collectivist interests are institutionalised within the policy process and therefore continue to be represented within the policy process despite changes of government.

In *From Public Housing to the Social Market* Kemeny (1995) uses this framework to explain how the Swedish labour movement has been able to construct the Swedish housing market according to collectivist principles so that low-cost housing options have endured (rather than been reined in) despite changes in housing market conditions. Specifically, Kemeny describes how the political construction of a 'deep collectivist' social democratic hegemony has ensured that cost-rental housing interests ('social landlords') became institutionalised alongside profit-rental interests ('private landlords') within the housing policy-making process. This resulted in the development of a unitary rental market, where profit-making landlordism is allowed but tempered by competition from cost-rental landlords whose growth was actively encouraged, thus acting as a 'brake' – through competition – on the extraction of profit from rental housing. The key to what happens next lies in understanding the policies that are formulated to respond to the 'maturation process', which takes root when the mortgage debt owned by cost-rental 'social landlords' begins to mature, thereby allowing them to set lower rent levels. Under a social democratic or 'collectivist hegemony', the maturation process is regarded as a 'historic opportunity' to 'capitalise' on competition between cost-rental and profit-rental landlords in order to lower rent levels across the board for the citizenry, even during 'normal' times, when, according to Harloe, the 'logical' imperative is to facilitate profit extraction from the housing market. In Kemeny's world, then, the so-called 'logic' of capital accumulation fails to explain the operation of housing markets, whose functioning is a consequence of the manner in which social democratic hegemony has – or has not – been constructed. This point is brought into even sharper focus if we examine the quite different case of Britain.

Kemeny argues that Britain is different from Sweden for a number of reasons. First, he argues that the British Labour Party made the historic mistake of using state intervention to tackle inequality but, unlike the Swedish labour movement, failed to follow this up by devising a political strategy that was designed to embed principles of collectivism in housing policy. Kemeny refers to the political strategy of the British Labour Party as 'statist' and therefore 'shallow' (that is, based on the Fabian strategy of using the state to 'correct' housing market failures) rather than hegemonic (that is, based on a strategy of achieving moral leadership concerning the principles that should drive the operation of housing markets). Kemeny (1995) argues that this resulted in the emergence of a 'dualist' rental market in which a 'command economy' of state housing was seen as an alternative ('safety net'), rather than a competitor, to profit-making housing forms, such as private renting and home ownership. Furthermore, since rental interests became more or less split along party lines (state renting associated with the Labour Party; profit-renting associated with the Conservative Party), support for them has been subject to the electoral swings of a two-party system.

Now, although the statist political strategy of the Labour Party resulted in a 'command economy' of state housing, this did not *initially* cause problems for the sector. This was partly because state rent levels did not threaten profit-making landlords and partly because a one-nation, statist instinct dominated the Conservative Party until the early 1970s. The problem came, rather, during the 'maturation process' when state housing rents began to fall. This created a 'policy problem' for the Conservatives because it threatened profit-rental housing interests and so was seen to produce a 'rent-differential crisis' as opposed to a 'historic opportunity'. The Conservatives therefore forced state landlords into rent rises, and thus profit-making, prior to the more strategic response of the Thatcher government, which was to subject state housing to a process of retrenchment, for example through the introduction of the 'right to buy' council houses. For Kemeny, then, housing markets in Sweden and Britain have not been driven by the logics that underpin distinct 'phases' of capitalist development. They are the product of 'collectivist' ideologies whose distinct (unitary, dualist) manifestations reflected the nature of the political strategies (hegemonic, statist) adopted by the labour movement in each country. The important point to note overall, though, is that housing markets are driven by ideas that are mobilised by institutions (labour movements etc.) that are constituted from within, and represent, social class positions.

Weberian theories of class and stratification

Weber's account of the *class structure* of capitalist societies differs from Marx in that he emphasises the 'life chances' associated with different 'market situations' rather than the exploitative nature of the social relations of capitalist production (Crompton 1998: 33). The distinguishing feature of Weberian class analysis is a deductive mode of analysis that makes no a priori claims about the ontological reality of class, which is treated as an empirical question: do classes exist and, if so, how do we know? Weberians therefore focus on processes of class formation, that is, the conditions in which individuals do, or do not, form into social collectives. Weberians are therefore open to the idea that the working class might not exist (Scott 1996).

As a methodological individualist, Weber argued that all human phenomena (including class formation) had to be reducible to their individual constituents and explained in these terms. Applied to class analysis, Weber argued that this meant that 'we may speak of a class when (1) a number of people have in common a specific causal component of their life chances, in so far as (2) this component is represented exclusively by economic interests in the possession of goods and opportunities for income, and (3) is represented under the conditions of the commodity or labour markets' (Gerth and Mills 1998: 181). Thus classes can emerge and be spoken of in terms of a 'class' when the life chances of a significant number of individuals are situated within a similar 'market situation'. The 'market situations' that determine 'life chances' are influenced by three key components: property (with property classes based on owners and non-owners of property), skills and education.[3]

A particular focus of Weberian class analysis has thus been on 'market situations' within the structure of employment, since this encapsulates each of the three situational elements identified above – property (e.g. ownership, non-ownership or management of productive capacity) and skills and education (e.g. hierarchical position within labour process). For example, Lockwood (1958) identifies three 'market situations': labour market situation (source and size of income, degree of job security, opportunity for upward occupational mobility); work situation (position in the division of labour or exercise of authority); and status situation (position in the hierarchy of prestige in society at large). This interpretation of 'market situation' as an 'employment situation' provided a key influence on Goldthorpe and his colleagues (1980, 1987), who based one of the most comprehensive exercises in British class analysis on the 'employment relations' or 'employment aggregate' approach (Crompton 1998).

This brings us to the second key aspect of the Weberian approach to class analysis. Since Weberians hold that, *contra* Marx, no substantive claims can be made concerning the ontological reality of class, it follows that they also argue that, once classes are identified, the question of whether they think and act as classes (i.e. as a class 'for itself' as well as 'in itself') is contingent rather than inevitable. Whereas a key tenet of cultural Marxism is the notion that being = consciousness, then, Weberian approaches to class analysis are based on a conceptual separation of social structure (i.e. the objective dimension of class derived from an analysis of 'market situations' or, rather, 'employment situations') and consciousness (i.e. the subjective dimension of class derived from analyses of attitudes held by individuals sharing the same 'market situation'). It is for this reason that Weberian scholars such as Lipset and Benedix (1959) distinguish between theories of 'class formation' (i.e. whether classes exist 'in themselves') and theories of class action and conflict (i.e. whether classes act 'for themselves'). This distinction opens up some important empirical questions because these Weberians are effectively saying that classes are not inevitably 'for themselves' but, rather, represent *possible* bases for collective action. This explains why so much Weberian research has been focused on the question of whether class consciousness can be said to exist and, if it does, on understanding the conditions in which class consciousness develops and translates into collective action.

The key Weberian work on class consciousness was undertaken by David Lockwood (1958), who argued that three key 'situations' (market, work, status) were the principal determinants of class consciousness. A key purpose of Lockwood's research programme was to show whether and how different norms and values arose out of different market situations. He referred to this as the S-C-A (structure – consciousness – action) Model since it sought to explain how market situations gave rise to different modes of class consciousness and class action. For example, his paper on 'Sources of Variation in Working Class Images of Society' argued that individuals

> visualise the structure of their society from the vantage points of their own particular milieus and their perceptions of the larger society will vary according to their experiences . . . in the smaller societies in which they live out their everyday lives.
>
> (Lockwood 1966: 249)

Empirical work led him to the conclusion that specific working-class attitudes towards society could be detected that corresponded to the work and community situations occupied by many working-class people. For example, he identified a 'them and us' attitude (which he referred to as a 'traditional proletarian' standpoint) and a deferential attitude (which he referred to as a 'traditional deferential' standpoint). Nevertheless, research undertaken in the 1970s and since has shown, on the contrary, that many people do not have clear class attitudes. Sociological researchers working in the 1970s struggled to find workers that were consistently proletarian or deferential in their outlook. For example Howard Newby (1975) found that both standpoints were articulated by the same people at different points in time, which led him to conclude that no clear class consciousness existed. He argued that these views (e.g. deferential, proletarian) tended to appear in, and were specific to, particular situations that people were in rather than indicative of a shared consciousness of people occupying a similar market situation. In the light of this and other falsifying evidence, Lockwood (1996) started to downplay the role of class.

Goldthorpe (1998), who had previously worked with Lockwood on the 'affluent worker study' (Goldthorpe et al. 1968, 1969) took a different turn from that of his colleague by seeking to defend the idea of the class society – refusing, in any way, to submit to the idea of a 'death of class' or the 'new' post-materialist programme in sociology based on issues of individualisation, self-identity and so on (see Chapter 1). To construct a defence of class analysis in the face of evidence of a lack of class consciousness, Goldthorpe (1988) invoked 'rational action theory'. This enabled him to argue that a 'class for itself' is best identified through an analysis of the rational responses that individuals formulate in specific market situations, rather than in terms of shared attitudes and values that might be considered to form a 'class consciousness' (Goldthorpe and Marshall 1992). Even in the absence of a shared consciousness, then, a 'class for itself' could be said to exist if specific forms of rationality could be identified in the thoughts and actions of individuals occupying particular market situations.

The most famous example of Weberian class analysis in urban sociology was undertaken by Rex and Moore (1967), who took the view that classes consist of people in a common 'market position' and that, critically, the labour market is not the only foundation for class formation. For Rex and Moore, the housing market provided an alternative site in which classes formed. Housing classes consisted of households that shared the same housing market situation. Rex and Moore identified six housing classes: (1) outright owners, (2) mortgaged owners, (3) council tenants, (4) private renters, (5) tenants in lodging houses, (6) owners compelled to let to meet loan repayments. Notwithstanding a variety of critiques of this 'housing classes' schema (see Morris and Winn 1990), it has stimulated a debate about housing classes *and* whether housing classes possess a collective consciousness or, at least, act rationally in relation to their housing market position.

Although there has historically been a strong correlation between tenure and voting, that is, between home owners and the Conservatives and council renting and the Labour Party, it has been difficult to substantiate claims that this is indicative of a shared consciousness (Heath *et al.* 1985, 1991). For example, it is methodologically difficult to determine whether shared consciousness influences tenure choice or vice versa (Heath *et al.* 1985, 1991). To complicate the matter even further, political attitudes do not necessarily map onto tenure anyway. This is because working-class culture has always been strongly associated with home ownership as well as council renting (Devine 1992; Gurney 1996; Fisk 1996), whereas the spread of home ownership during the last three decades has brought about an even more ambiguous relationship between housing and class (Saunders and Williams 1988).

So, Weberian scholars have found it difficult to substantiate the claim that housing classes 'in themselves' (e.g. owner occupiers, council renters) share a common world view that might transform them into housing classes 'for themselves'. However, they have faced less severe problems in establishing housing classes as 'rational actors'. This has been demonstrated by Heath *et al.* (1989, 1990[4]) in studies of housing tenure and voting patterns. These studies show that changes in 'housing market situation' result in a change in voting patterns, with Labour voting in the 1980s declining at a dramatic rate for tenants who had purchased their council housing. Importantly, Heath *et al.* also point out that households that had exercised their 'right to buy' occupied different positions in the employment structure when compared with those that continued to rent. This suggests individuals do act in ways that are rational to their 'market situation', but that 'housing classes' are sub-categories of employment classes (i.e. microcosms of the employment structure rather than independent variables), which remain the ultimate level of class analysis and explanation:

> This evidence further questions the validity of the position that ownership of domestic property creates a status group which cuts across and undermines class divisions [emanating from occupational situation].
>
> (Morris and Winn 1990: 72)

Nevertheless, further evidence in support of the notion that people behave in ways that are rational to the *broad* market situation that they are in is supplied by Johnston (see Morris and Winn 1990), who has shown that variations in patterns of voting are also a result of economic situation *combined with* tenure situation. Thus Johnston has identified that the Conservative Party tends to poll better among owner occupiers in prosperous areas, with the Labour Party polling better among people in the same tenure in depressed areas. Johnston claims that such voting patterns are perfectly rational given that they are driven by broad considerations of 'market situation', e.g. the material advantages associated with being an owner occupier living in a prosperous and therefore higher price area: 'local context was apparently an important influence on how people interpreted being working class, in both major housing tenures' (Johnston, quoted in Morris and Winn 1990: 73–4).

'New' sociological theories of class: consumption cleavages

Weberian scholars have primarily identified 'employment situation' (and therefore positioning within the production process) as the key indicator of social class. However Weberian scholars have also attempted to identify social class through analyses of 'consumption situations'. The most prominent example of this can be found in the work of Rex and Moore (1967). They identified how the occupation of distinctive 'housing market situations' resulted in the emergence of a series of distinctive 'housing classes'. Attempts to identify distinctive 'housing class rationalities' that would verify the empirical existence of 'housing classes' have been moderately successful, with some work showing consistencies in voting patterns amongst people in similar housing (and labour) market situations. So Weberians have not simply been satisfied with specifying class as a productive category, that is, a function of the labour market or work situation that individuals find themselves in. Some Weberians argue that social class formation also takes place within the field of consumption (e.g. housing market situations), which Saunders (1986) argues is becoming more rather than less important as a source of social stratification.

For Saunders (1986, 1990) the importance of consumption as a source of class formation and social stratification can be traced to the emergence and advance of the welfare state. Since then, the major axes of differentiation have been located not simply in the sphere of production but, because of welfare expansion, also in the field of consumption with some households being able to satisfy their needs and desires through personal ownership whereas others are forced to rely on collective provision via the state. That said, the 'new' focus on consumption within class analysis has resulted in the emergence of a research agenda that has been dominated by a concern with middle-class formation and fragmentation (Slater *et al.* 2004; Slater 2006). This is because middle-class households have the resources to devote to consumption, whereas for many working-class households a devotion to consumption remains a fantasy (cf. Bourdieu 1984; Charlesworth 2000).

Sociology of consumption and middle-class analysis

Middle-class analysis undertaken within a 'sociology of consumption' framework tends to invoke conventional conceptions and definitions of the 'middle class', i.e. derived from location within the employment structure. Weberian

understandings of the nature of this employment location are used to identify the 'characteristics' of the middle class, which are then used to explain its
associated patterns of consumption. The strength of the relationship between
location within the occupational structure and patterns of consumption is
therefore emphasised (cf. Hamnet 1989).

Theoretical debates about a 'service class' started as early as the 1930s
but really took off in the 1980s as the service class underwent a period of
massive expansion (Savage *et al.* 1992). Specifically, Marxists such as Renner
have argued that the decline of the 'family firm' and therefore owner manager,
especially in the 1930s, provided the context from which a 'service class' of
'salaried' managers emerged (Savage *et al.* 1992; Turner 1996). It follows that
this service class can be conceptualised in terms of the functions it performs for
capital or the capitalist class, that is, in terms of its functional importance for
capital accumulation and capitalism. Although the service class participates in
the exercise of authority, which is delegated to it by 'the firm', then, it does not
'possess' authority as such (Watson and Barth 1964). The 'delegated authority' that the service class exercises on behalf of capital includes the supervision
or surveillance of labour, control over the means of production, control over
labour power and control over investment (see also Braverman 1974). The distinct nature of this service relationship (to capital) has led Goldthorpe (1982)
to argue that 'trustworthiness' is the defining characteristic of the service class:

> [E]mployees to whom authority is delegated or to whom responsibility for specialist
> functions is assigned are thereby given some legitimate area of autonomy and discre-
> tion . . . . [It is] a matter of *trust* that they will act, i.e. will make decisions, choices,
> judgments, etc. – in ways that are consistent with organizational goals and values
> . . . . [This demands] their moral commitment to the organization.
>
> (Goldthorpe 1982: 169, quoted in Butler 1997: 22)

Although Marxists and Weberians agree that 'trust' is a defining characteristic of the service class, Weberians make additional points about the
characteristics of the service class that arise from its 'market situation' more
generally and not simply, therefore, its functional position as defined by the
'service relationship'. Specifically, Weberians such as Goldthorpe (Goldthorpe
et al. 1987) argue that 'service class' is a term that is used to describe a relatively
broad group of managers, professionals and administrators that occupy similar
work and market situations. As well as occupying positions that require the
exercise of authority, then, they have relatively high and secure incomes that are
likely to rise considerably during the course of their working life. Taken together,
then, these employment characteristics define the patterns of consumption of

the service class since 'political opinions, patterns of consumption, of work activity and so forth tend to fall into the bureaucratic net' (Presthus 1971: 151). And given this commonality of economic interest, the service class will act in defence of its economic privileges, which means that its general outlook will be conservative and supportive of the status quo (Goldthorpe 1982: 180). This is certainly a theme running through the work of Whyte (1957), who argued that 'organization man' has a tendency towards inconspicuous consumption and, therefore, a preference for the bland conformity of suburbia, where the priority is not to break ranks with the group norms and cultural practices. It is also evident in the work of Oliver *et al.* (1981), which paints a picture of 'organization man' living through the inter-war years in a semi-detached house on a suburban estate where he seeks to 'keep up with the Jones' but takes little interest in the distinctive character of his house.

Sociology of consumption and the formation of 'new' middle classes

What is clear from the above is that the service class has always been defined by its consumption practices as much as locations within the occupational structure, even though analyses of its consumption practices did not feature strongly in earlier analyses of class formation. Furthermore, the service class has grown from 5 per cent of the British population in the early decades of the twentieth century to approximately 25 per cent of the population by the end of the twentieth century (Butler 1997). The expansion of the service class has been so dramatic during the last few decades that Savage *et al.* (1992) have argued that it has become economically, socially and culturally the most dominant social group in contemporary Britain. (This will become apparent in my discussion of the 'Tyranny of Suburbia' in Chapter 4.) The expansion of the service class has occurred on the back of a growth and diversification of its occupational structure, with the rapid emergence and expansion of media, advertising, property services and so on (Lash and Urry 1994). The extent of this expansion has meant that the service class has had to recruit from other social classes. For example, Goldthorpe (1982) found that only one-third of a sample of people in service-class positions were the offspring of parents who had also held service-class positions.

Now we might expect that this expansion of the service class and, especially, recruitment from other classes could result in a diversification of consumption practices that would result in a fragmentation of the middle class. However, this is not straightforwardly the case. Work undertaken on the 'new' middle class by Wynne (1998) is instructive here. Nearly half of Wynne's households are best described as service-class households that have been recruited from the working class. Specifically, they were a recently affluent (socially and geographically mobile) grouping that owed their membership of the 'new' middle class to a series of promotions in the workplace that were made possible by the expansion of service industries and growth of white collar positions in the occupational structure. Although they had levels of educational qualification that were higher than for the general population, then, they had not amassed educational qualifications (i.e. there were few university graduates) and had progressed into the middle class as a consequence of occupational mobility rather than possession of educational capital. (We will see why this is important later in the chapter.) It is on these grounds that Wynne describes them as 'kids of the 1950s and 1960s' that had 'made good'.

An examination of the lifestyles and consumption practices of Wynne's 'new' middle-class households indicates a remarkable level of consistency with previous generations. Despite the recent diversification of household types, with many young middle class people either deferring or rejecting the idea of 'marriage and children' (Giddens 1992), Wynne's (1998) 'new' middle-class households were very conventional. They were predominantly composed of families with children and operated with traditional gender roles, with women undertaking most of the domestic tasks.[5] Conspicuous consumption was the hallmark of these households. They enjoyed a lifestyle based on the possession of consumer durables of a consistently high material standard, which demonstrated that they were materially successful. For example, they were all home owners with properties in the highest priced categories within a typical suburban development, 'The Heath'. Wynne's 'new' middle classes are therefore those for whom consumption symbolises their socio-economic position, that is, those for whom economic wealth is invested in forms of consumption that display economic wealth, thereby symbolising a socio-economic position that has been achieved within the employment structure. Yet, routes into the middle class have been more varied than those captured by the work of Wynne.

For instance Savage *et al.* (1992) have shown that the middle class is fragmented around three different middle-class lifestyles: (a) the 'indistinctive' lifestyles of 'organization man'; (b) the post-modern lifestyle of private sector professionals; and (c) the ascetic lifestyles of educated state professionals. We have already seen that a large element of middle-class growth has occurred as a consequence of the growth of the service class, that is, through the expansion of 'white collar' occupations such as insurance, finance and banking, which have been a major source of economic growth in many urban centres (Giordano and Twomy 2002). Savage *et al.* (1992) argue that this element of the middle class owes its class position to its possession of 'organizational assets', whose acquisition is a consequence of possession of characteristics such as 'trustworthiness'. This is why Savage *et al.* (1992) describe their consumption patterns as 'indistinctive', particularly those of 'managers'. However, Savage *et al.* (1992) go further than this and describe the consumption patterns of other 'private sector' professionals in possession of 'organizational assets' (that is, who owe their position to promotions within the career structure of private sector organisations such as banks and finance houses) as post-modern. They may opt for houses in suburbia, then, but they also use their economic wealth (relatively high incomes, bonuses, dividends etc.) to engage in a post-modern lifestyle based on the 'sampling' of a wide variety of cultural activities. Typical forms of consumption that are sampled are health clubs, windsurfing, water-skiing, tennis, golf, champagne drinking, the night-time economy – all activities that demand a relatively high income (Savage *et al.* 1992). Thus high incomes are used to engage in the type of 'conspicuous consumption', also identified by Wynne (1998), which is used to symbolise and buttress a 'middle-class' position that has been achieved in the labour market.

However, Savage *et al.* (1992) point out that the middle class has also grown as a result of the huge expansion of welfare fields such as health, social work and education. They argue that this professional element of the middle class is in possession of a distinctive asset base, which means that the new middle class is actually fragmented rather than cohesive. The expansion of higher education is particularly relevant to our concerns here. Now, the intention of successive governments in the 1960s and 1970s was to stimulate growth in science and technology subjects, yet the largest expansion took place in the humanities and social sciences, which, incidentally, ran parallel to the expansion of 'expressive professions', such as social work, in the same period (Butler 1997; Walter 1994). Since those who entered the middle class via higher education and subsequent careers in the so-called 'expressive professions' owe their social position to their possession of 'cultural assets' (e.g. education, knowledge), rather than 'organizational assets', they develop different orientations to consumption.

The consequences of this can be seen in the dramatic lifestyle differences between post-16 school leavers who owe their middle-class position to 'organizational assets' and those who complete their education after the age of 21 and owe their middle-class position to the possession of 'cultural assets'. The latter tend to indulge in 'things foreign' such as exotic restaurants and holiday in 'sophisticated' localities in Western Europe. Those completing their education after the age of 24 (i.e. after receiving a postgraduate education) are more likely to engage in older, high forms of culture such as opera, classical concerts, plays and art galleries as well as foreign restaurants (Savage *et al.* 1992: 112). With high levels of cultural capital and relatively modest levels of economic capital, this element of the middle class rejects the post-modern embrace of 'high living' (the preference for 'sampling', which they could not afford anyway) in favour of an authentic relation to cultural consumption that is incorporated into a lifestyle rather than merely sampled (Lash and Urry 1994; Warde 1994; Warde *et al.* 1999).

The important point to emerge from all of this is that middle-class positioning is no longer obviously 'linked either to property or organizational position . . . . [S]tyles of consumption and commitment [have] become socially salient as markers and delimiters' and therefore a key source of class formation and social stratification (Pakulski & Walters 1996: 156; also Lash and Urry 1987). This, in turn, produces its own dynamic, which creates a high level of instability in class formations. Specifically, middle-class households that owe their social position to the possession of 'organizational assets' are not able to straightforwardly assert their middle-class position through their mobilisation of economic capital in the service of conspicuous consumption. This is because the 'cultured' middle class (who are unable to assert their middle-class position through the possession of economic capital) engage in a struggle for recognition via engagement in 'authentic' forms of consumption that, by implication, challenge the hegemonic legitimacy of 'indistinctive' and 'conspicuous' forms of consumption preferred by other fragments of the middle class. Bourdieu (1984) refers to these as 'struggles for distinction', which Lash and Urry (1987, 1994) take to imply the succession of consumer capitalism constituted on the consumption of 'products' with a form of consumer capitalism that is constituted on the consumption of 'signs' (see also Clarke 2003). Key actors in contemporary consumer capitalism are the 'new' middle class (or 'sign producers'), who use their economic and cultural capital to establish new systems of classification. So how does this happen?

As 'positional goods' such as foreign holidays, designer sportswear or semi-detached houses in suburbia are brought within reach of an ever widening circle of consumers, they lose their value as sources of distinction. Conventional elements of the middle class have sought to maintain their distinction in the face of this by deploying their high levels of economic capital in new ways, for example, 'buying into' 'gated communities' that place ever greater *spatial distance* between themselves and generalised others (Atkinson and Flint 2004). However, as positional goods are brought within the reach of a wider range of consumers, elements of the new middle class who possess high levels of cultural capital (as opposed to economic capital) deploy their assets to achieve *cultural distinction* (Featherstone 1991). For this element of the new middle class, consumption is not contingent on their positioning within the employment structure but as a consequence of their socialisation within the education system (Butler 1997; also Savage *et al.* 1992; Reay 2001a, Reay *et al.* 2001). Consumption practices are not so much used to symbolise and embed class position that is a consequence of the acquisition of 'organizational assets' (e.g. by using a high income to purchase a home in an expensive 'gated community' development). On the contrary, they are a product of the possession of cultural capital which enables them to *construct* and *establish* 'new middle-class' positions despite having only relatively modest economic resources (Crompton 1998).

Now, although 'organization man' or 'post-modern' households can use their economic muscle to insert a *spatial distance* between themselves and generalised others (e.g. by living in a 'gated community'), they are less well equipped to meet the *cultural challenge* presented by the educated middle class who, as 'sign producers', denigrate their consumption practices (gated communities, mock Tudor houses) as 'crude' and lacking in 'taste'.[6] This potentially destabilises the 'conventional' middle class by undermining its claim to be recognised as *the* middle class. For the educated middle class, then, the sphere of consumption is the key site in which struggles for distinction are played out and not simply a site in which taken-for-granted dominance is asserted vis-à-vis generalised others. The consumption strategies of the educated middle class have ensured, then, that the significance of 'culture' has been elevated in the process of class formation and structuring (Crompton 1998). It is a key site in which class struggle is played out (Sayer 2002, 2005; Haylett 2003; Lawler 2005a). This is best seen in the middle-class analysis literature in urban sociology that focuses on the gentrification of housing within inner-urban areas of the major cities that host the 'cultivated' middle class in large numbers, such as London, Manchester and Bristol (Giordano and Twomy 2002).

Middle-class analysis in urban sociology

The term 'gentrification', which was originally employed by Glass (1964) to describe the practice of renovating and restoring houses, invites theoretical controversy between those who claim that it is a capital investment led process (e.g. Smith 1979) and those who claim that it is a consumption led process (e.g. Ley 1996). The former emphasise the significance of the emergence of a gap between the current rentable value of land and its potential value ('rent gap'), particularly within inner-city areas that have been abandoned by both industry and people, since this ensures that they are ripe again for capital investment and profit-making (Smith 1979). However, the 'rent gap' thesis has been subjected to critique for failing to appreciate the role that people have played *alongside capital* in the gentrification process (Hamnet 1984). This problem is addressed within the comsumption led approach, which rejects the notion that urban changes, such as gentrification of inner-urban areas, can be explained with reference to the logic of capital investment or via recourse to economic approaches to housing market analyses of supply and demand, which are equally problematic (Butler 1997). Consumption led approaches to gentrification are based on the critical claim that changes in the economic and social structure (in particular, the emergence of an educated middle class) has created a constituency that is relatively poor in economic capital but rich in cultural capital. Unable to afford to live in suburbia, and not very well disposed towards it anyway, this element of the middle class have placed themselves in inner-urban areas for a variety of reasons. This argument has been elaborated in the work of several urban sociologists and urban geographers such as Savage *et al.* (2005), Butler (1997; Butler with Robson 2003a), Ley (1996) and Zukin (1982), to name but a few.

For Butler (1997), changes in the structure of the middle class are critical to properly understanding gentrification. In work undertaken in London, Butler describes his respondents as highly educated and points to

> a particularly skewed occupational structure which comprises highly credentialised professional and administrative workers. It is a fascinating list involving not only the traditional professions, notably the law, but many of the newer semi-professions – welfare and education. Perhaps more interestingly is the large number working in design and marketing, the media and the systems side of new technology. It also includes more than a splattering of musicians, opera singers and therapists. What they share as individuals is many years of higher education and a belief in what Gouldner has termed the 'culture of critical discourse'.
>
> (Butler 1997: 95)

Ley (1996: 197) similarly notes how data from six Canadian cities shows that those who gentrify and occupy the central spaces of all of the cities are

> artists and related professions . . . . The artists are followed by: in second rank, social science professionals, third by religion, fourth by medicine and health, fifth by teaching, sixth by natural sciences and seventh, some distance behind the rest, by managerial and administrative occupations . . . . Graduates of business school, traditional in their values, and as primarily private sector managers and administrators [are] more likely to be suburban in their residential choice.

What is clear from this, then, is that households responsible for gentrification of inner-urban areas emanate from the element of the middle class that is highly educated and whose members tend to follow careers in 'expressive professions' such as art, performance, social work, health care and education (also Zukin 1982). What is less clear from this is why, specifically, this element of the middle class chooses to (re)occupy the central city *and* what implications this has for our understanding of class formation and fragmentation. Savage *et al.* (2005) are instructive here. Savage and colleagues employ the concept of 'elective belonging' to understand the relationship between people and place, both of which possess their own biographies, which, it follows, correspond in situations where people make choices to occupy a place and feel 'at home'. As places to which people attach their own biography, 'chosen' residential locations are sites for 'performing identity' (Savage *et al.* 2005).

The key thing here is that the housing choices of this element of the new middle class are said to be informed by 'cultural' considerations rather than conventional 'economic' considerations. On the one hand, it is clear that these new middle-class households tend to be vanguards of the critique of mass culture and thus stand in cultural opposition to suburbia, which they tend to describe as 'bland', 'boring' and so on (Ley 1996; Butler 1997). This comes through clearly in the testimony provided by one of Butler's respondents: 'We hate suburbia . . . . It's all the same, we have got for example some relatives who live in Southgate and we get lost every time we go there' (Butler 1997: 119). It also comes through in the way strictly labour or housing market reasons such as 'trading up' or job related moves were relatively unimportant to Butler's sample of 'new' middle-class households involved in the gentrification of Hackney. Fewer than 10 per cent of his respondents claimed to have regarded their move into a gentrifying area as an opportunity for capital accumulation, although under one-third agreed that it was a consideration and there was a general awareness of property appreciation about which some respondents were even embarrassed. Furthermore, although travel to work and cost reasons were not insignificant, they were rarely the deciding factors (Butler 1997: 113). On the contrary Butler argues that his sample of new middle-class households made a conscious decision to occupy the area *because of the feel of the area* (cf. Savage *et al.* 2005).

Research evidence suggests not only that this element of the new middle class rejects 'mass culture' but that the 'cultural competence' of its members ensures that they possess a form of cultural power that compensates, in the housing market, for a lack of economic power. Savage *et al.* (2005) thus describe their educated respondents as unusually reflexive and 'knowing' about why they wanted to move to gentrifying areas. They ignored 'brochure knowledge', which portrays neighbourhoods within a conventional hierarchy of area status and, instead, were able to tap into 'hot' knowledge and information about such areas from within their educated social networks. For Savage *et al.*, then, their incomer stories were rich with information derived from contacts within their educated social networks, which demonstrates 'the power of cultural capital to provide confidence in individual judgments . . . knowledge derived from social capital ties and connections allows [them] to exactly pick out where they want to live' (Savage *et al.* 2005: 92).

Although cultural power is *derived* from social networks that are laden with cultural judgments (friends from university and so on), cultural power is also manifest in the way that it is mobilised within the urban economy. Cultural power can be seen to be mobilised within the sphere of consumption in two inter-related ways. First, members of the new middle class who are well endowed with cultural capital possess the conceptual instruments of appropriation that enable them to know *what* forms of consumption are 'correct' and *how* to engage with those forms of consumption (Lash and Urry 1987, 1994). A good example here would be a 'taste' for classical music born of the knowledge that it is the 'correct' form of music and the knowledge of how to engage with it, i.e. how to appropriate it, appreciate it, talk about it to others etc. Mobilising cultural capital in the service of appropriating distinctive forms of culture is integral to new middle-class positioning strategies, as we have seen. Second, cultural power is mobilised to valorise 'new' practices of consumption and thereby establish new systems of classification that become a focus for establishing new modes of distinction (Lash and Urry 1987, 1994). This is nowhere more apparent than in the gentrification literature, which is replete with references to the way some middle-class people are able to mobilise their cultural capital and, in doing so, impose new cultural interpretations and judgments on buildings that were previously lacking in social and economic value within a housing market context. This certainly comes through in the work of Zukin (1982), who discusses how artists appropriated – as living and work space – and thereby transformed the cultural value of 'ugly' warehouse lofts in New York. It is also evident in Allen's (2007b) work on the 'renaissance' of Manchester city centre in England and Ley's (1996) work on the gentrification of Canadian cities, which discusses how the valorisation of ugly landscapes constitutes an important strategy for the new middle class, whose members have

> an aesthetic eye that transforms ugliness into a source of admiration, that reshapes common, scorned, and used objects into icons of desire. Aesthetic distancing, a quality well-developed among social and cultural professionals, contains the creative power of transformation. Such an aesthetic sensibility is found particularly among social groups rich in cultural capital but poor in economic capital. At the core of such groups is the urban artist.
>
> (Ley 1996: 310)

Savage demonstrates the distinctive nature of this ability to valorise the ugly in his work on Manchester (Savage *et al.* 2005), which discusses how different elements of the middle class were divided in their views on the city. Elements of the middle class that were low in cultural capital identified negatively with the city, citing problems such as the ugliness of the urban landscape or crime. Residents with high levels of cultural capital, on the other hand, felt very differently about the city and were more likely to 'pick out' its aesthetic qualities as well as the quality of its cultural infrastructure, which includes classical music venues, foreign restaurants and so on (Savage *et al.* 2005; also Ley 1996). This is demonstrated in the work of Butler (1997), who talks about how key reasons for living in Hackney were related to its aesthetics ('the style of the architecture') as well the importance of heritage to this element of the middle class, which has a particular distaste for modern imitations: 'preservation and gentrification thus appear to be inextricably linked' (Butler 1997: 109)

The notion that cultural power is constituted upon the mobilisation of what Bourdieu (1984) calls the 'judgment of taste', which has involved the appropriation of ugly spaces within the urban economy, highlights another aspect of gentrification. Appropriating and transforming 'ugly' urban spaces implies that new middle-class housing strategies of gentrification are also strongly associated with the restoration of architecture (Glass 1964). This has led Zukin (1982) to argue that the historical urban fabric has become a commodity that the 'cultured' middle class 'work on' to express their distinction and thereby 'achieve' their elevated position within the class structure through the mobilisation of their 'judgment of taste', which is the exclusive preserve of 'the likes of them' (see also Butler 1997). The manner in which the judgment of taste is mobilised is evident in several gentrification studies that have identified the level of aesthetic renovation work that is associated with gentrification. For example, Butler (1997) notes how 10 percent of his sample of new middle-class households had totally 'gutted' their homes and how a further one-third had carried out more than five improvements. Copious amounts of money had been spent on improvement by his respondents, a key motivation for which was related to aesthetics and a concern to impose a sense of style (Butler 1997: 128). To this extent, Lash and Urry (1987, 1994) are quite right to suggest that consumer capitalism is about the consumption of 'signs' rather than the straightforward mobilisation of economic wealth in the market for goods, which is why Bauman (1988) refers to those who lack the conceptual instruments that would enable them to identify and appropriate the 'correct' consumption practices as 'failed consumers'. Nevertheless it is also important to note that some scholars contest claims made by members of this new middle class that capital accumulation is not a key motive for gentrification, by suggesting that artistic and cultural values can be a useful smokescreen for more blatant financial motives (Zukin 1998; Smith 1996).

What is clear from the discussion above, then, is that consumption of the urban fabric is critical to the ability of the new middle class to position itself within the class structure. The elements of the new middle class that are low in economic capital but well endowed with cultural capital cannot afford to achieve their class position by mimicking the suburban consumption practices of 'organization man'. (Many would not want to mimic these consumption practices even if they could afford to anyway.) This means that class position cannot be achieved via the mobilisation of economic capital in a way that symbolises (for example, via a house in the suburbs) a class position that has already been achieved as a consequence of a high salaried position within the employment structure. On the contrary, the element of the new middle class that is well endowed with cultural capital 'achieves' its class position via the value that its members are able to impose (through the mobilisation of their cultural power) on their own urban consumption practices. Urban consumption is not intended to symbolise position within the employment structure, then, but is a sphere within which the new middle class struggles to impose itself within the class structure and, in doing so, challenge the legitimacy of 'organization man' to be recognised as the dominant symbol of the middle class. This is recognised by Ley (1996), who argues that the act of valorising inner-urban space is indicative of the way in which struggles for distinction – within the middle class – are being played out between elements with different portfolios of capital:

> the assertion of such positional goods (including homes and neighbourhoods) represents conscious attempts by some members of the new middle class to separate themselves from landscapes of mass consumption, quintessentially the suburbs.
>
> (Ley 1996: 313)

Conclusion

This chapter has shown that social class has been theorised in a range of different ways. Conventional approaches to theorising class focused on positionality within the employment structure. The Nuffield paradigm and Marxist approaches to class analysis exemplify this approach. However, recent theorising in the field of class analysis has switched the focus of attention from positionality within the employment structure to the ways in which people from different social class backgrounds engage in consumption. We have seen, then, that class struggles take place within various fields of consumption, such as the market for houses. The conventional middle class has sought to establish its middle-class credentials by locating itself in expensive suburban areas whereas elements of the 'new' middle class have been associated with increasing levels of gentrification activity. Their valorisation of inner-urban areas represents a challenge to the cultural dominance of the suburban middle class, which shows how the market for houses has become an arena in which class struggles for cultural hegemony are played out. This analysis provides the context for the next chapter, which argues that the consumption focus of contemporary class analysis has skewed research attention towards those groups that can devote themselves to consumption, namely the middle class (Skeggs 2004, and in an urban sociology context Slater *et al.* 2004; Slater 2006). The purpose of the next chapter is to develop an insight into the constitution of the contemporary working class.

Part II

Social class and the market for houses

Chapter 3
Social class and the question of 'being'

Introduction

The notion that social class position is secured through housing consumption practices has been captured in the literature on gentrification of inner-urban areas of cities as varied as Manchester, New York and Toronto. Chapter 2 discussed how this literature has provided insights into processes of middle-class formation and fragmentation within urban housing markets. Although insightful, this literature nevertheless provides a partial and limited analysis of processes of social class formation within the context of the housing market. A number of lacunas are pertinent.

First, the gentrification literature focuses on the housing consumption strategies of the middle classes and, through this, processes of middle-class formation and fragmentation in the market for houses. Insofar as the working class appears in the gentrification literature it is as 'victims' of displacement. There is, then, a stark absence of literature that provides an insight into how working-class people relate to, and exercise agency within, the market for houses. Second, urban sociological and geographical accounts of gentrification emphasise how middle-class formation within the market for houses occurs through the mobilisation of various forms of resources that are referred to as 'capitals'. The overwhelming emphasis here has been on the way in which elements of the 'new' middle class have mobilised their 'cultural capital' within the housing field. Specifically, they have changed the dynamics of the housing field by imposing value on inner-urban spaces that were previously devoid of 'residential credential'. The nature of the impact that this has had on the market for houses is exemplified by the way in which the Chicago 'zone model' of the city has been inverted by these middle-class housing consumption practices: socially valued areas can now be identified within zones I (the Central Business District) and II (the inner-urban ring of working-class housing) that now possess 'high-value' places of residence. However this approach is less than useful to a project that seeks to understand how working-class people relate to the market for houses, not least because working-class people are 'lacking' in both economic and cultural resources (Charlesworth 2000).

My argument in this chapter is that an understanding of how working-class people relate to housing requires a theory of 'being' that must extend beyond an understanding of the resources (i.e. capitals, assets) that some households mobilise to secure a position for themselves in the market for houses. This requires an understanding of what it is like 'to be' working class, namely how the social world is experienced, perceived, felt *and most importantly grasped* by people occupying that class position. This chapter provides such an insight.

The limits of new sociological theories of class

Theories of class discussed in Chapter 2 have two key limits. First, the consumption focus of the new cultural sociology of class represents a welcome change from the narrow focus on class as a productive category. However, a focus on patterns of consumption in diversifying product markets (including housing) has, perhaps inevitably, resulted in a focus on consumers who are *actively* engaged in negotiating their way through those complex product markets. In other words, the sociology literature on consumption and class is largely a literature about consumption and the middle class. This is most apparent in the work of sociologists such as Mike Savage and colleagues (e.g. Savage *et al.* 1992, 2005), who have invested serious effort into understanding what the consumption patterns of the middle class mean for middle-class formation and fragmentation in contemporary Britain. Insofar as working-class people appear in the sociology of consumption literature, this is as 'failed consumers'; that is, they are represented as a social group that *desires* and *tries* to adopt middle-class styles of consumption but, as a class that lacks cultural capital that would enable them to decipher the 'correct' way to consume, their consumption practices are inevitably doomed to failure. This approach is clearly evident in the work of Skeggs (1997, 2004) and others. The sociology of consumption literature tells us little, then, about how working-class people consume *on their own terms* because their consumption is always situated in relation to other groups, as 'failed'. Yet the material presented in the remainder of this book will show that working-class people do not always situate their consumption practices in relation to other (middle-class) social groups. Working-class consumption practices have their own internal economy that needs to be understood *on its own terms* (Haylett 2003).

This brings me to the situation with class analyses of housing consumption, which is the particular form of consumption that I am addressing in this book: the sociological focus on middle-class consumption is replicated in urban sociology, which has been narrowly concerned with the issue of middle-class gentrification (Slater *et al.* 2004; Slater 2006). Insofar as working-class households appear in this gentrification literature, they do so as victims of the actions of middle-class households ('displacement') rather than agents in their own right. So, again, we are told very little about how working-class people feel about, and consume, houses. The purpose of the remainder of this book, then, is to understand how working-class people relate to their own houses, as well as the market for houses more generally, *on their own terms.*

Now to the second issue to emerge from my discussion of theories of class in Chapter 2, which is epistemological. Sociology literatures on consumption and class formation have, perhaps inevitably, been influenced by Bourdieu's work in this area (especially Bourdieu 1984). This has involved an overt focus on the portfolio of capitals (economic, social, cultural etc.) that make up the class habitus. For example, the work of Savage *et al.* (1992) distinguishes between elements of the middle class that are rich in 'organisational capital' and those that are rich in 'cultural capital'. Work in urban sociology is similarly focused on the class habitus as a mechanism for the accumulation, storage, transmission and deployment of capitals. Thus middle-class households involved in inner-urban gentrification (rich in cultural capital, poor in economic capital) have been distinguished from suburban middle-class households (rich in economic capital, less well endowed with cultural capital) by virtue of their portfolio of capital. Since working-class households are, by definition, less well endowed with most of the 'capital' assets and resources that middle-class households possess, the question arises of whether an epistemological focus on 'capital' is appropriate to a study of how working-class people relate to the market for houses.

Now, although I am arguing that Bourdieu's capital schema is less than appropriate to studies of how working-class people relate to the market for houses, I want to suggest that it is limiting for other reasons too. Specifically, studies of middle-class formation and fragmentation – especially those studies that have focused on gentrification and middle-class formation – primarily treat habitus as a product of positioning within systems of production or consumption. This is probably a consequence of the way in which debates about class formation have been played out in relation to positionality within the changing employment structure and, more recently, consumption practices. Indeed recent studies have tended to connect position in the employment structure *to* styles of consumption. We must acknowledge, of course, that education has also intruded into the relation between employment and consumption in most recent studies of class formation. For example, gentrification studies have made much of the occupational and educational origins of those involved in the gentrification of inner-urban housing. Yet, for Bourdieu (1977), habitus is a form of 'being-in-the-world' that is *not* simply a product of positioning within systems of production, education and consumption but, rather, social space *writ large*. We need to discuss this conception of 'being' in more detail before we can move on.

Social class and the question of being

The question of being has been addressed by existential phenomenologists such as Heidegger (1962), Merleau-Ponty (1962, 1964) and Bourdieu (1977, 1990, 2000), for whom everyday 'involvement' in social space produces perceptions and concerns that are products of, and oriented towards, objective positions occupied in social space. These involvements and concerns provide human beings with a 'practical sense' of what it is *to be*, which becomes manifest in a background structure of intelligibility that is oriented towards, and compatible with, involvement in the social space that is occupied. This correspondence between involvement, concern and intelligibility results in a form of intentionality that is projected towards what is 'there for me' in social space and so, conversely, refuses the things that appear to exist beyond grasp (Heidegger 1962; Bourdieu 2000). This is what Bourdieu (1977, 1990, 2000) means when he refers to habitus ('being') as a 'generative scheme' that only allows us to grasp what is there 'for the likes of us' who occupy such positions in social space:

> As an acquired system of generative schemes objectively adjusted to the particular conditions in which it is constituted, the habitus engenders all the thoughts, all the perceptions, and all the actions consistent with those conditions, and no others . . . . [T]he habitus is an endless capacity to engender products – thoughts, perceptions, expressions, actions – whose limits are set by the historically and socially situated conditions of its production.
>
> (Bourdieu 1977: 95)

Thus 'being' is a way of existing that becomes manifest (embedded and present) in schemes of perception and bodily senses, which orients the manner of our concerned involvement in social space *to what it objectively is* and, therefore, provides us with a sense of our 'place' in the world: 'Being is being in, it is belonging to and being possessed' (Bourdieu, quoted in Charlesworth 2000: 80). This means that human beings, in their being, ordinarily comport themselves towards *their being* – not the being of others – in the way they realise themselves *in their own terms* in the social spaces that envelop them (Heidegger 1998).

Turning to our interest in social class, then, we can now say that we need to avoid conceptualisations of 'being' that are consonant with the middle class intelligentsia's 'concern' with *their own being* (accumulating capital, position-taking within the space of positions etc.), which is a product of its 'concerned involvement' in struggles for position in social space. On the contrary, we now need to concern ourselves with understanding the primary condition that constitutes working-class forms of being, which is present in the way working-class people talk about how they feel about, and encounter, the social spaces that devour them on an average-everyday basis. When we seek to understand the manner in which working-class people are primordially 'involved' in the world we are exposed to a level of proximity to economic necessity that the women below describe in terms of a constant 'struggle' for day-to-day survival.

> Everything costs money. We go shopping and then it's [husband's income as a chef] gone. I've got nothing, that's it. It's all gone straightaway before I've even thought about anything else. I mean we were just saying it's gone in one hand and straight back out the other.
>
> JA35

> We didn't really ask for anything, well we didn't because we always knew my mum was struggling. We were quite good kids, I think, you know when I think back, we were very considerate of her needs. We knew she didn't have money, so we didn't have to think about things we couldn't have.
>
> MP47

What is clear from this is not simply that working-class 'involvement' with the world is defined in terms of a *struggle for survival* (not a *struggle for position*), but also the manner in which this struggle for survival leaves its teeth marks firmly embedded within the being of working-class people. This is exemplified by the way in which one of the women, quoted above, talks about not even bothering to think about 'things we couldn't have'. This infinite level of complicity with the objective probabilities that are inscribed into working-class positions in social space is constitutive of the most basic aspect of working-class being, which consists of a circumscribed way of 'knowing' and 'living' that is inherited – through the occupation of marginal social spaces – rather than chosen (Charlesworth 2000, 2004, 2005, 2006; Allen 2007a).

'Just being'

Working-class complicity with the objective conditions that constitute their existence provides an insight into the manner in which the economic world consumes and possesses the being of working-class people. The brute fact that there is nothing other than what little is 'there for them' characterises what it means to 'be' working class, which is best articulated as a form of 'just being'.

By 'just being' I mean a form of being toward the world that is inscribed with the limited set of possibilities that are 'just there', and a form of comportment that 'just' grasps what is 'there' without reference to the wider set of possibilities that might exist but are hidden from the view of a form of intentionality so circumscribed. This is most evident in the form of comportment and intentionality that working-class people exhibit towards the labour market. Proximity to economic necessity and the urgent requirement to work that this implies had become so inscribed into the subjectivities of working-class people that the only relation to the labour market that they could articulate emphasised the perceived necessity for them to 'just take whatever work is there' in order to 'get by', rather than regarding their 'job prospects'. This meant that they were occupying some of the lowest and most insecure positions in the labour market (see Appendix II). Working-class people were, then, complicit in the reproduction of the insecure condition of their basic existence in the labour market. But that is not all. The historical conditions in which this working-class intentionality was constituted reinforced, in quite specific ways, the intentionality to 'just take whatever [low paid and insecure] work is there'. This is an important point that needs to be discussed in more detail.

Conventional wisdom within economic thinking is that the 'full employment' that existed in Liverpool in the 1960s and 1970s was beneficial to the working class and, to the extent that it provided the economic conditions in which working-class people could 'just work' to meet their basic needs, this is true. Yet a phenomenological view of full employment provides a very different insight into the working-class condition. Specifically, 'full employment' provided an economic context that was compatible with the imminent necessity for working-class people to 'just take whatever work was there' in order to 'get by'. This means, of course, that an economic context of full employment facilitated the realisation of the working-class intentionality to 'just work' in order to 'keep the wolf from the door'. Now, as Heidegger (1962) warns us, such a harmony between intentionality and the social world in which it is realised results in the adoption of a 'ready-to-hand' relation to what is 'there' in the social world. That is to say, we treat the limited possibilities that exist as 'ready and waiting' for us, which explains why, in a context of full employment, working-class people describe 'just falling into' whatever jobs 'just happened to be there' for them.

> Not a clue [about what job I wanted to do]. I had a job before I left school, to go to. The minute I left, I was working the next week, which you did in them days, but I didn't have any idea [about what I wanted to do].
>
> MP47

Yeah oh I couldn't wait to leave school. I just wanted to earn money . . . . I had no trouble [getting a job], you know . . . . I mean the jobs I had, they weren't I never really had good jobs 'cos I've never had qualifications so.

CS47

Oh yeah I was up there . . . . It was easy then wasn't it 'cos you could leave one job in the morning and start another one in the afternoon.

KB55

These working-class respondents' relation to the labour market was not simply governed by their proximity to economic necessity and concomitant availability of jobs that enabled them to manage their proximity to necessity on a day-to-day basis. Since a situation of 'full employment' was compatible with the imminent necessity for them to 'earn money' in order to 'get by', and little else, the situation of full employment reinforced the working-class intentionality to 'just take' whatever work was 'there' for them without needing to 'think about it'. Moreover, 'just taking' whatever work was there (rather than considering long-term 'job prospects') also reinforced working-class respondents' imminent relation to the future ('you just live from day to day'), which had required them to 'just take whatever work was there' in the first place. The significant point here is that working-class people who entered the labour market in the 1960s and early 1970s were simply not required to objectify their position in the labour market on leaving school ('no idea about what I wanted to do') because, quite simply, there were 'jobs there' for them. Although they 'could probably have done better' in principle, then, their intentionality to 'just work' (which was a product of their imminent relation to economic necessity) compelled them to take whatever jobs that were 'for the likes of them' rather than 'think about' the 'job prospects' that they might have otherwise had.

Q   Did you want to leave school when you were 15, then?
FS62   I think everyone did then 'cos there was jobs for you, you could choose your
        job, I could have done better maybe, I just didn't try hard enough maybe.

The corollary of the intentionality to just work 'out of necessity' is working-class indifference towards education: 'I think the attitude in them days . . . . I think my parents' attitude was, you know, you leave school, you get a job, you'll be alright then once you'd got a job.' Nevertheless, although full employment provided a context within which working-class people were able to manage proximity to economic necessity, the economic restructuring of the last few decades has resulted in the decimation of the industrial economic complex to which working-class dispositions were so oriented (Charlesworth 2000).

The industrial complex now lacks full employment opportunities that provide working-class people with a context within which they can realise their intentionality to 'just take' whatever work is 'there' for them. In its absence, working-class people are increasingly faced with an urgent requirement to objectify their relation to a post-industrial economic landscape that is now constantly moving beneath their feet. Within this changing historical context education has been elevated in its importance both in policy terms (e.g. 'widening participation' within higher education so that the workforce is prepared for the challenges of the new 'knowledge economy') and across the social classes. For example, recent studies have shown the extent to which middle-class households have become so preoccupied with schooling and education that it is now a driver of housing market behaviour as middle-class households seek to locate themselves within the catchment areas of 'good schools' (Butler and Robson 2003b; Savage *et al.* 2005). This literature also shows that these middle-class households understand the dynamics of the educational field, that is, the forms of capital and assets that can be extracted from it – and subsequently 'cashed in' to secure privileged positions within the labour market – as a result of making the correct investments in the right parts of the field.

The same is not true of working-class people in Kensington who have progressed through the education system during the last three decades. Although these working-class people can no longer be indifferent towards schooling (because performance therein is no longer dissociated from their ability to secure a position within the labour market), their attitudes towards school are very different from the attitudes towards education that the middle class have been reported to articulate (Butler and Robson 2003b; Savage *et al.* 2005). Specifically, with lives characterised by proximity to economic necessity, working-class people in Kensington described the urgency of their entering the labour market at school leaving age and, therefore, an instrumental relation to education, which they regarded as something that they just needed to 'get through' in order to secure 'a job' ('You've got to get your Maths and English'). This instrumental orientation to the perceived 'necessities' of education (that is, to simply achieve whatever is necessary to secure a position in the labour market), rather than a lack of 'talent',[1] resulted in working-class respondents' securing minimal levels of qualification (see Appendix II).

The consequences of this are manifest in the low and insecure positions that these working-class people occupy within the post-industrial labour market, for example call centres. Positionality in the contemporary labour market, then, is a consequence of a form of 'just being' whose concomitant lack of 'concern' for educational assets and 'job prospects' is a product of an imminent relation to necessity ('you just live from day to day'), which ultimately ensures that working-class people are complicit in their labour market positioning ('any job that pays the bills'). This can be seen in the way working-class people position themselves within the range of contemporary labour market opportunities that are 'for the likes of them' as the young woman below indicates in a discussion of her desire to work for a bank call centre rather than the National Trust call centre.

> I work for the National Trust, it's not very good, I'm actually looking to try and change it at the moment, I'm trying to get more into banks, 'cos I want to try and work my way up the ladder 'cos I haven't got an education behind me, so try and get into a bank call centre.
>
> AC19

This sense of possession by a world that inscribes its limited possibilities into the being of working-class people constitutes a very different form of being-in-the-world from that of the middle-class 'project of the self', which, on the contrary, implies possession of a world that consists of a infinite series of possibilities that are strategically incorporated into a 'life plan' (cf. Giddens 1991). Whereas middle-class people leave their mark on the world (as we saw in the earlier discussion of how 'new' middle-class gentrifiers have left their mark on the residential landscape of the contemporary city), we can now see how the world leaves its mark on the being of working-class people. These differences in classed forms of being are nowhere more apparent than in the way working-class respondents are unable to construct individualised narratives about their lives ('me-being') in the way that middle-class people do.

We-being

Skeggs (2004) and Robbins (1986) argue that the potential to construct 'personhood' and 'character' is a trait of the middle-class habitus and not a characteristic of late modern individuals more generally (cf. Giddens 1991). Only from the position of (and with access to the resources of) the middle class, then, can a presumption be made that there is a possibility, first, to construct an individualised project of the self, second, to assume the power to construct an individualised autobiographical narrative and, third, to assume a significance to the individualised autobiographical narrative (Skeggs 2004). Individualisation theory and the autobiographical methodologies that it sustains therefore represent the bourgeois privilege of self-possession in which being the competent author of one's life is a privilege of individualised forms of personhood (Marcus 1994). Indeed, for Skeggs (2004), this provides us with a way of understanding the post-class programme in late modern sociology. Skeggs (2004) rightly argues that individualised forms of being are actually *classed* forms of being that, unrecognised as such by some social theorists, are inappropriately universalised as *late modern* forms of being.

> [A]cademic agenda setters can be seen to embody what [Bourdieu] identifies as a *middle class habitus*. So, for him, a retreat from class is just the expression of the class interests of a group of relatively powerfully placed professional intelligentsia . . . . The knowledge class's own interests are actually based upon representing their own position, their perspective, their own cultural politics openly and without embarrassment. As Savage (2000) observes, this suggests that the kinds of [individualising] forces that Giddens sees as systemic, background features of late modernity might be better seen as exemplifying the embodied habitus of particular types of socially located individuals . . . . This exposes Beck's and Giddens' arguments as a particular kind of intellectual manoeuvre, a celebration of a cosmopolitan intellectual ethic, that can only be realized by a small minority of people. These 'new' speculations of Urry, Beck and Giddens, therefore, should be seen for what they are: that is, projects for intellectual aggrandizement. Class is displaced and effaced in these new modes of mobility and individualization, by the very people whose ideas are institutionalized and help to reproduce class inequality more intensely.
>
> (Skeggs 2004: 54)

Theories of individualisation are, then, constituted on an ontologically founded mode of knowing, that is, a middle-class form of being and therefore knowing. Moreover the representation of the *individualised* being of the middle class occurs 'openly and without embarrassment' because the privileged conditions in which middle-class life is conducted govern the perception of the intelligentsia that emerges from that class never more subtly than when they fail to recognise their social situation as especially privileged. This is because it leads to their production of grand theories of 'being' ('individualisation theory') that are constituted on their neglecting to recognise the particularity of the social conditions that constitute their own privileged forms of being and through which their theorising is mediated. The corollary of this is that the potential to narrate experience is unevenly distributed within the population, with working-class people (lacking in resources etc.) less able to present themselves as the subject of narrative. This comes across most clearly in the work of Byrne (2003), who has shown how women from different social class backgrounds in London were differentially able to resource the telling of themselves, with working-class women unable to draw on narratives of transformation and agency in accounting for their experiences.

Working-class people in Kensington were equally unable to articulate an autobiographical narrative of their lives. In contrast to middle-class people, who are well versed in articulating biographical accounts of their lives and for whom there is even an institutional requirement to do so (for example, the need to maintain a CV that demonstrates a coherent career trajectory), working-class people in Kensington were unable to respond to interview questions about their 'personal history'. Such questions met with either silence or the response that they were 'just an ordinary bloke' who had 'just had an average childhood' or a feeling that they had 'nothing interesting to say', resulting in concession of the social science interview to the social scientist: 'I'm in your hands'. The notion that working-class people position themselves as such in the social science interview ('I'm in your hands') is indicative of the recognition that they, the dominated, afford to the epistemic devices mobilised by the dominant (i.e. 'individualisation theory', e.g. 'tell me about yourself'), thereby ensuring the dominance of the dominated by the conceptual language and representations of the dominant, which, as I have argued, are separate in both social and linguistic terms from the working class.

Nevertheless, although possession by the *severely circumscribed* probabilities inscribed into the social spaces that working-class people occupy produces a 'just' form of being that is exemplified in barriers to their articulation of autobiography ('I'm just an ordinary bloke', 'I've never known what I wanted to do', 'you just live from day to day'), working-class people in Kensington are eminently able to articulate a narrative account of their lives-with-others. Despite being 'stumped' by questions about their own lives then ('My life is not very interesting. I haven't done anything'), working-class people in Kensington are able to provide free-flowing accounts of their lives-lived-with-others without much interruptive prompting ('there's so much I can tell you, some funny stories about this street', 'I could tell you lots of stories about the neighbours'). Working-class people articulate such narratives from a 'we' point of view that decentres themselves, the author, from the narrative. The 'we' in the narrative consists of family, neighbours and friends who have lived in close proximity to each other for their entire lives, that is, in the same street or 'community'.

> In any discussions of working class attitudes much is said of the group sense, the feeling of being not so much an individual with a 'way to make' as one of a group whose members are all roughly level and likely to remain so . . . [this feeling] arises from a knowledge, born of close living together, that one is inescapably part of a group.
>
> (Hoggart 1956: 68, 70)

There is nothing surprising about this because most accounts of working-class communities characterise them with reference to the strong 'social bonds' that are said to exist therein.[2] Indeed, this characterisation of working-class communities shaped much of the early sociological research programme into 'the working class', which consequently became focused on the working-class 'culture' of collectivism (Savage 2006). Although this eventually gave way to a focus on the 'occupational structure' of the working class and, in particular, the patterns of social mobility that led some to proclaim the death of the working class (see Chapters 1 and 2), the assumption that working-class communities can be characterised by strong social bonds remains canonical in contemporary social science. This was evident in the high level of 'neighbourliness' and inter-household cooperation to which working-class people from Kensington make constant reference. Now the important thing to note here is not the conditions of sociality themselves, but the form of being-in-the-world ('we-being') that is constituted in these conditions of sociality, as the respondent below suggests.

> I think it's the way you're brought up. We're just friendly with everybody. I mean we wouldn't turn anybody away you know, you wouldn't not speak to them or like 'You're from Manchester, you're a Man United fan, I'm not going to talk to you'. It's not like that. We're just born to be like that.
>
> SJ35

Urban sociology has conventionally focused on identifying whether conditions of sociality have endured in working-class communities (e.g. Forrest and Kearns 2001; Kearns 2004) rather than understanding the form of being that is constituted in, and constitutes, conditions of sociality. This is exemplified in the tendency of urban sociologists to examine the prevalence of inter-household cooperation in working-class communities rather than the form of working-class intentionality that produces such sociable practices (see Bridge *et al.* 2004 for a review of this literature), which is arguably more important to understanding working-class culture. What we are saying here, then, is that working-class people in Kensington possessed a 'we' form of being, that is, ethical dispositions towards their lives-with-others. The other important thing to note here is that the practical intentionality that is projected through 'we-being' actually reinforces 'just being' and therefore the occupation of marginal social positions. This can be seen if we examine how 'we-being' manifests itself in the practical intentionality that working-class people exhibit towards the education and labour markets.

Now we already know that working-class people in Kensington had an instrumental relation to education ('Just get your Maths and English') and that this was a consequence of the manner in which proximity to economic necessity provided them with an urgent need to secure a position within the labour market. However this instrumental relation to education was not simply a consequence of proximity to economic necessity. It was also enforced by 'we-being', since this compelled working-class people to judge schools according to their sociability rather than simply educational criteria, to which they exhibited distance (Reay 2001a, 2004; Reay *et al.* 2001). So, whereas middle-class people are known to make judgments of schools via reference to league tables and the type of subjects taught (e.g. literature, classics), working-class people are more likely to judge a school according to its 'friendly atmosphere'. Indeed the importance of the 'friendliness' of school is so important to working-class people that they even persevere with schools when the education provided therein is regarded as falling below acceptable standards.

> At the moment they're ready to go like into another class when they go back in September and now for like the third year I think it is running Jake hasn't had a stable teacher. Jake is like going into Year 4 now and this will be his second or third year where he hasn't had a teacher. They just keep bringing in like a supply and then after a couple of weeks she could be gone or she could be there for three months and then she'll be gone . . . . I'm sort of panicking over his education because I'm a bit too scared to take him out of school because he gets on with everyone and we've just had no problems, I've never had any problems with him in school . . . . I'm just scared that if I took him out of the school and put him in another school, you know, it could just change him.
>
> JE42

The point here is that 'we' forms of being require educational institutions to be 'friendly' and to make working-class people feel 'comfortable'. Since 'friendliness' is a key requirement, working-class people make 'choices' to remain at educational institutions where they feel comfortable even when they are not 'high performing'. This is something that Diane Reay has written about in a whole range of papers containing reams of data showing how working-class people judge educational institutions according to the level of comfort they feel even when the middle-class judges of educational worthiness might regard them as 'low-grade' institutions whose qualifications carry little value in the market for credentials (Reay 2001a, 2004; Reay *et al.* 2001). Moreover, in the same way that this form of 'we-being' towards schooling is enough to maintain working-class people 'in their place' in education markets, as this suggests, the same applies to positioning within the labour market. Thus working-class people who occupy even the apparently worst (low paid, insecure etc.) jobs define them as enjoyable so long as they are working in places that are populated by 'good people' and where they can 'have a laugh':

Q	How does that suit you being in a call centre?
AC19	Yeah I like it, it does suit me, I think it's like being . . . all just sitting there because I love my job.
Q	Do you? What is it about it that you love?
AC19	It's just all my workmates and everything.
Q	So you like the kind of social aspect of it?
AC19	Yeah.
AR39	It was good, factory . . . we'd all have a laugh.
Q	So did you like make friends there with the people you were working with?
AR39	Well I used to go out with quite a lot of them you know what I mean like, with the lads and all that from work.
Q	Yeah, after work kind of thing?
AR39	After work yeah, and every Friday.
Q	Right, was that more of a lads thing though?
AR39	Whoever wanted to tag along, you know what I mean it was one of them. From work like to the pub. There'd be some of the girls there and we'd end up in town and that like, so just who ever was up there. It was quite sociable actually, Bibby's.

Conclusion: social class and the housing question

This chapter commenced by arguing that an analysis of working-class being in the market for houses requires, as a first step, an existential understanding of working classness. The purpose of this chapter has been to provide an insight into working-class forms of 'being' in the world. The chapter commenced by showing that working-class people characterise their lives in terms of a close proximity to economic insecurity and necessity. This was shown to produce a form of being (or intentionality) that primarily encounters the world as an entity that makes an endless series of urgent demands on them, for example, to 'get by'. And as forms of being that are absorbed by the urgent demands that economic insecurity and necessity impose, working-class people talk about 'just' taking jobs 'to keep the wolf from the door' because they were 'there'. This is hugely significant because it implores us to recognise how 'just' forms of intentionality and comportment, which are constituted in the marginal spaces inhabited by working-class people, produce their complicity with their own marginality ('just' took that job because it was 'there') thereby ensuring the reproduction of their own class position.

Moving on, the chapter showed that 'just' forms of intentionality char-acterised a *wide range of working-class practices*, such as 'just' going to the local school because it was 'there' and 'ready and waiting' for them. The purpose of the next chapter is to show how working-class people also talk about 'just' buying their houses because they were 'there', dwelling spaces that were 'ready-to-hand' to them in all of their matter-of-factness. They were simply demanding to be bought by people who simply needed somewhere to live. That said, working-class forms of being cannot simply be characterised in terms of a disposition to 'just' grasp the world in terms of its basic essentials. Working-class testimonies also point to a form of 'we-being' that decentres the author of biographical narrative from the narrative itself. This point also has significance when we come to analyse working-class forms of being-toward housing in the next chapter. The essence of the point that will be made then is as follows: middle-class people have been said to use the market for houses to secure their class position. Working-class people, on the other hand, see houses in terms of their practicalities (dwelling space) and therefore 'just' buy what is 'practically there'. But they also regard their houses as sites where their lives-with-others are played out. Their houses are comfortable and welcoming ('we-being') rather than like the 'display houses' ('me-being') that middle-class households are said to prefer. This understanding of working-class forms of being-toward the market for houses becomes particularly important when we move on to discuss 'housing market renewal' in Part III of the book.

Chapter 4
Being in the market for houses

Introduction

The level of 'interest' in the market for houses is arguably at an all-time high. This is reflected in the sheer number of programmes about house purchase, selling and renovation that can now be seen on TV screens. The content of such programmes demonstrates that housing is now regarded as a form of consumption that transmits the social identity and position of the owner (Bridge 2001). In other words, the dwellings that we live in are no longer supposed to be simply 'for us', that is, places to live in. They are supposed to communicate something about our social identity and social position to a generalised other.

We already know the reasons for the contemporary importance of housing as a means of social classification, of course. As the importance of our location within the employment structure has receded as a class identifier, social classification increasingly occurs within the field of consumption (Saunders 1986, 1990; Crompton 1998). The key argument here is that late modern capitalism no longer involves the consumption of 'things' (houses to live in, food to eat and so on) but rather 'positional goods' that act as 'signifiers' ('city centre apartments', 'Edwardian town houses', 'proper' Italian restaurants etc.) (Lash and Urry 1987, 1994; Featherstone 1991; Clarke 2003). The other key part of this argument is that fragments of the new middle class have used their 'cultural capital' to establish new systems of classification and, in doing so, developed into the main sign producers ('specialists in symbolic production') who have displaced the commodity producers of 'organized capitalism' (Lash and Urry 1987; Featherstone 1991; Bourdieu 1993a). Thus Chapter 2 discussed how fragments of the 'new middle class' have used their 'cultural capital' to establish a 'gentrification aesthetic' in previously 'run down' inner-urban neighbourhoods, which now occupy distinctive positions in the market for houses. What we have here, then, is a middle-class form of being that is 'interested' in the market for houses as a 'space of positions' and that engages in 'position-taking' in order to secure social class position.

Now I have argued that the tendency for contemporary sociology to represent this 'interested' relation to the positional aspects of consumption as universal obscures the fact that it is actually particular to the social groups that practise and write about it (cf. Skeggs 2004). This is why I argued earlier that there is now a need to understand the working-class relation to (housing) consumption *on its own terms*, which means avoiding the assumption that working-class people are 'interested' in (housing) consumption in the same way as other social groups. That brings me to the content of this chapter, which seeks to problematise the dominant view that the market for houses consists of a 'space of positions' by examining and elucidating the working-class relation to the market for houses. The chapter shows that not all households objectify the market for houses as a space of positions, nor do they engage in position-taking. Working-class people who articulated a 'just there' form of intentionality towards the labour market in Chapter 3 are now shown to experience their housing and neighbourhoods in the same matter-of-fact way: their houses and neighbourhoods are 'just there' for them. In the words of Merleau-Ponty (1962), they constitute a 'lived space' that is understood in terms of the way it presents itself to them 'in the thick' of their everyday lives and not something that should be positioned within a space of positions. This results in distaste for the idea of housing as an investment.

Although the primary purpose of the chapter is to understand working-class forms of being-toward housing *on their own terms*, it is nevertheless important to understand how working-class people feel about their own relation to houses when confronted with the dominant view of the market for houses. This is important because the dominant view of the market for houses, as a space of positions and position-taking, is represented on a daily basis in the media. For example, Sprigings *et al.* (2006) counted 20 programmes about moving up the housing ladder on terrestrial television during one week in 2006. Although the second part of this chapter shows that working-class people take an 'interest' in such programmes, the nature of this interest is 'disinterested'. This is because their 'interest' in TV programmes about the market for houses is disconnected from any concerns about their positionality in the housing market, which, quite simply, they are not really interested in. Working-class people tend only to be concerned with houses as a 'lived space' that is 'there for them'. Nevertheless, their 'interested disinterest' in the market for houses is shown to result in their recognition (admiration) of 'the suburban ideal' that so often features in such programmes. Since working-class people only really admire the suburban ideal that they cannot have ('fantasy is the word', 'maybe if I won the lottery'), they are confronted with the stark inevitability of their own housing situation. This becomes manifest in their accommodation to 'the inevitable', which is expressed in terms of their 'happiness with what we have got'.

The market for houses as a space of positions

A key argument in the social science literature is that housing is no longer 'an end' in itself, that is, a 'thing' that enables the satisfaction of the basic need for shelter and dwelling space (Clapham 2005). It has become a 'means to an end', that is, a symbolic site through which the cultural competence and social position of the occupant can be expressed (ibid.). In Bourdieusian terminology, the market for houses is now seen to comprise a 'space of positions' (Bourdieu 1984) within which houses are socially situated. This dominant view of the housing market as a social space of positions on the urban landscape is encapsulated in the concept of 'elective belonging' in the work of Savage *et al.* (2005). For Savage *et al.* (2005: 29) elective belonging 'articulates a sense of spatial attachment [and] social position . . . . Individuals attach their own biography to their "chosen" residential location, so that they tell stories that indicate how their arrival and subsequent settlement is appropriate to their sense of themselves'. It is for this reason that the advertising of dwellings has recently assumed so much importance.

> Advertising and marketing has become an increasingly important part of the selling process. The portrayal of lifestyles and other forms of imagery associated with the house are relied upon heavily. Brochures advertising housing will put a lot of emphasis on the lifestyles the future occupant might enjoy.
>
> (Evans 1990: 13)

Yet this characterisation of the market for houses as a space of positions is articulated from (middle-class) social positions that are separate in social and epistemological terms from the 'lived' reality of housing for a lot of 'ordinary' people on an average-everyday basis. Indeed the dominant view that the market for houses consists of a space of positions violates the whole way of being-toward houses that working-class people possess, which, as a product of proximity to necessity, construes consumption, *in general*, in terms of the satisfaction of basic necessities and housing, *in particular*, according to the 'reality principle' (i.e. as a 'thing', e.g. 'bricks and mortar', 'shelter').

> The problem is that the conditions of practicing the techniques of disinterested contemplation, a fascination with questions rendered speculative, conspicuous, posed purely for the pleasure of the fruition of the process where by one satisfies oneself with the correctness of a solution or interpretation as opposed to the practical working out of a problem in the world, seems to have no sense to people who are too

wedded by necessity, urgency and position to the principle of 'reality' and a world that brooks no interpretation, which is always simply, 'there', insisting to be dealt with. The problem for [these people] is that culture . . . and the understanding it requires are existentially foreign in that they belong to a form of existence to which [they have] no primary, domestic access.

(Charlesworth 2000: 45)

Although Charlesworth is referring to distance between working-class people and culture, the same principle applies to the working-class relation to housing, which is immersed in the 'reality' of dwelling rather than the hyper-reality of the market for houses as a space of positions, for which they have neither the time nor the inclination. Working-class people talk about their relation to housing only in a matter-of-fact form of language that emerges from – and unselfconsciously communicates – the reality of their existence and the proximity to necessity that envelops and characterises it. Housing is 'bricks and mortar', 'shelter', 'where you live' and little more:

A house is basically four walls with a roof on, just as a shelter.

JS67

It's just, like, bricks.

SN24

Q	You didn't see it as sort of buying something and then hoping to move on?
MB70	To move on, no, no, I never did. It was a roof over our heads, that was all.
Q	I mean what is this living here meant to you then, in this house I mean?
LR55	It's just my house, it's my house. It's where I am.
Q	So tell me about living in this home, I mean what has it meant to you?
JC54	I don't know, we just like the house.

There are two things to note about the manner in which the people above refer to their houses. First, these people are essentially articulating the view that houses are 'things' that serve as 'equipment' (four walls, bricks and mortar, a roof etc.) rather than positions within the space of positions. In other words, they are articulating a practical economy of housing consumption. Second, working-class people who relate to houses as 'things', rather than positions within a space of positions, demonstrate a distaste for the contemporary penchant to use housing as a form of investment. These are important points that should be discussed in more detail.

The practical economy of working-class housing consumption

We have already seen how the idea that houses are positioned within a social space of positions (or, in common parlance, situated on a 'housing ladder') works its effects into the subjectivities of middle-class households who seek to use their housing consumption practices to establish their class position (Savage *et al.* 2005). Position-taking within the space of positions in the market for houses represents an ontological necessity to these social groups, which can only properly impose themselves in social space via their housing consumption practices (ibid.). That is to say, these households need to understand the market for houses in order to position themselves within it in a way that is consistent with their middle-class position.

The contrast with working-class households is stark. Working-class households governed by the urgency of a world that demands to be dealt with ('bills to be paid') are so preoccupied with managing their proximity to necessity ('you just try to get by from day to day') that housing presents itself to them in terms of its average-everyday practicalities rather than as situated in a space of positions. This can be seen in the way the criteria of legitimate or worthwhile housing consumption for working-class households is informed by the 'reality' principle which values houses as, straightforwardly, a 'place to live' or 'where I am'.

> My house doesn't mean a lot to me. My home means a lot to me because that's where I am. That's where my kids and my husband is.
>
> JA35

> It's just my house . . . . It's where I am. It's where the family know to find me.
>
> LR55

JS67   At the end of the day you can't take out of this world anything that you've made.
AC63   You come in with nothing, go out with nothing, don't you.
JS67   You come in with nothing then go out with nothing. So at the end of the day *what's the value of it except to live?*

Although middle-class households' reflexive orientation to housing compels them to situate houses within the space of positions in the market for houses, working-class households' imminent relation to necessity impels them to regard housing as a 'thing' that is 'there for me'. That is to say, working-class households tend to perceive housing as something that is 'ready to hand', which means that it is simply 'there' ('a place to live') on an average-everyday basis (Heidegger 1962). This imminent relation to housing is also reflected in the forms of articulation that working-class respondents employ to describe the primary importance of their house in terms of its ability to provide a space for 'peace', 'comfort', 'relaxation' and so on.

JS67	You turn your house into what you believe is—
AC63	Your own comfort.
JS67	Your comfortable space, and then, if you like—
AC63	You add the luxuries.
JS67	And then, yes, add the luxuries later. *But really and truly it's where you live* . . . . When you open the front door and you come into your home, you can relax and be comfortable.

Somewhere where I relax and, you know, shut my front door of a night and that's it. I'm quite happy. I love that feeling when everyone's in and I lock up.

CS47

Yeah. It's your little patch really, isn't, it, it's your territory type of thing where you come for a bit of peace with your wife and that. Whereas your house is just your house, isn't it, you know, it's just bricks and mortar; somewhere you're actually living like.

RM32

Comfortable I think, more than anything else I just know that it's my own little corner of the universe . . . . It's understated but it's functional. We decorate but everyone makes their house nice.

TP26

The important thing to note here is that working-class people articulate a primary orientation to housing as a 'thing' that is 'there for me' (rather than a signifier of social position) but, crucially, also 'with others'. This is particularly important to working-class people for whom 'we-being' forms a critical part of their existential make-up. The following people articulate it as such.

My house is where my family comes. It's a place for your family, friends, neighbours to come.

LR55

I think, I just think of it more for the kids really, it's somewhere for them to come back to. Sounds a bit . . . but not about me, it's about my children. Yeah, it's just about the kids coming back to me, if they need to be somewhere that's really comfortable. . . . it's just the general feeling of the place.

MP47

SJ35	I don't want to move house.
Q	You've made choices, obviously?
SJ35	'Cause we've got the best neighbours in the world next door, haven't we?
JJ37	Yeah.

I love it. I always lived around here. It's 'cause we know everyone. I get on with everyone round here . . . . I've always been very much just a people person.

AC19

This 'we-being', which necessitates that houses are *for me with specific others*, compelled working-class households to denigrate the middle-class orientation to housing as a signifier of social position, in particular by criticising the way in which middle-class households use their houses to display their distinctive class tastes to *generalised others*. Such an orientation to housing ('like a display house') was incompatible with the working-class orientation towards houses that were 'comfortable' and 'welcoming' to others.

JS67	But if you get a house where people just want a house for status, sort of thing, you know, it's not a home.
Q	Right.
JS67	A home, as far as I'm concerned, is my base, where I live, where I relax, where I can basically feel at peace.
AC63	And people are made welcome.
JS67	And to say that an Englishman's home is his castle, this is my little castle.

It's not big to have somewhere where everyone goes 'Oh have you seen that? Oh, it's really something, you know.'

TP26

This preoccupation with houses as 'lived space' that is understood in terms of the way it presents itself in the thick of everyday life, rather than a position in the space of positions in the market for houses, circumscribes the 'interest' that working-class people take in the market for houses in Liverpool. This becomes clear when we confront the words of the people below, who, like others, were absorbed in Kensington ('I am happy where I am') and who expressed no interest in living in other neighbourhoods in Liverpool which 'meant nothing' to them personally.

> I never wanted to know about other areas. I was happy where I was, there was every shop you needed on Wavertree Road, we were near town really, you can walk into town from here.
>
> RH65

> I see myself here really. I can't picture myself in any other area to be honest.
>
> DH26

Q	So what about the areas that are mentioned there?
MB70	I don't know those areas, I mean they're part of Liverpool, and the city, but I don't know them, they don't mean anything to me those places.
Q	Right, so do any of them, do you know any of those areas, like Norris Green, or any of the others?
MB70	Well, I know Fazakerly, and I've visited Fazakerly, and I've visited in Garston, in Croxteth, in Dingle . . . . But they don't mean anything to me.
Q	Because you don't know them, is it?
MB70	I don't know them.

> If I found myself where I liked the area and I like the house, I would stay. I wouldn't pack up and leave. I think I am settled . . . . I do like where we live but I do like our house as well. I like our neighbours so moving would be daunting, I think, moving to a different area . . . . I'm so used to living here, where I am now, that you don't want to move to another area, really, if you like where you are and you are settled.
>
> SN24

For people like this, who are possessed by a form of being that is conditioned by the imminence of their relation to a social world that devours them with its urgent demands ('you just live from day to day, I can't see beyond that really'), and preoccupied with the practicality of an average-everyday life in Kensington, the urban landscape can only really be understood in terms of the way it presents itself to them on an average-everyday basis; not as a space of positions in which the impetus to engage in position-taking is paramount. This point is articulated by the person below, who rejects the dominant point of view of the urban landscape as a space of positions because it is parasitic on the possibility that a panoramic view of the landscape is possible when, in fact, this is not possible for working-class people who possess a form of being-toward the landscape as a 'lived space' and not a space of positions. In contrast to middle-class people, then, whom Savage *et al.* (2005) describe as reflexive and 'unusually knowing' about the space of positions on the urban landscape, interview questions to working-class people about the residential desirability of other parts of Liverpool are met with responses such as 'I'm not there, so I can't voice an opinion':

Q   I'm just wondering if you know sort of, if you have any idea of what other parts of Liverpool are like to live in?

NL67   Not for me, no.

Q   But I mean if you were kind of to make a general—

NL67   No, because I'm not there, I'm not in the heart of the community, so I couldn't voice an opinion on that.

Q   No, I don't mean even for anybody in the community, I just mean, you know, sort of what your view of the areas are.

NL67   No, the areas just don't appeal to me at all because I don't want to live there in the first place, so I wouldn't be looking in areas like that.

This orientation to the urban landscape as a 'lived space' was also evident when respondents were asked to pick a house that appealed to them from a range of estate agents' advertisements presenting properties of all shapes, sizes and prices across the city. Possessed by forms of 'just' and 'we' being that oriented them to the market for houses, our working-class respondents picked out small terraced houses in locations such as Kirkby and Old Swan because they were 'familiar' with them or because this would place them near significant others.

RH65   I would probably go for the terraced in Old Swan.

Q   What number is that, the terraced in Old Swan? Okay, that's number 31, why would you go for that one?

RH65   I suppose I'm just familiar with the area.

Q   Anything else there that you fancy?

LR55   That one in Kirkby's quite nice actually.

Q   What about Kirkby that you like?

LR55   My sister lives there, our Amanda lives there, I used to live there, that's where I met Kenneth, in Kirkby.

Q   How far away is it from here?

LR55   Ten miles.

Q   So it would be good because you're, you know, you know people there?

LR55   Oh yeah, well Kenneth grew up in Kirkby, as I say, Amanda's lived all her life in Kirkby.

Q   Your step daughter?

LR55   Yeah. I was there not yesterday, the day before.

This shows, again, how working-class people exhibit a primordial relation to houses as 'lived space' ('what's the value of it except as a place to live?'), which proscribes the formation of a view that situates housing within the space of positions in the market for houses. Insofar as working-class respondents talk about the position of housing on the urban landscape, they only really do so in terms of the practicality of its geographical (not social) position on an average-everyday basis.

Q   Do you feel any kind of attachment to this area?

CS47   If I could be anywhere, I think I'd still like it. It's just handy for like town and me mum's.

Q   I know what you mean, yeah. So what aspect about living round here makes it worthwhile staying here?

CS47   I think it's just like handy when I go to Old Swan, town, me mum's, you know, the bus routes. I mean I know I drive but if I go into town I just catch the bus at the bottom of the street, it's easier, you know, and you can get a bus at the bottom of the street to almost . . . if it doesn't go anywhere you want to go you've only got to get it into town and pick another bus up. It's, you know, it's on a good route.

Q   What about things that are good about living around here, I mean it's got a lot of problems?

MP47   My job is walking distance, it's a great little part-time job and it's good wages.

Q   That doesn't cause you any stress?

MP47   No, I don't drive, it's convenient.

Oh it's important where it is, yeah. And this one, I can just go down the street and I can go into town. I'm right on top of the hospital, which is convenient, or I can go to Belle Vale. I mean the other Sunday my nephew and niece picked me up and we went to scatter my brother's ashes in the Mersey.

RH65

RM32   A lot of mates, yeah. Like I say it's handy to get into the city centre, it's handy for me for work.

Q   Where do you work?

RM32   In town. It's only ten minutes away from there in the car. It's handy for the football, happy days like . . . . What more do you want?

Although it could be suggested that 'convenience' informs the relocation decisions of most households, there is a key difference in the way it informs the decisions of households from different social class backgrounds. Middle-class people might desire convenience, but their being-toward housing as a 'signifier' of their class positioning means that the convenience of their location is a product of this reflexive orientation towards housing and neighbourhoods, i.e. middle-class people tend to desire 'convenience' for the cultural facilities of the city centre, which are consumed for the purposes of constructing a distinctive lifestyle (Savage *et al.* 2005). On the other hand, working-class people valorise 'convenience' and 'handiness' because it facilitates the performance of the basic tasks (walking to work, walking to the supermarket etc.) that are 'just there' demanding to be dealt with on an average-everyday basis.

The manner in which working-class people related to houses as 'practical things' rather than 'positional goods' was also exemplified in their testimonies about purchasing houses. Now, although housing is *apparently universally* regarded as a 'major life decision' and 'the biggest thing that you will ever buy', this characterisation of such statements is based on the misrecognition that they are neutral in origin. Yet such statements are primarily articulated by social agents occupying social spaces that compel them to view the market for houses as a space of positions (estate agents, the middle classes etc.) and so are anything but neutral. The pertinence of this point becomes clear when we examine the matter-of-fact way in which working-class people in Kensington 'just' bought houses without reference to any criteria other than their use as dwelling space. In a manner consistent with the way working-class people in Kensington talk about houses for 'what they are' ('bricks and mortar', shelter, dwelling and so on), they describe 'just buying' or 'just ending up' with the first house they saw that met their practical requirements rather than 'searching' for houses within the space of positions.

Q	Why did you move here?
MP47	I don't know, to be honest. I think we thought we were going to, we were getting a good deal when we came to see the house, because it's a pretty big house, and it was only £8000. And we thought it was a good deal. We didn't really look round. We sort of liked the first thing we saw: 'yeah, we'll live here'. We just sort of jumped in without really thinking about it.
Q	Did you get a mortgage?
MP47	Steve's dad had got made redundant and he gave us the deposit for the house, you know, 'go and get yourselves a house', and things like that, and that's what started the ball rolling. But we didn't really seriously think about it very much, just jumped in without thinking about it.

RM32   I was just thinking of terraced and that, but the way we stumbled on this two
           bedroom new build semi-detached: we were actually going to the pictures one
           night and . . . we seen these and wrote the number down, so we thought we'll
           go and have a look in there, you know, see what it's like, how much they are
           and all that. And at the time this was only £40,000 at the time . . . . I was
           originally looking at moving up to by Anfield in like a terraced, out that way.
Q   Near the football ground?
RM32   Not for that like . . . I went to school up that area.
Q   Oh, did you?
RM32   Yeah, and like a lot of my mates are from up there anyway. I know the area
           through working round there on the Post and that and I always thought it was
           a decent sort of area and the parks like. So I was going to look up there. . . I
           think we were going to the pictures one night and we happened to turn down
           here like and we seen these. So we'll go and have a look and we just ended up
           with one, this was the first one we looked at to be honest. A bit silly really when
           you look back but this is the only one we looked at and we got it and that was
           that. Never really looked anywhere else . . . . It's handy for like the city centre,
           it's handy for where I work, it's handy for where she works and all my mates are
           around here.

There is literally nothing in the above quotations that indicates an 'interested' relation to the urban market for houses as a landscape of positions. Such a relation to housing is possible only for those who possess the requisite levels of cultural and economic capital that not only enables them to objectify the market for houses as a space of positions but also provides them with the instruments of appropriation to correctly decipher housing market signals, that is, by knowing where to invest and where not to invest. I am referring here to middle-class households that take an interest in, and invest in, the market for houses as a matter of ontological necessity.

The distaste for housing investment

The idea that housing represents an 'investment opportunity' makes sense only to those whose 'existential actuality' (cf. Heidegger 1962) enables them to relate to housing in such terms, that is, those who have money to invest. It is anathema to working-class people who live their lives in close proximity to economic necessity and insecurity. For these people, the notion that housing is an investment is existentially foreign because it speaks only to those with a form of being that is enthralled with the use of money ('investment').

Q	Some people see housing as a bit of an investment as a way to sort of accumulate. I mean is that how you see it?
RM32	Not really, no.
Q	Do you think that a property ladder exists though?
RM32	Oh yeah, definitely yeah.
Q	Yeah, but I mean do you see yourself being on that ladder?
RM32	Not really, no.

It is important to note that these working-class people are not simply articulating a 'lack of interest' in the market for houses that is a consequence of their 'lack of money' to invest (in which case they would have made statements such as: 'I'd like to climb the housing ladder but I haven't got the money'). Working-class people such as the man quoted above are articulating a 'point of view' on housing that is a product of a form of being literally *unable* to comprehend the idea that housing is anything other than somewhere to live and that, therefore, the notion that it should be valued for its investment potential is alien to their existential actuality (cf. Heidegger 1962).

JC54	I don't really see it as an investment, because I think any house, whatever you do is an investment if you look at it that way. I'd look at it investment wise if I was planning to be moving all the time, yeah, but.
Q	But you're not?
JC54	No, I don't look at it as an investment. I mean obviously it's going to be at the end of the day sometime or other, but to us it's a home for us to live in, what we want to live in.

To perceive housing as a potential investment, one needs to possess a privileged form of being-towards housing as a means to an end (equity accumulation, social status) rather than an end in itself (shelter, dwelling space). Now although different elements of the middle class have distinct (property, cultural, organisational) asset bases that they are able to deploy to negotiate their way through the uncertainties of the post-industrial labour market (Savage *et al.* 1992), thereby enabling them to take risks with mortgage debt, this is not true of working-class people, who are left to negotiate those risks without the 'insurance' of a distinct asset base that could secure their place in the post-industrial labour market (Charlesworth 2000). It is instructive to note that most working-class respondents had felt the brute force of the economic restructuring of the last few decades through experiences of prolonged unemployment as well as through their repositioning in insecure employment. So, although middle-class households tend to regard mortgage debt as a source of investment, mortgage debt induces feelings of terror in working-class people because it reminds them of the insecurity of their economic positioning and their absence of an asset base that could enable them to manage the uncertainty of their position in the post-industrial labour market. For example the respondent below articulates a being-toward housing consumption ('material things, they don't bother me') that is indicative of the fear that mortgage debt strikes into working-class people who *feel* the insecurity of their labour market position.

AC63   I mean you can buy all these material things just to – that doesn't bother me. Because material things, I mean, I like to have a decent home and that, but I wouldn't go out and say 'oh, I want that, I'm going to get that'.

JS67   But in monetary terms, yes, I can see the point of going up, using it as an investment, and I can see that. But what happens when suddenly somebody's taken ill, can't pay the mortgage, then they're facing bankruptcy, or all sorts of other problems, and stress, and – all caused because in the first place, they fell ill and couldn't pay, and these days, you know, if you're in that sort of situation you are chucked on the scrap heap. There's very few things that you can do to be looked after.

AC63   I think it's greed . . .

JS67   The prime objectives of people are getting on, getting ahead, one step better, better than, you know, keeping up with the Joneses and all that sort of thing.

AC63   I think that's why they've got problems.

JS67   I think that's the cause of a lot of problems.

> Everyone would change their lives if they had the money to do it, wouldn't they? That's what everything boils down to at the end of the day. Putting yourselves up to the hilt with a mortgage, which I would never ever do. I'd rather have a life. Have a massive big mortgage and packet of fish fingers between four of you of a night. No, I couldn't live like that.
>
> JC54

We have already seen that these working-class households do not regard themselves as located on a housing ladder because they possess being-toward housing as a 'thing'. We can now see that their being-against housing as a field of opportunity is a product of a form of being that, lacking in the assets necessary to manage and improve their position in a post-industrial labour market, is terrorised by the prospect of mortgage debt and, thus, the house price inflation of the last few decades. The person below articulates this in terms of 'being scared' to 'go after other property' because, like the respondent above, they are 'terrified if anything went wrong' such as falling ill and being unable to maintain mortgage payments:

It's horrible to think that like, you know, when you look at your rent book each month and like at the end of the year all that rent you've paid, you know, could have been like another couple of thousand off [a house] but I know realistically there's just no way we could afford it then. And *even if we did afford it I always think even if we did afford it to buy it I'd be terrified if anything went wrong . . . . I'm too scared . . . .* I'd be scared of that, you know, like because you hear of so many people now don't you getting like can't keep up with the payments and you know what I mean. No, I think I'm just happy.

JE42

These people are not saying that they could not secure a mortgage that would enable them to engage in position-taking in the market for houses. The respondent above indicates that many working-class people probably could obtain such a mortgage. But an orientation to necessity, the corollary of which is a distaste for the superfluous luxury of housing investment, means that working-class people experience mortgage debt as a 'burden' (rather than 'investment') that they seek to minimise ('not living beyond your means', 'only borrowing what is necessary') and rid themselves of at the first opportunity. In a society with the highest levels of personal debt ever recorded, this says something very particular about these working-class people.

Q	How do you feel about your mortgage?
RM32	Yeah, just pay it. It doesn't bother me. I don't really miss it that much. It's got to be paid and that's that.
Q	So you don't see it as being anything very negative?
RM32	No, *I wouldn't have lived beyond my means* because we still like to do things outside the house.
Q	I was going to say is that because it's a manageable mortgage?
RM32	Yeah. That's another thing, yeah.
Q	With yourself and your wife working?
RM32	Yeah. *I don't see the point of living beyond your means and getting like this big fancy house and all that and you end up having to sit here looking at it, don't you,* you know what I mean, I like to still get out as well, which you wouldn't be able to do if you had a mortgage for like, I don't know, £600 a month or something . . . . I mean don't get me wrong, I'm not out all the time, but I like to get to my football. I like to do that but if you have this big fancy house you're just paying for that constantly aren't you, you end up sitting here looking at it, looking at four walls. No good to me that.

Symbolic violence and the 'love of the inevitable'

The working-class relation to housing is not simply a consequence of the form of being that emerges from an imminent relation to necessity. It is also a product of the symbolic domination of working-class people that results in their acceptance of the legitimacy of dominant ideas about the market for houses as a space of positions, even though they feel unable to partake in such position-taking, for reasons outlined in the first part of this chapter. This compels them to 'know their place' in the market for houses. So, rather than releasing them from the constrictions of their own world view of the market for houses, thereby compelling them to play the housing game, the symbolic domination of working-class people actually reinforces their being-toward houses as a 'thing' that is 'there' for them. This is an important point and so will be discussed in detail in the remainder of this chapter with reference to the way in which the media and other institutions manufacture working-class 'interest' in the market for houses as a space of positions – even though working-class people feel unable to engage in position-taking – as well as their recognition of, and admiration for, particular positions (the 'suburban ideal') that are simply out of their reach.

Symbolic domination and 'interested disinterest' in the market for houses

Bourdieu (1993a) refers to the way in which some middle-class groups exhibit a 'disinterested interest' in cultural goods (that is, one that refuses the 'commercial' value of culture) in order to accumulate the symbolic profits that accrue from having a 'genuine' interest in the cultural worth of cultural goods. That is to say, a 'disinterested interest' in artifacts, such as housing, demonstrates the legitimate 'taste' of the interested party whose interest in the artifact is 'pure' rather than sullied by economic considerations. The most obvious example of this is provided by the 'gentrification aesthetic', which gentrifiers present as a 'disinterested interest' in the architectural features of a dwellingscape that, constituted on risk, is purported to be divorced from and therefore unsullied by economic considerations. This relation to artifacts such as housing is crucial to middle-class households who are rich in cultural capital but poor in economic capital and who, therefore, are dependent on their deployment of cultural capital to 'achieve' a status position within the class structure.

Such strategy within the market for houses has resulted in a complex and increasingly differentiated market, with price rises in 'hot spots' providing the most obvious evidence of the presence of such position-taking (Cole *et al.* 2004). Moreover the extent to which the market for houses has become a site in which class position can be secured is indicated by the intensity with which discourses about distinctive consumption possibilities within the housing market circulate in media and social space. For example, we noted before that 20 programmes about moving up the housing ladder appeared on terrestrial television in one week in 2006 (Sprigings *et al.* 2006). The extent to which such programmes have succeeded in imposing the dominant view of the market for houses as a space of social, economic and cultural possibilities (rather than a place to simply dwell) is evident in the way that working-class households who primarily relate to houses as a place to 'live' now take what I will call an 'interested disinterest' in the market for houses as a space of positions. By this I mean that working-class households took a 'general interest' in the market for houses (particularly prices) but, at the same time, exhibited a 'disinterest' in the market for houses, which was not 'for the likes of them', for whom housing was a practical matter rather than an opportunity for investment or consumption.

Q	Would you look at, say for example, the property sections of the local newspapers?
JC40	Well, I do that anyway. I have, I do that every Wednesday night when the *Echo* comes, and the *Daily Post* comes, I do, and I look at the prices of houses.
Q	Why do you do it?
JC40	I don't know, I just take a general interest in it.
Q	And do you look at houses around here?
JC40	Yeah, and I'll say 'such-and-such a house is going for this, look how much.' But I wouldn't just go out and say 'oh it's worth this, I'm going to go and look for a smaller place and that's it.'
Q	Do you look at property programmes on television?
JC40	Yes, I do, when they're renovating them.
Q	Do you sort of get ideas from that or do you get information from them?
JC40	Well, I'm interested to know the prices of houses in different areas, and I like to see what's happening, I do take an interest in that.
Q	Would you sort of look at the property section in a newspaper?
FS62	Well, we do look, occasionally, I mean I don't study it sort of thing, I'll have a look. We'd look in estate agents or wherever, compare prices. Two weeks ago we were in Stratford on Avon for the day, so we were having a wander round, so we had a look in the estate agents, I said '£300,000 for that!'
Q	I know.
FS62	It's absolutely horrendous. Then we like to go to Llandudno in North Wales, and we always have a look when we're wandering round the shops, oh, we'll have a look at the estate agents. Sort of comparing prices to Liverpool, what we look at say in the *Echo* or estate agents here. *But we're not actually looking to move.*

The fact that working-class people in Kensington took an 'interested disinterest' in the market for houses as a space of positions is indicative of what Bourdieu (2000: 170) refers to as 'symbolic violence', which he defines as

> the coercion which is set up only through the consent that the dominated cannot fail to give to the dominator (and therefore to their domination) when their understanding of the situation and relation can only use instruments of knowledge that they have in common with the dominator, which, being merely the incorporated form of the structure of the relation of domination, make this relation appear as natural.

The symbolic domination of working-class households by the social agents that structure the market for houses was nowhere more apparent than in the speech of the person below, who exemplifies the nature of this 'interested disinterest'. This person articulates a level of interest in the market for houses by referring to estate agents as 'magnets' for her interest yet, at the same time, iterates that her interest in the market for houses is actually 'disinterested' because she has no intention of 'playing' the housing market.

> I can't help myself, as I walk past estate agents now, it's like a magnet. Not that I want to move, I just want to see what the house prices are.
>
> LR55

All this indicates that the social agents (estate agents, media etc.) that promote the dominant view of the market for houses as a space of positions have the ability to secure legitimacy for their view, which, when misrecognised as the legitimate view by dominated groups, results in a form of symbolic violence that is manifest in the 'interested disinterest' that dominated groups take in the market for houses. Thus 'interested disinterest' is simultaneously a product of symbolic domination (resulting in a 'general interest' in house prices and so on) *and* a form of being conditioned by proximity to economic necessity (which circumscribes that 'interest' in house prices to such an extent that it lacks instrumentality), which means that working-class people might know the house market in terms of its generalities but have no reason to relate this to their own position – which, in fact, they do not see as a position.

This point about symbolic violence is reinforced when we consider the idea of a 'housing ladder', which is the vernacular expression often used to represent the market for houses as a space of positions. The concept originates from social agents (estate agents, media etc.) who take an 'interest' in the market for houses as a space of positions, and who produce discourse about the market for houses ('housing ladder') that reflects the nature of their 'interest' in housing.

Moreover, these social agents' misrecognition of their 'housing ladder' view of the market for houses as self-evident (rather than an arbitrary view articulated from a particular position in social space that is separate in social and economic terms from the average-everyday use of housing) leaves no conceptual room for any other legitimate view of the market for houses to emerge, e.g. as a mechanism for exchanging spaces to dwell. This becomes problematic when the 'housing ladder' view of the market for houses becomes so dominant that working-class people acquiesce to it (they acknowledge that houses are situated on a 'ladder') yet are unable to *practically* relate to housing in this way.

Q	Do you think there is such a thing as a property ladder?
MB70	Oh yeah, there is a property ladder.
Q	Have you ever been on it?
MB70	No, it's never entered my head. Never.

Now since the vernacular concept of 'housing ladder' is so powerful in British culture, the denial of an interest in climbing the housing ladder can seem hard to understand. Readers may, indeed, be sceptical of such comments. Yet, as Bourdieu consistently warned us (Bourdieu 1977, 1990, 2000), the privilege of social position is never more powerful than when the perception that emerges from it goes unrecognised as a privileged perception, and is therefore universalised across social groups as if perception were, itself, floating free from social position, i.e. 'what everybody knows' (Berger and Luckmann 1966). Although working-class people recognise the idea of the 'housing ladder' that has been imposed on the market for houses by dominant groups, then, it is crucially important to acknowledge that they have no interest in locating themselves on it, let alone climbing it. Indeed the idea of being located on a housing ladder is so unthinkable for many working-class people that the very thought invites a laugh.

Q	Do you see housing as a ladder, I mean is it like that for you?
RH65	No.
Q	Why not?
RH65	Why don't I want to?
Q	Yeah, why have you never?
RH65	Because I'm contented the way I am.
Q	Yeah.
RH65	I'm contented. I never wanted a big, posh house, what would you do with a big posh house? I need a house big enough to accommodate the family a couple of times a year, but if I didn't have it, then I'd have to go to them wouldn't I?

Q	You would, and is that how you've always felt about housing?
RH65	Yeah, it's just a, it's just somewhere to live for me. I've never been that ambitious, you know, that way about wanting to make myself, well, better.
Q	Yeah.
RH65	Because I feel all right as I am. And like I said, I'm one of those people.
Q	So would you see housing in terms of a housing ladder?
JR77	Yes indeed, yes.
Q	And do you think that you've ever been on that ladder in any sense?
JR77	No, I could have been, but never did, never did, like I say foolishly, we intended to move but you get comfortable.
Q	Yes, and you were happy where you were?
JR77	Oh yes, yes.

Although working-class households accept that houses (but seldom their houses[1]) are located on a 'ladder' and that there is a social expectation that housing consumers will 'move up the ladder', then, their being-toward housing is such that the idea of playing the housing game 'never enters their heads'.

Q	You've never been on that ladder?
MP47	No, this is my first. This is still my first house. I bet you're thinking 'you mad lunatic'.
Q	No, you must be joking, I'm not on any housing ladder myself.
MP47	I think it's just down to laziness, to be honest, couldn't be really bothered, I think it probably was that . . . . We were just plodding along doing other things.

Symbolic violence and the 'tyranny of suburbia'

We have already seen how social agents (media, estate agents, etc.) have imposed the dominant view of the market for houses, as a space of positions, onto dominated social groups, such as working-class people, and how this resulted in working-class people taking an 'interested disinterest' in the market for houses. However, this is not the only way that symbolic violence has been wreaked on working-class people in Kensington. The suburban middle class has been equally successful at achieving recognition for their own modes of housing consumption from working-class people in Kensington, who recognised the cultural dominance of this suburban mode of residential consumption as legitimate. Specifically, the testimonies gathered from Kensington suggest that *total* recognition was accorded by the working-class people living there to *a* dominant 'suburban ideal' (Silverstone 1997) and that, furthermore, these working-class people recognise no other form of residence (e.g. the gentrification aesthetic) as ideal or desirable. For example, the person below refers to how her desire, in an ideal world, is to possess a house in a 'nicer area with a garden, *just like everybody wants*' thereby assuming that the suburban ideal, and no other form of residence, constitute *the* legitimate form of residence.

Q   And where would you think of moving to if you could?
JC54   Oh I don't know, anywhere that took my fancy really.
Q   Would it be a bigger house?
JC54   Not so much bigger 'cos these are quite big, but maybe in a nicer area with a garden, *just like everybody wants*. If you move house you move to improve not to downgrade.

The significance of the above testimony lies not simply in the recognition that working-class respondents give to the forms of residence occupied by dominant social groups, such as the suburban middle class. Significance also lies in the way working-class respondents articulate their 'desires' through a form of language ('nice house', 'lovely house', 'bigger house', 'better house' etc.) that is indicative of a primordial relation to housing that encounters it for 'what it is' or 'how it appears' rather than through a form of reflexive articulation that situates it within a complex field of positions.

FS62   If I was going to, I'd be looking for a nicer area.
JS63   We'd go to Llandudno . . .
CS47   I suppose if I was married I'd like to own my own place and then go on to bigger and better but.
Q   But?
CS47   I'm quite comfortable as I am. It's always nice if I could have a bit more money like but, you know.
Q   What do the words 'moving home', 'moving house' conjure up for you then?
MP47   Moving into a nicer house, that's it. . . . . It would just mean moving to a nicer house.

> I would like it if [our children] could afford to get on like the property ladder and then by the time they're like mine and Colin's age they could afford somewhere nice, like up in Childwall [suburb of Liverpool] type of thing.
>
> JE42

The form of working-class perception that situates houses with reference to a primordially generated set of binary oppositions ('nice area'/ 'bad area', 'big house'/ 'small house') is not without consequence. For example, we know that 'new middle-class' households that are rich in cultural capital have been successful in deploying it to create new tastes within the housing field such as 'the gentrification aesthetic' (Butler 1997; Butler with Robson 2003a; Bridge 2001) and that, when recognised by other social groups as 'desirable', this produces economic profits that have enabled gentrifiers to move up the 'housing ladder' to places such as suburbia (Allen 2007). But working-class households do not possess the cultural capital that could enable them to impose their 'taste' on other social groups, and have no other way of relating to the market for houses than through the primordially generated series of dualisms that juxtapose what they have (a terraced house in a 'run-down area') with what they are encouraged to recognise as culturally desirable (a 'nice house with a big garden in suburbia'). Herein lies the nature of the problematic for working-class people, who recognise what they are encouraged to recognise but do so primarily through this series of binary oppositions that juxtaposes what they have with what they should have – which is a consequence of the ability of some social groups to impose their tastes onto the housing market so that those tastes, and only those tastes, are regarded as 'legitimate taste' by dominated groups ('everybody wants that'). Specifically, their recognition of what they should have (a 'nice house with a big garden in suburbia') in relation to what they have (a terraced house in a 'run-down' area) is a consequence of their symbolic domination by a culturally dominant suburban middle class, which, crucially, ensures that working-class people only really desire what they cannot have. This was evident in the way people in Kensington articulated a desire to live in a nice house with a garden in suburbia but, at the same time, acknowledged that this was a 'fantasy' that was 'never going to happen' and that they were 'happy where they were anyway'.

RM32   I mean don't get me wrong, if I ever won the lottery or something like that I'd get well out of here like to be honest.

Q   Okay, so where would you go?

RM32   We were out on Saturday with the baby and we went to Eastham Woods, I don't know if you know over the water?

Q   No, I don't.

RM32   There's some lovely places over there, you know, the likes of Hoylake or West Kirkby and all them. You'll see them in there sometimes for like 500 grand a house and all that. Somewhere like that would be great but it's not going to happen. But if we stayed in Liverpool, probably the nice areas: the likes of Aigburth, Halewood, parts of it like, Walton, Mossley Hill, places like that are quite nice. Formby, Crosby.

FS62	Because if, when you sell your house, you want a bigger and better one, it's going to cost you more.
JS63	Yeah, so really cost is . . .
FS62	And unless you win the Lottery.
Q	Would you look at property programmes on the television, or do you?
MP47	Fantasise is the word.

Moreover working-class households' recognition that they only desired what they could not have (a semi-detached dwelling in a suburban location) resulted in their tendency 'to make a virtue of necessity, that is, to refuse what is anyway refused and to love the inevitable' (Bourdieu, 1977: 77), which was expressed in terms such as 'I am happy here anyway'. This is why Bourdieu and Passeron (1977) argue that symbolic violence actually reinforces (rather than disrupts) our being-toward the social world, which we have characterised in terms of a doxic complicity with the objective probabilities that are inscribed into the positions we occupy in social space and that, ultimately, engender aspirations that correspond to this structure of objective probabilities. This doxic complicity ('love of the inevitable') can be detected in the forms of articulation used by the respondents below, who talk about being 'happy', 'contented', 'comfortable' etc. in Kensington even though they are living in an area that is denigrated on a daily basis by the local newspaper

> I've always been a very happy lassie living where I am; maybe that's the answer. Maybe I don't expect or demand a lot out of life. I think happiness is your first priority . . . . I would be quite happy to stay exactly where I am now. I've got everything I require. I'm very happy with what I've got.
>
> NL67

> I could still pinch myself because I just cannot believe, you know, God help me if I got like a mansion or you know something with like rambling gardens I'd be just like in awe because I just absolutely still can't believe that we've got this one.
>
> JE42

Q	What kind of aspects of living round here make it worthwhile staying because you say you're content and that you've no plans to move?
JJ37	Well, going back to the other thing you were saying about problem areas, it's like when people say, 'Where do you live?' and you say Kensington and that, and they go, 'What?' Because I've lived here like for thirty-odd years I'm used to it anyway . . . . So, you know, it's just normal to me like. Yeah. It's normal. Whereas like if someone come from outside, I mean say like yourself, I don't

know you might live in a nice posh area somewhere and you come here and it might be like a shock to you, do you know what I mean, but it's not to me it's quite normal . . . . Like saying about positives in the area, I don't know, I'd say like just because I'm used to living here that's one thing.

Q   So have you any strong feelings about living on X Road?

RM32   Just that I'm quite happy here really.

Q   Content?

RM32   That content feeling, yeah. Quite happy with it.

I feel comfortable living around here.

SN24

You just plod along, one foot in front of the other, and I try, but I don't always succeed, take each day . . . . I wouldn't feel as happy living in another road, because I'm used to this road, you know.

JR43

Q   Yeah, and thinking about where you live now, how do you feel about it now?

JS63   Fine.

FS62   I'm quite happy really, although we do go about a bit now, don't we, since I've finished work . . . . It's never bothered us living here . . . it's what goes on inside your four walls.

We're alright where we are, we're in the house we want to be in.

JC54

Q   And how does living here make you feel?

NL67   I feel great. It makes me feel great. The only time I get stressed about living here is when people aren't listening to us like the likes of the council or the planning department.

I'm always a great believer in destiny, so whatever happens, happens, you know, it's not as if we've made everything happen, you know. I mean I'm not disappointed in my life, I mean I've got a really good husband and he's good with children and his family and I wouldn't trade that for anything.

SJ35

Symbolic violence, regret and resistance

We have already noted that the working-class relation to the market for houses is a complex one. Thus we cannot simply understand working-class people as passive victims of the symbolic violence wreaked by dominant groups that seek to impose their own relation to the market for houses, as a space of positions, on other groups. Although working-class people recognise the market for houses as a space of positions, they possess a form of being-toward houses (as a 'thing') that we have seen to perforce necessitate their refusal to 'play the game', for example by refusing to locate themselves on the 'housing ladder'. But this is not all. The symbolic dominance of working-class people by social agents and social groups that structure the market for houses as a space of positions also complicates the working-class relation to the market for houses in other ways. Specifically, working-class recognition of the legitimacy of the view that the market for houses consists of a space of positions entices them into regretting that they have not 'played the game'. Yet it also induces a sense of resistance amongst working-class people, who, possessed by a form of being-toward housing as a 'thing', which proscribes any relation to the market for houses as a space of positions, fail to see the point of 'moving up the housing ladder'. They express this resistance by ridiculing the futility and superficiality of position-taking ('they call it an apartment, I call it a flat'). The remainder of the chapter is devoted to a detailed discussion of these key points.

Symbolic violence and regret

Although working-class respondents were 'happy with their lot' they neverthe-less referred to how they wished they had 'done things differently' when they 'looked back' on their lives. There appears to be nothing remarkable about this on the surface because most people would probably say that they harbour regrets when they 'look back'. However, to leave things there would be to overlook the sociological significance of this regret. The sociological signifi-cance of regret emerges out of the gap that exists between what people do *at the time* and what they *think* they would have done when *looking back*. This is because the 'benefit of hindsight' enables individuals to observe what has hap-pened in the housing market, how other people have constituted and benefited from what has happened in the housing market, how what these people did in the housing market was different from their own practice, and the differential nature of the outcomes it generated.

The 'benefit of hindsight' cannot be accomplished within the context of a 'lived view' of the housing situation because this consists of a primor-dial relation ('just being') towards houses as they present themselves in their average-everydayness. This is why households articulate their sense of being 'happy' with houses that provide them with what they need on an average-everyday basis, that is, dwelling space. The 'benefit of hindsight' can only be accomplished when this sense of 'being at home' is existentially disrupted, resulting in what Heidegger (1962) refers to as a 'call of care', that is, an impetus towards reflexivity that releases 'being' from its 'lostness' to the grip of its determinacy on an average-everyday basis. When the dominant view of the market for houses as a field of investment and position-taking is recognised, as legitimate, by working-class people who therefore derive their 'benefit of hindsight' from within the parameters of this dominant view ('We should have moved to a better house when prices were lower') it entices them into a sense of regret. By recognising the dominant view of the market for houses as *the legitimate view*, then, working-class people produce the means of their own domination by familiarising themselves with a way of perceiving the market for houses (as a field of investment) that exposes their own 'lived view' as an arbitrary and 'failed' form of perception that has resulted in 'missed opportunities'. This 'failure' of the 'lived view' of housing, which was a source of regret, was articulated by the person below, who is now critical of the way she had 'just bought' her home without 'looking around'.

MP47   But we didn't really seriously think about it very much, just jumped in without thinking about it.

Q   Why, what do you feel now on reflection?

MP47   I think we made a mistake, I think we should have took our time, looked around. You know, just stupid things like that . . . . We could have probably afforded much more of a mortgage than we did. We should have gone for a, sort of a, better style home if you like, you know a bigger . . .

Q   A semi, something like that?

MP47   Yeah, a semi. Because we could have probably afforded it. But we just didn't think.

The articulation of regret in terms such as 'I wished I had done something else' is all too apparent with the 'benefit of hindsight', which, in an act of symbolic violence, was enforced in the social science interview (i.e. 'what do you feel now on reflection?'). The subtext to this interview question was: 'knowing now "what everybody knows" about house price rises, how do you feel about moving here?' The notion that working-class people 'wished they had done something else', then, is indicative of their submission to the dominant view of housing when it is imposed on them by researchers like me, whose very pronouncement of the term 'housing ladder' ('So would you see housing in terms of a ladder then?') provides the concept with a hegemonic legitimacy against which the respondents are impelled to judge themselves. Such questions reinforce the symbolic violence already wreaked on working-class households by social agents (media, estate agents etc.) that have the power to structure the market for houses and the meanings that circulate within it and have an interest in the dominant view of the market for houses as a space of opportunities, since this is what generates the house moves that produce economic profits for the house sales industry.

We also know that the 'failure' of these respondents to do what they now say they wished they had done (i.e. moved up the housing ladder rather than stay put) was an inevitable product of the gap between opportunities that existed in the housing field at the time and the intentionality of working-class respondents who 'just didn't think' to grasp them. The notion that these respondents 'just did not think' recalls the point that Bourdieu (1977) makes when he refers to habitus as a set of dispositions that structure what is thought and render some things 'unthinkable', resulting in 'missed opportunities'. This is evident in the testimony of the person below, whose 'missed opportunities' in the field of housing investments (which was the source of her regrets) emerged because she had 'never seen it like that' until now.

> I didn't see it as accumulating capital in that way, I never saw it like that. Now I do . . . . I do now, yes, it was said to me a couple of months ago, friends who came in said if your house was in a better district, you'd get twice as much money for it, and I thought, yes, I know that, it was a foolish buy, but it was the case of Hobson's Choice at the time. And it was more foolish staying.
>
> JR77

The other interesting aspect of this persons' narrative is the internalisation of 'failure' to act 'correctly' in the housing market. This is evident in the way she describes her actions as 'foolish'. This is possible, of course, only because the respondent recognises the dominant 'investment view' of the market for houses as the legitimate view and, as such, her own 'lived view' as arbitrary and 'failed'. She is the archetypal 'failed consumer' that Bauman (1988) refers to *and she knows it*. And she is not the only one. People living in Kensington articulate their 'regret' in a variety of forms, e.g. by describing themselves as 'foolish' or saying that 'I must be a mad lunatic' not to have moved up the housing ladder. Informed by an apparently legitimate point of view on the market for houses that they could not live up to, these people not only described their *consumption practices* as 'failed' ('lunatics', 'foolish'). They also internalised these failures when they articulated reasons ('I'm too lazy', 'too set in my ways') for their failure.

JS63   This house we paid for quite quickly.
FS62   Yeah.

JS63   We might have moved then.

FS62   But you get set in your ways.

JS62   And I think we were too, we were too set in our ways.

Such is the power of symbolic violence that it not only labels working-class housing practices as failures, but results in the inscription of that failure onto the bodies of those that have apparently failed. It goes without saying, of course, that these working-class people are anything but failures. They are misrecognising what are actually class processes (different classed forms of being-toward the market for houses) as personal traits and lamenting their own 'personal failures' to live up to the dominant view of housing as a field of opportunities. Moreover the symbolic violence wrought on these households' relation to houses ('a space to dwell') by social agents that structure the field of housing ('a space of positions') not only results in their internalisation of failure ('I'm a lunatic', 'I am foolish' for not playing the housing market) but brutally reinforces their sense of their own domination because it makes them acutely aware of how socially and economically distant they are from the housing market, as the respondent below indicates.

> Yeah, and I always look at the property pages, and me and my boyfriend, the two of us, like I said before, Kevin, these are £75,000, how on earth are we going to get on the property ladder?
>
> DH31

Symbolic violence and resistance

This is not to suggest that working-class people submit to this symbolic domination in its entirety, which is why it is inappropriate to simply constitute the working-class as 'failed consumers'.[2] Working-class people do not submit to symbolic domination in its entirety because, as Foucault (1977) notes in a discussion of sovereign and disciplinary power, the point at which the disciplinary power of discourse applies its force also becomes the nodal point for a strategy of resistance:

> what makes power hold good, what makes it accepted, is simply the fact that it doesn't only weigh on us as a force that says 'no'; it also traverses and produces things, it induces pleasure, forms of knowledge, produces discourse. It needs to be considered as a productive network that runs through the whole social body much more than as a negative instance whose function is repression.
>
> (Foucault 1994: 120)

That is to say, the very act of mobilising truths (about the market for houses) produces a field of discourse from which other truths can 'find their voice'; in this case, the working-class 'truth' about housing as a 'thing' rather than a 'signifier' of social position. This is exemplified in the way the person below articulates a revulsion at the middle-class tastes that have been imposed on housing by TV 'makeover' programmes, which she refers to as 'over the top'.

Q	Do you look at the property section of the newspaper?
MB70	No.
Q	Never?
MB70	If somebody points them out to me, and some of my colleagues do, they look at them – the homeowners – and they say 'look at them' and they say 'did you see the house in such and such a street went for £60,000?'
Q	Do you ever look at the TV and property programmes, you know, like doing up houses and selling them on?
MB70	Only very, very occasionally because I'm sick to death of them now. And to be honest, those I've seen, if they came into this house and did what they've done to them, I'd throw them through the door. You know, some of them are way over the top. That's not me. I'm, you know, from a personal point of view, that's just not me.

The next quotation similarly refutes the forms of truth that institutions, such as estate agents, circulate about housing, which, in this case, are communicated through 'signs' that are attached to the *same* forms of dwelling in order to differentiate the spaces occupied by middle-class households (apartments) and council renters (flats). Discursive strategies that seek to differentiate between dwellings do not impress this person, who sees dwellings for 'what they are': with reference to the matter-of-fact way they present themselves to her (e.g. as a multi-dwelling building) rather than a lifestyle choice that she has no access to and no 'interest' in (e.g. 'loft living').

Q	And you know, would you ever for example look at the property section of the newspaper?
RH65	Oh I do, just out of curiosity, yes.
Q	Is that something you do on a regular basis?
RH65	Oh no, no, no. Because I don't see the newspapers that often. Only if I go to one of the kids' – they get the *Liverpool Echo*, and I'll go through it, and say 'ooh, that house in such a street, fancy it being worth that much'. Because they are amazing prices, they really are.

Q   Yeah.

RH65   I mean flats up the road here, 100 and odd thousand pounds for an apartment,
         as they call them now. I call them flats.

Resistance to the dominant view of the market for houses, as a space of
positions, does not simply occur through the ridicule of TV programmes and
the language that is used to describe middle-class dwelling space. It is also
articulated through a form of politicised discourse that exposes position-taking
for what it is (futile) from the point of view of working-class people that possess
a form of being-toward houses as a 'thing' or 'lived space'.

> I consider this to be where I am rather than just flit from house to house.
>
> SP26

This can be seen in the way working-class people referred to the futility of
investing in housing as a 'signifier' of social position, which is little or no use to
someone whose being is toward 'things' that have 'use value': 'if you have this
big fancy house you're just paying for that constantly aren't you, you end up
sitting here looking at it, looking at four walls. No good to me that.' Adherence
to this 'reality principle' – which, of course, is not a matter of 'choice' but one
born of proximity to necessity – is never more manifest than when articulated
in terms that so unselfconsciously present the futility of the 'housing ladder'
for what it really is: pointless, to a form of being that is engrossed in a struggle
for survival rather than for social position. 'You come in with nothing, you go
out with nothing. At the end of the day, what's the value of it except that it is
somewhere to live?' These articulations represent resistance to the dominant
view of housing by exposing it 'for what it is', that is, a 'game' that, as such, is
distant from the reality principle that governs working-class lives and that provides them with their legitimate criteria of judgement of worthiness: 'it doesn't
bring you happiness in the end', 'no use to me that'.

Conclusion

Chapter 2 and this chapter have discussed how middle-class people 'play' the
housing market to secure and defend a class position. However, this chapter has
also shown that working-class people do not relate to the market for houses in
this way. The chapter has shown how working-class people in Kensington were
immersed in the reality of dwelling rather than the hyper-reality of the symbolic
economy of housing: they did not locate themselves on the property ladder,
nor did they regard their houses as an investment. Nevertheless, working-class

economies of housing consumption were not simply born of a form of being constituted at close proximity to economic necessity.

The ferocity with which the dominant view of the market for houses (a space of positions) circulates in media and social space means that working-class people simply cannot escape it. Indeed the dominant view of the market for houses is imposed so successfully in social space that working-class people in Kensington took what I termed an 'interested disinterest' in the market for houses as a space of positions. Since this equips them with a form of knowledge about the market for houses, which they accept as constituting legitimate knowledge, it provides the basis of their domination (symbolic violence). Thus working-class people make reference to the dominant perception of the market for houses, as a space of positions, when engaging in *post ante* reflections on the adequacy of their own housing consumption. This is why they articulate 'regret' about their own economy of housing consumption even though, quite simply, they could hardly have consumed houses in any other way and certainly not in the 'middle-class way'. Further, their recognition of forms of residential consumption that they could not have (the suburban ideal), and no others, was shown to result in a 'love of the inevitable', which was expressed in terms of 'contentment' with their own house and neighbourhood. Working-class people relate to the market for houses in a practical matter-of-fact way and are happy to do so. They did not seek a position within the space of positions because to do so would require their assumption of housing debt. Mortgage debt is a burden (not a source of investment) to working-class people, whose proximity to necessity proscribes views of consumption that are constituted on anything other than the need to satisfy basic necessities. Housing investment in order to secure a position within the space of positions in the market for houses is, quite simply, a luxury that working-class people cannot afford. Further it is one that does not even occur to them. It is crucial to understand all of these points if we are to properly understand the impact that housing market renewal has on working-class people. The relationship between housing market renewal and working-class people is the focus of the remaining chapters of the book.

Chapter 5
Being in a 'depressed' market for houses

Introduction

Neighbourhoods such as Kensington are commonly referred to as 'failed', 'problematic', 'run down' etc., as if this were self-evident. Yet these neighbourhood perceptions constitute arbitrary views, no matter how such 'problem areas' may appear to the 'naked eye'. The thing to note about these arbitrary views of Kensington is that their constitution from methodological distance (that is, from the social and spatial distance of the town hall research and statistics office) is what provides them with their legitimacy. Indeed this is what has provided the justification for regeneration initiatives such as 'housing market renewal' (HMR), which is discussed in the next part of the book. Suffice it to say, for the time being, that knowledge constituted at such a social and spatial distance from Kensington has no justification for presenting itself as objective. On the contrary it is born of a form of involvement that, as distant, can understand Kensington only through the knowledge that is produced at such a distance. Such knowledge constitutes little more than 'representations' that are particular to the positions in social space from which they originate as forms of understanding.

Now practitioners of these 'official views' denigrate understandings born of practical involvement in the everyday life of Kensington as constituted through 'arbitrary experience' rather than the formal procedures of social science that generate 'knowledge'. But if we treat these resident views as legitimate *on their own terms*, this helps us to expose the arbitrary nature of the 'official' view of Kensington, which is shown to be constituted on little more than a series of representations that fail to accurately reflect the experiences of people living there. Specifically, working-class understandings of Kensington, constituted through involvement in it as a 'lived space', represent the place as largely unproblematic. Kensington people simply do not recognise the representations that circulate about Kensington ('dirty', 'run down', 'crime ridden', 'drug ridden' and so on) and that have been used to justify the imposition of regeneration programmes, such as HMR. It is crucially important to understand these key points before we proceed, in Part III of the book, to examine the imposition of HMR programmes on working-class people living in Kensington.

The policy view of Kensington

If one were to compile a 'profile' of Kensington that drew exclusively on 'official reports' it would read something like this:

> The Inner Core of Liverpool has a number of distinctive weaknesses including low house prices, high turnover levels and high void rates. During the 1980s social housing became difficult to let. More recently the phenomenon of 'low demand' has spread to private housing, especially in the inner ring of nineteenth-century terraced housing that surrounds the city centre, and within which Kensington is located. Kensington was adversely affected by the economic situation in the 1970s and 1980s, which saw a loss of manufacturing and a general recession in Liverpool. For an area so dependent on manufacturing the closure of household names including Meccano and Crawfords was particularly damaging and the loss of railway-related employment was also significant. The extent of the problems that Kensington faces is indicated by its inclusion in the Merseyside Objective 1 programme (1994–99) as an area in need of special assistance. More recently, it qualified for New Deal for Communities (NDC) status because it has been identified as the second most deprived area in the city.
>
> The general environment in Kensington is poor, with 10 per cent of properties empty and many neglected and derelict sites in the area. The percentage of vacant dwellings in Kensington (8.9 per cent) is double the average percentage of vacant dwellings (4.4 per cent) in Liverpool as a whole. The New Deal for Communities Delivery Plan highlights a number of issues that indicate the weakness of the Kensington housing market. The area is characterised as having a 'monolithic provision' of dense terraced housing, which is increasingly providing for a high turnover market in the social and private rented sector. 83 per cent of the houses are terraced and 87 per cent of these have two or three bedrooms. As turnover and void levels increase the market for owner occupation continues to weaken. The ageing population is also a factor. Thirty-three per cent of residents are elderly, a figure which is above the national average. The demographics of the area combined with the dominance of terraced housing are the main constraints on the housing market.
>
> Another factor holding back the local housing market is the dominance of the social rented sector, with Housing Associations owning 28.6 per cent of the stock and the City Council owning 16.5 per cent. There is also a surplus of social rented housing. There is an average of only one applicant registered for each void that occurs during the course of any one year in Kensington.
>
> In recent years Kensington has accommodated a significant proportion of the student population in the city. Around 6,000 students live in the L7 area. However, their continued presence in the area cannot be taken for granted because the market for student accommodation has broadened to include 2,000 new bed spaces in and

around the city centre. The supply of low-cost accommodation within Kensington will continue to increase if students choose to vacate the neighbourhood in favour of a city centre location.

Analysis of house prices reveals that house prices rose by 31.9 per cent across the city between 1995 and 1999. However, within the inner core of the city prices only rose by 14.9 per cent, and in the L7 postal district, in which Kensington is situated, prices increased by only 1 per cent over the same period. In addition to having marginal growth in values over this five year period, the absolute value of properties in Kensington was the lowest in Liverpool. More recently, between 2002 and 2003, the average price for a detached property in Kensington fell whereas the average price for a terraced house increased by 12.5 per cent in the same period.[1]

The 'lived view' of Kensington

Practitioners of the 'official' view of the market for houses claim that Kensington and other similar areas within the inner-urban ring of Liverpool have undergone profound social and economic changes during the last few decades. 'Official statistics' produced by state agencies problematise the area as having a depressed housing market and poor neighbourhood conditions. Media interest in the area has grown in line with this apparent growth of 'problems' within the area. The extent of this media coverage (particularly from the *Liverpool Echo*) has reinforced the 'official view' by telling stories about the area that, taken together, constitute a 'narrative of decline'. Kensington, it seems, is a 'neighbourhood in decline' with a depressed market for houses.

Although the media narrative of decline corresponds with the 'indicators' of decline that have been produced by other agencies (local government, regeneration agencies, research consultants), from which it derives its much of its legitimacy, it is exactly that: a narrative. And as a narrative it can only be understood as a particular – not objective – way of 'knowing' that emerges from the social position from which its form of knowing is made possible and articulated, that is, from the social and spatial distance of the statisticians' office. This point has been made more than adequately by Merleau-Ponty, who argues that:

> Analysis has no justification for positing any stuff of knowledge as an ideally separable 'moment' and that this stuff, when brought into being by an act of reflection, already relates to the world. Reflection does not follow in the reverse direction a path already traced by the constitutive act, and the natural reference of the stuff to the world leads to a new conception of intentionality, since the classical conception, which treats the experience of the world as a pure act of constituting consciousness, manages to do so only in so far as it defines consciousness as absolute non-being, and

correspondingly consigns its contents to a 'hyletic layer' which belongs to opaque being.

(Merleau-Ponty 1962: 283)

Merleau-Ponty is saying much the same as Heidegger (1985: 161), which is that 'official' narratives of decline emerge from a form of 'involvement' with the social world which structures 'knowing': 'Every act of knowing always already takes place on the basis of the mode of being . . . which we call being-in, that is, being-always-already-involved-with-a-world'. Since officials' involvement takes place at a social and spatial distance from places such as Kensington, they rely on statistics and other sources of 'objective' information to enable them to 'observe' and 'understand' such places, which they objectify as depressed areas. That such 'official views' constitute particular forms of 'knowing', which are separate in social and spatial terms from the 'lived view' of Kensington, was well understood by working-class people living there, who argued that 'representations' of their area were partial to the position from which they were produced and articulated.

> When I saw that, and even when you see stuff on the news like that, yeah technically it is my area but *none of it really applies.*
>
> TP26

RM32	I'm quite proud to come from round here like, yeah. It gets a lot of stick like, to be honest.
Q	I'm going to ask you about that actually.
RM32	Yeah, it gets slated, yeah.
Q	But before that, I mean what's it like living on Y Road on a day-to-day basis? What's it like to . . . ?
RM32	Alright. Like I say it's very quiet really . . . . Well, I knew it'd be pretty quiet, as I say, it's not the greatest road and that like but we know at the top end it's a bit grim but actually here is pretty quieter [sic], it's very quiet.

These people above make an important point when they draw on their own 'experience' to denounce representations of Kensington. Now, although their experiences are particular to them, the point being made is that constitutive acts of knowing are products of the positions in social space from which they originate. There is, then, nothing in the official and policy points of view of Kensington that provides them with any more legitimacy than any other point of view – other than, of course, the fact that official points of view are articulated from institutional spaces that provide them with symbolic power. Indeed the person below goes even further than this by suggesting that legitimate acts of knowing can only be constituted from within the social space of Kensington, that is, constituted from 'lived experience' of Kensington as a social space.

NL67   It's easy for anyone to say that if you don't live in this area. If you live here you've got a right to voice an opinion. But when you don't live here, how do you know? You're only going on facts, and sometimes people put the facts there that aren't true.

Q   So you don't go along with their sort of representation?

NL67   No, no, no. I will stand up and defend this area to anybody. I have done.

Q   Because you're living here?

NL67   It's passion. It's my area; I was born and bred here. It's no different to me . . . going back to the *Liverpool Echo*, let's be honest, if anybody believes everything that they read in the press then, television, any media, come on, wake up, smell the coffee, or get out there and find out the truth for yourselves.

Kensington as 'lived space'

We have already noted that middle-class people reflexively interpret the market for houses as a space of positions inscribed with possibilities 'for the likes of them'. The neighbourhoods that they occupy become understood via reference to the definitions that middle-class households impose on them ('bohemian', 'urban village') rather than according to the everyday reality of life therein. On the other hand, working-class people do not tend to situate their houses or neighbourhoods within the space of positions on the urban landscape and judge them accordingly ('an up and coming area', 'a bohemian area', 'a deprived area' etc.). On the contrary, working-class people whose being-toward is conditioned by, and immersed in, the urgent necessities that average-everyday life imposes on them, and who characterise their lives as a struggle for existence rather than position ('you just live from day to day'), tend to formulate pre-reflexive judgments about neighbourhoods that are a product of their primary experience of those spaces as 'there' for them on an average-everyday basis ('a place to live', 'where I am'). And their primary experience of their own houses and neighbourhoods as 'lived spaces' results in their production of a discourse about these neighbourhoods that describes them in the way they present themselves in everyday life rather than within a system of signifiers. Although the official 'signifiers' that circulate about Kensington denigrate it as a 'deprived', 'run down', 'crime ridden', 'drug ridden' etc. area, then, this discourse seldom finds its way into the mouths of working-class people who live there and relate to it in terms of the way it presents itself to them 'in the thick' of their everyday lives.

This is evident in the way the people below refer to Kensington as 'unproblematic' in their experience.

> You sort of walk around with rose coloured glasses *because you still see it as it is* [i.e. not how it is represented].
>
> JC54

> I'm quite happy here like, I've been here seven years and *I've had no problems*, no break-ins. The old girl got broke into just before . . . , next door, money like. Apart from that it's been okay.
>
> RM32

> No problems personally. It's fine. I'm not saying 'It's great' but . . .
>
> SN24

And as a space that *they* had 'no problem' with, they articulate a sense of being 'comfortable' with Kensington, even if regeneration agencies were not particularly comfortable with it.

> I feel comfortable living around here . . . . I've never felt threatened at all.
>
> SP26

Q	What feelings does it conjure up for you when you think about living here?
JR77	Being comfortable and safe, it is a very safe little spot, never had any trouble. So I get the feeling, and I always, when we're away, even if it's only for a day, I always come back and thank God I'm home.
Q	And what's it like living in this neighbourhood?
KB55	Fine, great, no problems. Everybody looks to everybody else and helps everybody.
Q	Is that just on this street do you think or is it . . . ?
KB55	No, no, it's within the neighbourhood, yeah. You have your problems, so does everyone else, but you get them sorted out. You do get them sorted out.

Indeed the problematic nature (in the 'eyes of outsiders') of their unproblematic relation to Kensington only really became apparent during enforced acts of reflection within the social science interview. For example the people above refer to their 'lived view' of Kensington as unproblematic to them but as potentially problematic when subjected to the gaze of an outsider from a 'better area'.

If someone come [sic] from outside, I mean say like yourself, I don't know you might live in a nice posh area somewhere and you come here and it might be like a shock to you, do you know what I mean, but it's not, to me it's quite normal.

JJ37

So although all of the 'signs' indicate that now is the time to 'get out' of Kensington this was not how working-class people experienced it. Indeed their feeling that Kensington was unproblematic to them (because, in reality, it was unproblematic to them) was *actually reinforced* by the constant circulation of stories about the endemic nature of crime and anti-social behaviour in the media. Thus, although working-class people formulate judgments about their neighbourhoods according to their primary experience of it, and not the 'narratives of decline' that have been attached to them by media and other institutions, they are acutely aware that the media characterises contemporary society *writ large* as riddled with crime and anti-social behaviour. This media representation of contemporary society *writ large* infested with crime, drug use and anti-social behaviour provided little incentive for our respondents to move to other areas that were 'much dearer' because it was clear that 'all places have these problems'. So working-class people did not only experience Kensington as a 'lived space' that they had no reason to vacate because it was unproblematic to them. They also lacked the desire to move to other, more exclusive, neighbourhoods that were potentially equally problematic.

RM32   They're all the same, big cities, they're all the same. If you chose to live in a big city you're going to get problems here and there, aren't you, it's a fact of life.

Q   Yeah, because it's wherever you visit?

RM32   Yeah, you're going to get like gangs, drugs; it goes with the thing of living in a city, don't it, it's part of city life.

Q   So in the grand sort of scheme of things do you think it's a problem area to live in?

RM32   I just go about my own thing but I wouldn't say it's any worse than say Anfield or the south, down Toxteth, The Dingle, that way. I think there's equally as bad areas if not worse areas.

JJ37   I mean no matter where you go, there's always drug problems, whether you're in Woolton or Kensington or wherever, you'll always get a problem with drugs
        . . . .

SJ35   Wherever your big cities are you'll get trouble, won't you?

JJ37   Croxteth, and the nearest ones of course are . . . there's a lot of new estates over there but I think they would have the same problems. Well they will start having them now, as what we've had . . . . So we're very happy living round here . . . . I mean it has deteriorated, ... But I'd find it hard probably now to move away, but I don't know, keep saying maybe one day, but I doubt it. 'Cos where would we go, you know, there's good and bad wherever you go so.

This is not to suggest that there was literally nothing wrong with Kensington in the perceptions of those who occupied it. Working-class people in Kensington acknowledge that it has changed (increasing unemployment, a decline of 'community' and so on) but their 'lived experience' leads them to suggest that, despite these changes, it is 'still a decent area' that, contrary to media representation, is populated by 'decent working-class people'.

Okay, I know with Littlewoods and one of the firms that went off Edge Lane and . . . and the bus sheds and what have you, that did take a lot of work away from the area, which of course does cause unemployment which there was high unemployment, still is. But it was still and it still is fundamentally a decent area . . . . It's amazing how every one of these houses basically had decent select people in them or perhaps not so much select but, you know.

LR55

There are still a lot of very good kind honest people, I like people around here. Yes, a lot, and it's not only the older generation, it's the youngsters as well . . . . There's a lot of really good caring youngsters around, they're not all bad, no way. I know they're not . . . . They will stop and will part to let you go through, the boys. I go, 'oh thank you lads'. And if they're playing football in the streets, they'll stop [to let me walk by], or if they're on their bike, they will stop [to let me walk by]. But there again to my mind that's the way they've been brought up by their parents.

SH78

Q   What about your neighbours?
AC63   I mean the area has changed, but, you know, it's a quiet road, but there are still young ones that are [daughter's] age that are rearing their families and they're doing that discipline because they've been taught respect and discipline. You're still getting it from those and their children.

These examples are not being presented as aberrations, which would, of course, serve to validate the legitimacy of official views of Kensington. They are presented within the context of an urban narrative that is articulated from the point of view of 'lived experience', which suggests an unproblematic relation to the area. These working-class people are suggesting that there is nothing unusual about the presence of 'decent' people in Kensington because, indeed, they were the people who had a historical relationship with the area.

Problems of being in Kensington

Although most working-class people have an unproblematic relation to Kensington on an average-everyday basis, some respondents articulate a problematic relation to it. However even those who do articulate a problematic relation to Kensington do so from the point of view of their 'lived experience', which, consisting of a series of direct encounters with Kensington, was articulated as 'mixed'.

Q   So how would you describe your own experience then of living here at the moment?

LR55   A nightmare at times, it's an absolute nightmare. Other times it's great . . . .

Q   So how do you feel about, you know, where you live, I mean what kind of . . . ?

LR55   I want to see it go back to the way it used to be. Okay, everyone's entitled to live their life their way, I am a great believer in live and let live, but something should be done about number 4, . . . we are trying to get it done.

For these people, there is nothing inherently 'bad' about Kensington, which is 'no worse than anywhere else' because 'all areas have their problems'. On the contrary, these respondents are simply articulating what they perceive to be a 'realistic' perspective of Kensington as a counterbalance to the hyper-reality of official views that are articulated through an unambiguous 'narrative of decline'. This is clear in the 'lived narrative' provided by the man below, who articulates a matter-of-fact description of some problems encountered on an average-everyday basis whilst acknowledging that they 'do not particularly bother' him. This is very different from the feelings of panic that media representations invoke about the same phenomena that he describes in the testimony below.

Q   You know the *Liverpool Echo* every now and then run a story about Kensington and you know it might be painting the place as not a very nice place to live, the area in general. I mean, how does that make you feel?

RM32   They've got a point in some things they say. It isn't the greatest area. I mean I go out a lot round here and you can see it for yourself, it's not hid away, it's in your face half the time like.

Q   What is that, I mean what kind of things would you see that would be in your face?

RM32   I see drug dealing for a start, prostitution, poor housing, gangs, poor shops, all kinds.

Q   Where would you see those? I mean on a day-to-day basis.

RM32 On a day-to-day, yeah.

Q Say you're just going round in your normal everyday life and you're going to work and you're coming home and you might be going out taking your wife, I don't know, would you see that kind of thing?

RM32 Yeah, you would, yeah, on most days.

Q And is it near here or is it somewhere else?

RM32 If I was walking up Z Road I'd say most days you'd see one or maybe two prostitutes working every day, guarantee it. I'll go and pick my wife up after and I'll guarantee I'll see a prostitute there. Or you'll see smackheads waiting for a car to pull up with the gear and stuff like that, or smackheads just walking up and down like, you know, space cadets, like.

Q And does that cause you any problems?

RM32 It doesn't bother me particularly. I just don't think it should be there. Really like I don't think it should be so open like that, particularly the prostitutes like.

Q So I mean would you talk about it with your wife say or would you just blank it out?

RM32 Probably say 'Look at the state of her', or 'What's going on there?' like. There's no need for it, is there? I mean my Dad's been coming home from the pub of a night and been asked or propositioned and things like that. You know what I mean? He's like 70 years of age. It's not on like, is it? I see them when I'm driving to work of a morning down Edge Lane, so you see them then as well.

Q So I mean is that the kind of thing that would make you think maybe you should move?

RM32 Well, it wouldn't want to make me move particularly like. I think something should be done about it like. They're supposed to be looking at that now; different areas with a red light areas type of thing. Whether that comes off I don't know because you're going to upset someone, aren't you?

Q And what about the drug dealing and all that, I mean would that sort of impinge on you in any way?

RM32 Not really. I mean don't get me wrong you don't see that every day, although you know it goes on and whatever.

This is not to say that all working-class people are so 'balanced' in presenting an account of their 'lived experience' of Kensington. Working-class respondents also talked about the problems that confronted them in a way that was indicative of the direct and uncompromising way that some 'problems' in the area imposed on them. This can be seen in the way people present and analyse some of the problems that exist for them in Kensington in a primordial form of language that is indicative of their social and spatial proximity to those problems.

> So the thing that brought this area down is housing associations, and the families they put in, that's what started the decline definitely. You can tell, you can walk up any road, there again there's a lot of people I know live in housing association houses that have done for a long, long time, but not the new breed who are living in the new housing associations. You could walk up any of these roads and I bet you, you could point out which was owned and which was housing association or rented by private landlords even worse. We've had some terrible families in this street, absolutely horrendous, and we've had murder with private landlords.
>
> JC54

CS47   About the last five years [housing associations] moved every bit of scum from anywhere, loads of drug addicts, prostitutes, oh it was terrible, it was really terrible. You couldn't go outside the door and they'd be asking for money and it was right facing our house there was, the house was actually boarded up but they took the boards off.

Q   Who?

CS47   All drug addicts, but prostitutes, but you know, dirty, stinking, god knows who'd pay to go with them, they never had a tooth in their head, minging and oh god they were terrible, disgusting but on the game you know with men.

These descriptions do not constitute 'primitive' understandings of the problem, even though this is how regeneration agencies describe them when they refer to such descriptions as 'miserably expressed' (see Chapter 8). As Bourdieu and Passeron (1977: 116) have pointed out, the 'liberal' world views and sanitised language of the middle-classes tend to 'abstraction, formalism, intellectualism and euphemistic moderation' because they exist at a spatial distance from social problems that present themselves in 'run down' neighbourhoods. On the other hand, the language of the working class emerges from bodies that exist in close proximity to problems as they present themselves and therefore tends towards 'expressiveness or expressionism . . . which manifests itself in the tendency . . . to shun the bombast of fine words and the turgidity of grand emotions, through banter, rudeness and ribaldry' (Bourdieu and Passeron 1977: 116). Charlesworth (2000) provides an excellent analysis of why the profane language used by working-class people should be valued for the unique insight that it provides into problems so directly encountered (and not as exemplars of 'primitive thought') when he explains why some of his working-class respondents described Rotherham using one word, 'crap', coupled with a refusal to elaborate.

> When asked for an opinion of Rotherham this woman felt the one word, 'crap', uttered with a blank face, as though the question was one of an imbecile, in the tones of tolerant self-evidence and complete seriousness, was a satisfactory description of the place . . . . She reaches spontaneously for 'crap', the immediacy of her response shows that the response is not one that issues from a careful weighing of possible responses; she is not contemplating different aspects of her perception of experience, but feels 'crap' captures the experience of stultifying banality the town engenders . . . . It crystallizes in a condensed meaning, a whole relation to the world, attitude to existence and being, and instantiates this in a sense that relates to the referential-whole of their lives . . . . Rotherham–crap is a direct expression of her experience . . . . [This] description takes the form of direct expression of experience that is primordially encountered. Instead of reports of a reflective, deliberative, aesthetic kind, one finds expressions that are closer to pain behaviour in form.
>
> (Charlesworth 2000: 114, 119)

It is for this reason that Merleau-Ponty (1962: 178) distinguishes between 'second order' expression and 'first order' or 'authentic' speech. Second order speech is essentially 'speech about speech' and therefore a representative form of speech that 'sees itself' rather than the legitimate thoughts and feelings of a speaking subject within a certain style of being-in-the-world, which it actually conceals. First order speech consists of the originating expressions that are formulated *for the first time* and capture how the interlocutor is enveloped by the situation. These first order articulations are primary meanings that 'feel themselves' rather than 'see themselves' and, as such, are prior to the second order thoughts that they arouse and which actually conceal the primacy of experience. Capturing this 'authentic' form of speech as it is formulated unconsciously 'on the spot' offers us a way of appreciating how perception emanates from the density of lived experience. It is this that leads the person below to deny the label of 'racist' that she feels those who are positioned at a social and spatial distance from her experience may impose on her. On the contrary, she is simply articulating the situation as it would appear to anyone so fixed in social and geographical space.

JC54   I'm sorry if you're offended but tough shit, basically, sorry. I go to work every morning and I'm about the only white person walking up the road, or if I'm not the only white person, I'm the only person who's not a smack head . . . . We're the outcasts, we're the outsiders. It's not our community anymore. And

I don't mean it should be, this is our community, nobody can come in here strange or anything like that, I don't mean that. But when you feel as if you're just being overtaken and not considered, and just, you keep paying all your bills and let everyone else come and wreck the area, it's wrong, totally wrong. These over here, this is the fourth week on the run, they've thrown fridges out, they've thrown three piece suites out the back. If I had done that, I'd get fined. I just can't stand it now. Not just here, the whole of the country. And everyone I speak to feels exactly the same. There's no consideration for people in this country anymore, absolutely none. None whatsoever. And I am so disillusioned now. Because with this Regen you kept thinking 'oh things are going to get better, it's going to improve the area, it's going to . . .', you know, all the plans. It's never come to that at all. They've just deliberately run it down.[2]

Q   So do you feel any attachment to the area?

JC54   Not now, because it's not the area anymore. It's been overtaken, by arseholes who don't pay any rent or tax or nothing. And immigrants. It's not a community, it's not an area anymore. It's a dumping ground . . . . It's got nothing to do with racism, nothing whatsoever. But it does bring the area down, I'm sorry it does, it's a fact of life. If they were proper refugees who fled from a war torn country, I'd open my own front door to them. But they're not, they're all the gypsies. . . . they're getting everything paid for them. And people on the social, never intended to work. And I'm paying £80 a month in mortgage. It's not right. It's not who they are or what colour they are, that's got bugger all to do with it. It's just like they were second-class citizens and even third-class now.

The same person claims that her response to this situation has been to 'shut the door' ('basically I've just got the attitude I go to work, I come in and shut the door and that's it'), which, of course, would provide some legitimacy to the official view that Kensington is in social decline. But this would be to overlook the way in which the 'we-being' of working-class people actually compels them to continue to cooperate with households that, paradoxically, they denigrate within the context of the social science interview. This suggests, therefore, that a quite different social situation exists in Kensington to that promoted by the official view.

JE42   Yeah and we got the house and then she moved in, private landlord moved her in and, at first, she was fine. But then she used to have like gangs on the steps. And then he was in prison, her fella. Then he come out after about two years, and I used to think 'oh god'. And she was one of these. She'd have everybody and anybody at the door, and she was fighting in the street. She had a mouth like I don't know what. She'd be screeching all over and the language and I used to think 'oh god'. Then they'd be on the [front door] step at all hours of the night, and then she started selling the weed. And then he come out of prison after about two years and it went quiet. But then, one time, my husband and my little boy were in bed and then my husband come running down the stairs and I thought 'oh'. He come running, he was like pulling his pants up and he was like 'Jane, Jane quick', and I thought 'oh, something's happened to the baby'. But he ran out into the street and she was getting murdered outside the door [by her fella].

Q   Literally?

JE42   Literally battered, I mean on the floor getting kicked in the head. Anyway my husband ran out to this fella. But he was like bigger and everything and went like 'keep away, otherwise, you know, you'll end up getting it'. Anyway he [my husband] went out and picked her up and what have you and her face was a mess. Her little lad was hysterical and I was trying to calm him and she went 'it's alright. He's seen it all before, what his dad used to do to me.' I try my best to sort of get on with her. I'm not a snob but, you know, when you know you're in a different league to somebody else.

Q   Would your kids play with her kids?

JE42   Yeah, yeah, the little girl like 'cos she ended up having another baby then who was, she's about three now, four maybe and like my little girl she'd play. I'd never stop the kids, I'd never dream of stopping the kids playing with like them next door.

Conclusion

The representation of Kensington as an area of 'urban decline' is deeply problematic. Such representations simply do not correspond with the 'lived view' of Kensington that is articulated by working-class people who live there. The problem here is not that there are contrasting views of Kensington. The problem is that official views of Kensington obtain their legitimacy from the practices of objectification (gathering statistics etc.) that are employed to construct them. Despite their legitimacy, the official view is not unproblematic. Far from it. Official views that are constituted from the social and spatial distance of the statisticians' office have no way of understanding Kensington as a 'lived space' at all. They simply understand it through a series of statistical representations ('low demand', 'high void rate') that are constituted by urban professional elites whose 'interest' in Kensington is as a position in the space of positions. Hence terminology such as 'low demand' is relational because it speaks of Kensington only in relation to other areas; it has lower demand for its houses than other areas, more empty dwellings than other areas and so on. Yet working-class people, who relate to Kensington as a lived space and not a position within the space of positions, experience Kensington as largely unproblematic. It is important to understand this because the next part of the book discusses how the legitimacy that is accorded to the official view has 'necessitated', from the policy point of view, the imposition of the HMR programme on Kensington.

Housing market renewal is underpinned by the dominant view of the market for houses and so problematises neighbourhoods that have become disconnected from the space of positions in the market for houses because of, say, a 'low demand' for houses in those neighbourhoods. The purpose of housing market renewal is to reposition these neighbourhoods within the space of positions in the metropolitan housing market. It seeks to do this in Kensington by demolishing terraced houses and replacing them with 'high-value products' that 'people want to buy'. Yet this violates a whole way of being-toward Kensington, that is, the working-class experience of Kensington as largely unproblematic. Moreover, restructuring of the market for houses in Kensington, so that it is positioned within the space of positions in the metropolitan housing market, violates a whole way of being-toward houses as, quite simply, a place to dwell. These issues are taken up in detail in the next part of the book.

Part III

The class politics of housing market renewal

Chapter 6
Housing market renewal and the 'new' market logic of urban renewal

Introduction

In the introduction of this book I argued that literatures on housing and class formation have paid too much attention to habitus and not enough to the field. This is evident in the existing scholarship on middle-class formation (especially gentrification studies), which has largely focused on how the forms of capital possessed by middle-class people are mobilised within various fields of consumption. I think it is fair to say that nothing like the equivalent effort has been invested in analyses of the institutional constitution of these various fields of consumption. For example, gentrification studies have overwhelmingly focused on how middle-class gentrifiers have imposed their habitus upon inner-urban neighbourhoods, such as by mobilising their cultural capital to appropriate, valorise and secure parts of the inner-urban landscape for themselves. Insofar as gentrification studies focus on the institutions that structure the inner-urban housing market (e.g. developers, estate agents, regeneration agencies), they tend to appear late on the scene (see Ley 1996). In 'staged' processes of gentrification, then, these institutions are represented as agents that *follow* housing market trends and enter inner-urban housing markets to exploit the profit-making opportunities that have been created in the inner city as a result of the efforts of 'urban storm troopers' who have valorised those areas at an earlier stage of the process of gentrification (e.g. Zukin 1982; Feinstein 1994). Thus we have been told very little about the institutional constitution of the market for houses in which social groups, such as gentrifiers, operate. What is needed, then, is an approach that places housing market institutions at the centre of analysis.

Analyses of the institutional constitution of the market for houses have been undertaken before, of course. For example, Harloe (1995) and Ball (1983) have analysed the 'various combinations of agents involved in the structures of housing provision'. However, their account of the institutional constitution of the market for houses is underpinned by an underlying logic of development. What we are presented with, then, is an insight into how institutions constitute housing markets *with a bias towards owner occupation* for the purposes of ensuring capital accumulation. Now there is nothing inherently wrong with this. It is simply limiting as a frame of reference (see Chapter 2). The limit of such Marxist accounts is that they tend to theorise housing development with reference to a *political economy of tenure*, that is, in terms of a 'logic of capitalism' that supports owner occupation over social renting. Yet this overlooks the fact that the market for owner occupation is itself constituted in distinct ways. That is to say, there are distinct *markets for owner occupation*, each of which is constituted in particular ways by the agents involved in them (estate agents, regeneration agencies, house purchasers etc.). We saw this to be the case in earlier chapters, which referred to two distinct economies of housing consumption: middle-class households relate to the market for houses as a space of positions, whereas working-class households tend to exhibit a practical economy of housing consumption. Now we already know something about how housing market institutions constitute the market for houses as a space of positions, e.g. through advertising of lifestyles (see Chapter 4). The purpose of this chapter is to examine how housing market institutions are reconstituting local housing markets, such as Kensington, that have become disconnected from the space of positions within the wider market for houses because they offer little symbolic and economic value to middle-class purchasers, who consequently refuse to buy houses therein. It does this by examining the motivations and practices of institutions involved in 'housing market renewal'.

Conventional forms of 'urban renewal' primarily focused on improving the physical fabric of urban areas (Roberts and Sykes 2000). This conventional vision has been rejected by architects of HMR, such as Ian Cole, who denigrate it as the 'sticking plaster' approach (Cole and Flint 2006: 17). The architects of HMR argue that it is an entirely 'new' form of urban renewal initiative (Cole and Nevin 2004) because it seeks to 'renew' the *market for houses* in inner-urban areas, such as Kensington, rather than simply *the houses themselves*. Thus, they problematise the market for houses in Kensington because, in their terminology, it has become 'unpopular' with middle-class households and therefore 'disconnected' from the space of positions in the wider metropolitan market for houses. The key purpose of HMR, then, is to 'reconnect' neighbourhoods such as Kensington to the space of positions in the market for houses.

> The word market is what makes this a different programme. This is not about pumping a lot of money into the physical fabric of homes. This is a regeneration project, *it's about linkages, not housing conditions.*
>
> (Manchester Housing Director, quoted in Cameron 2006: 6)

> This isn't a housing renewal programme, it is a market renewal programme.
>
> (Managing Director, Newheartlands HMR[1])

The chapter discusses how housing market institutions have created and mobilised *an arbitrary form of knowledge* about Kensington, in the space of positions, which is being used to legitimise a programme that is reconstituting the market for houses in Kensington in a very specific way. Specifically, these institutions are demolishing 'low-value' working-class housing and replacing it with a 'high-value' dwellingscape that is attractive to middle-class households in order to reposition Kensington within the space of positions in the metropolitan market for houses. The chapter argues that this renewal strategy should be challenged for two reasons. First, it 'speaks' only to the interests that the house sales industry and middle-class people have in the market for houses ('an investment') because it provides them with opportunities to extract economic profits from places such as Kensington. Second, this institutional pursuit of a 'class remake' of Kensington violates working-class forms of being-toward houses as 'dwelling space' and not a position in the space of positions.

The 'evidence base' for HMR in Liverpool

In April 2002 the government announced the creation of an HMR programme in nine areas of the North and Midlands that were exhibiting signs of 'housing market failure'. Housing market failure was said to be evident in high vacancy rates, increasing population turnover, low sales values and, in some cases, neighbourhood abandonment (Cole and Nevin 2004). The New Deal for Communities (NDC) area of Kensington was identified as a 'failing' housing market and incorporated into the 'Newheartlands' HMR area of Liverpool. Housing market renewal will require the mass demolition of approximately 50,000 'unwanted' dwellings in Merseyside (Nevin and Lee 2001). Between 20,000 and 30,000 of these dwellings are located in Newheartlands (Cole and Nevin 2004; Crooks 2006) with at least 11,000 of these being located in the inner-urban ring of the city of Liverpool (Ecotec 2005). The purpose of this mass demolition programme is to provide large parcels of land to developers, who will be charged with the task of creating an inner-urban dwellingscape that is attractive to middle-class house purchasers. To put this in context, 39,000 dwellings were demolished in the City of Liverpool, between the years 1951 and 1966, to make way for a high-rise dwellingscape (Dunleavy 1981).

The 'housing market renewal' programme exemplifies the New Labour penchant for 'evidence based' policy making. It was formulated in response to research undertaken on 'changing housing markets and urban regeneration in the M62 corridor' (Nevin *et al.* 2001), which provided an analysis of 'housing market change' in the North West. This research focused on a number of areas in the North West, including housing markets within the inner-urban area of Liverpool, such as Kensington. The programme to demolish working-class housing in Kensington is informed by this research study as well as a range of other research studies undertaken by one of the architects of the HMR programme, Brendan Nevin, in conjunction with a range of housing research consultants. The justification for the HMR programme that involves the demolition of working-class houses in Kensington can be found, then, in a range of research reports produced by Nevin and his colleagues (for example, Nevin *et al.* 1999; Nevin and Lee 2001; Lee and Nevin 2002; Nevin *et al.* 2001; Ecotec 2005) as well as a series of other supporting documents that lawyers acting for Liverpool City Council submitted to a public enquiry into its proposed compulsory purchase of working-class houses in Liverpool.[2] This public enquiry was convened to consider the justification for the housing demolition programme, which has met with significant opposition from working-class people living in the inner-urban ring in Liverpool.

The research reports that have informed the HMR programme in Liverpool claim that the housing market has failed in the inner core of the city for a number of reasons. First, economic and income growth, coupled with residential development in suburban areas within and outside Liverpool, has resulted in the abandonment of inner-urban areas. As incomes grow, then, people leave the city to live in more 'desirable' suburban areas. Second, this process of suburbanisation (and 'emptying out' of the inner core) has occurred because income growth produces rising housing aspirations. Third, these housing aspirations can be satisfied in suburban developments, which provide for a better quality of life. The research reports argue that the quality of life in the inner core is poorer than that found in suburban areas, according to a range of 'key indicators' such as crime and anti-social behaviour. Fourth, 'low demand' for houses in the inner core is also a consequence of the 'monolithic' predominance of specific dwelling types, namely 'outdated' terraced housing. The rising aspirations that accompany rising incomes have resulted in a desire for 'modern' and 'contemporary' houses, which are defined as new build detached and semi-detached houses with gardens. Fifth, the relative unattractiveness of the inner core has resulted in a polarised housing market. House prices have been growing in areas that have soaked up rising aspirations, whereas the inner core has 'suffered' from stagnant or even negative house price change. The consequences of this polarised market are said to manifest themselves in an unequal distribution of housing wealth, with owner occupiers living in the inner core seeing the value of their homes 'fall behind' those in the wider market. Finally, the reports claim that neighbourhoods such as Kensington are 'holding back' the regeneration of Liverpool because they lack the type of housing that the middle classes, who presumably drive urban economic performance, seek. The Newheartlands Pathfinder has stated as its key purpose, then, the

> need to *reconnect* our pathfinder areas to their surrounding markets and to the renewed, vibrant city centres that lie next to many of them – so that the benefits of urban renaissance are enjoyed more widely . . . . We need to ensure that these areas provide homes fit for the twenty-first century . . . . [S]ome of the housing in the pathfinder areas has reached the end of its useful life – it no longer meets modern needs or aspirations . . . . Creating functioning housing markets within a sustainable framework is a key part of achieving sustained economic growth . . . [so that] the housing market supports broader regional economic aims. But a housing market that provides quality and choice for everyone relies on more than just the provision of attractive houses . . . . Involving the community is important because people who live in areas of low housing demand are suffering the consequences . . . . Ensuring that there is the right amount of housing which meets people's needs and expectations is a central aim of our work. Pathfinders will work to raise house prices in the pathfinder areas so that they match regional averages.
>
> (Elvin and Litton 2006, emphasis added)

The idea that inner-urban housing markets have become 'disconnected' from 'surrounding markets' is based on the notion that places such as Kensington *should* occupy a position within the space of positions on the urban landscape:

> housing market restructuring [is] required to ensure that the older urban areas compete at a regional, national and international level.
>
> (Cole and Nevin 2004: viii)

> Housing market renewal will not be seen to have succeeded unless it brings about a 'reconnection' between their local housing markets and those of the wider area.
>
> (Leather *et al.* 2007: 56)

The relative lack of controversy surrounding the view that places such as Kensington *should* occupy a position within the space of positions on the urban landscape is indicative of the manner in which this 'definition' of the market for houses, as a space of positions, is taken for granted as self-evident within academic and housing policy communities.[3] Yet it is a product of the hegemonic view of housing markets mobilised from social positions (government agencies, regeneration agencies, academics, consultants, estate agents etc.) that are separate, in social and economic terms, from the manner in which ordinary working-class people experience the 'reality' of housing on an average-everyday basis. Thus housing consultants who occupy social spaces that enable them to perceive and analyse the market for houses as a space of positions (rather than in terms of the way in which they are experienced by ordinary people) are compelled to problematise positions that have become 'disconnected' from the space of positions. Thus Lee and Nevin, summarising the findings of their eight studies into the Liverpool housing market, claim that their research

> has revealed a highly complex and polarised housing market within the city of Liverpool . . . . Notwithstanding the positive market characteristics outlined above [economic growth in Liverpool, rising house prices], the fact that 24 per cent of properties are situated in neighbourhoods experiencing acute decline has a signifi-cant negative impact upon the regeneration effort within the city. Within these areas individuals are seeing their major asset depreciate and experiencing negative wealth distribution.
>
> (Lee and Nevin 2002: 50)

What is interesting here is the articulation of this problematic in the *name* of the poor ('individuals are seeing their major asset depreciate') so that its resolution appears to be self-evidently 'in the *interests* of the poor'. Yet such claims-making only makes sense when viewed from the position of the narrators, who view the poor as negatively situated in relation to other people within the market for houses. These claims are anything but self-evident from the point of view of the poor, in whose name Lee and Nevin articulate them in order to justify the 'housing market renewal' programme to demolish working-class houses in Kensington. The *views* of the poor are that their houses are not a form of economic wealth and that their neighbourhoods are not positioned within a space of positions on the urban landscape. This should have become apparent in Chapters 4 and 5, which discussed how working-class people relate to their houses and neighbourhoods as 'things' that are 'ready to hand' rather than in terms of their symbolic or investment value within the space of positions in the market for houses.

Understanding Kensington within the space of positions

The representation of Kensington as a position within a space of positions within the market for houses emanates from social agents (local authorities, hous-ing developers, estate agents etc.) whose 'interest' in Kensington is primarily economic (see Box 6.1). Yet the economic nature of this interest is obscured by reference to the research that provides 'housing market renewal' with an 'evidence base'. This point was articulated by the legal team acting for Liverpool City Council during an enquiry into the issue of compulsory purchase orders on working-class households in Kensington in July 2006. One of the key elements of the city council's case was that:

> The *evident* decline of the inner core was confirmed through research carried out by CURS which issued a series of 8 reports from 1999 to 2002. That research was concerned with assessing the sustainability of neighbourhoods in Liverpool and assisting in the development of a strategic framework for addressing the issues identified by that research.
>
> (Elvin and Litton 2006, emphasis added)

The purpose of presenting the case in this way is to suggest that proposals for demolition and renewal have emerged following a process of 'stakeholder' reflection on evidence that has been collected in an unproblematic way. Yet this belies the fact that the eight reports to which the city council refer have been produced from the standpoint of consultants whose 'involvement' and 'interest' in the market for houses is as a market for houses, that is, as a space of positions. These consultants' misrecognition of their views as 'objective', rather than particular, is indicated by the extent to which they constitute their particular view of the market for houses, as a space of positions, as self-evident ('doxa'). This is apparent in the way in which the research that led to the declaration of the HMR 'initiative' was undertaken *in response to changes in local housing markets* using a definition of the 'housing market' as a 'space of positions' (strong demand for this; low demand for that) that was taken for granted.

> This study was commissioned by the Housing Corporation, 18 local authorities, the National Housing Federation, the National House Builders Federation, the Chartered Institute of Housing and 24 RSLs [Registered Social Landlords]. These agencies were *responding to changes in local housing markets* in the North West which were experiencing *strong demand for newly built accommodation for sale* and *increases in vacancies in the social rented sector and owner occupied terraced sectors.*
>
> (Nevin *et al.* 1999: vi, emphasis added)

The problematic for those who seek to critique housing market renewal is that the 'evidence base' that is used to justify it has emerged from a conception of the market for houses that, as doxa, appears to be neutral rather than a point of view articulated from the standpoint of social agents who seek to reposition

Kensington within the space of positions in Liverpool's market for houses. The power of this doxa is evident in the way new languages that emerge from it, which describe the nature and extent of the 'disconnection' of working-class housing in Kensington from the space of positions, have met with little or no controversy. Two new languages of the market are pertinent in this respect. The first concerns the 'discovery' that there has been an inflation in housing aspirations to match growing economic affluence, which has resulted in a demand for 'modern' and 'contemporary' houses as opposed to Victorian and Edwardian terraced houses. This is presented as a 'fact'. The second concerns the implication of this, which is the contention that working-class terraced housing has now become 'obsolete'. This is also presented as a 'fact'. I will now address the manner in which these two apparent facts have been linguistically constructed.

Box 6.1 Economic interests in Kensington

The political economy of 'interest' in housing market renewal

A key concern for Liverpool City Council is that 93.4 per cent of homes in the HMR area, Newheartlands, are in council tax bands A and B, because this reduces the revenue-raising capacity of the council (Green 2006). Liverpool City Council has an economic interest in maximising the number of 'high-value' dwellings in the HMR area because this will increase the number of properties that fall within higher council tax bands, thereby increasing the revenue-raising capacity of the council.

Thus the Assistant Executive Director for Housing and Neighbourhoods within Liverpool City Council has stated that a key motivation for housing market renewal is 'transforming Liverpool's housing, alongside its economic renaissance, [to] ensure that economically successful people can obtain housing quality and choice within Liverpool rather than leave the city'.

The local authority can make this happen by issuing compulsory purchase orders (CPOs) on 'low-value' houses. This enables the local authority to purchase houses at their current market value when the CPO is issued. The housing market renewal programme was initiated at a time when the market for houses in Kensington was 'depressed',[4] which means that Liverpool City Council has been able to purchase working-class houses at low cost. Moreover, since these houses stand on land that is adjacent to the city centre, it possesses a large 'rent gap', which means that the potential value of the land (when redeveloped) far outstrips its current value. This potential land value now accrues to the city council, which now owns it, rather than working-class people from whom it has been forcibly taken.

Rhoades (2006) has explained how land that has come into the ownership of Liverpool City Council is now being developed to ensure that profit-making opportunities, which exist as a consequence of the large 'rent gap', are split between the city council and developers.[5] The agreement between Liverpool City Council and developers states the following:

- The city council will be obliged to offer all housing land in its owner-ship [as a result of CPO] to the appropriate lead developer for housing redevelopment.
- Once the development agreement is signed the developer will pay the council a percentage of the estimated land value and an appropriate portion of the remaining land value as housing units are completed.
- A building licence will be granted to the developer upon payment of the initial sum.
- If the land value turns out to be greater than the estimated land value then the extra profit is split equally by the city council and the developer. If the actual value is less than the estimated land value already paid to the city council, the deficit will be carried forward to the next development site. It will effectively act as credit to the developer.
- The developer is allowed a minimum rate of return on the Gross Development Value of each development and the agreed form of the final appraisal is attached to the Overarching Agreement.

'Modern' and 'contemporary' aspirations

The research reports that 'necessitate' the demolition of working-class houses in Kensington emerged out of a survey of consumer preferences that sought to add flesh to statistical evidence of a shift in housing demand from inner-urban terraces to new build houses with gardens in suburban locations. This consumer survey was undertaken by Nevin *et al.* (2001), who polled the views of 233 residents living on the Wirral but with work ties to Liverpool as well as two focus groups undertaken in the Croxteth Park area of Liverpool. The key findings of this research were that suburban households possessed anti-urban attitudes, preferred living with 'like minded' people and felt that the quality of their own suburban dwellings was better than those in Liverpool (only 3 per cent suggesting that housing in Liverpool was of better quality). This compelled the authors to suggest that 'if urban renewal of Liverpool is to be successful . . . it is reasonable to predict that considerable inducement in terms of the physical fabric and the social climate would have to be addressed' (Nevin *et al.* 2001: 31). Official policy documents have used this analysis of statistical trends and 'consumer preferences' (showing that increasing affluence has been accompanied by large-scale movement from inner-urban terrace houses to new build houses with gardens in suburban locations) to suggest that housing market renewal needs to provide for:

- 'rising aspirations', 'modern day aspirations' (Green 2006: para. 2.12);
- 'homes fit for modern living standards' (Elvin and Litton 2006: para. 35);
- 'modern contemporary homes' (Green 2006: para. 1.23).

Before we proceed any further, it is instructive to note that we have been here before, with disastrous consequences. Patrick Dunleavy (1981), writing about the politics of mass housing, notes how a key turning point towards the high-rise experiment came in 1963 when:

> Keith Joseph decided to seek industrialists' views on the ways to tackle Britain's urban problems, with a view to encouraging private enterprise to take on a larger share of the urban renewal effort. The MHLG [Ministry of Housing and Local Government] invited Taylor Woodrow Ltd., the second largest construction group in Britain at the time, to undertake a study of Fulham and produce proposals for the urban renewal policy to be pursued in the study area, which covered some 480 hectares with a population of 40,000 people. Taylor Woodrow's team responded by calling for '*large scale rebuilding rather than piecemeal development* of worn out housing areas'. The necessity was argued not in terms of acute housing need – 'there are very few slums in the area' – but in terms of *a need for modern, purpose-built accommodation.*
>
> (Dunleavy 1981: 109, emphasis added)

The corollary of the claim that twenty-first-century housing consumers want to live in 'modern and contemporary homes' is the implication that Victorian and Edwardian terraced houses are 'obsolete' and 'unwanted'. This view was articulated by Nevin *et al.* in their first report on the Liverpool housing market, which interpreted statistical evidence of movement to the suburbs to mean that terraced houses had become 'life expired and unsuitable for modern living' (Nevin *et al.* 1999: 8) and that:

> Inner city housing built in the Victorian era may be less appropriate for housing contemporary households and lifestyle arrangements. At the same time, housing designed to accommodate an industrial working class (high density, flatted accommodation, for example) will be less appropriate for contemporary 'flexible' service sector households who are increasingly influenced by a consumer driven society.
>
> (Nevin *et al.* 1999: 41)

Terraced housing at the 'end of history'

At a public enquiry into the compulsory purchase of terraced houses in Kensington, Liverpool City Council argued that the proposed demolition of these houses was 'evidence based' by pointing to the eight reports produced by independent consultants. Yet the terraced houses occupied by working-class people in Kensington were initially denigrated by the *first* report published by these consultants in 1999 and continually thereafter. The notion that terraced housing is 'obsolete' and 'unwanted' is not a hypothesis or fact that has been subject to empirical testing by other researchers but, rather, a conceptual language that has been used by the same consultants from within the parameters of the official view that Kensington has become disconnected from the space of positions in the market for houses in Liverpool. Specifically the notion that terraced houses are 'outdated' and 'unsuitable for modern living' has emerged as a result of these consultants' interpretations of population movements scanned across a range of housing market areas at an arbitrary point in time, coupled with their interpretations of the views of a number of suburbanites whose survey responses to questions about housing quality have been interpreted to indicate a desire for 'modern' and 'contemporary' houses, which, presumably, terraced houses are not. But that is not all. The consultants have not simply attached labels ('outdated') to terraced houses. They have created an 'end of history' narrative about terraced houses, which unfolds in the following way:

- Terraced housing in neighbourhoods such as Kensington was built for an industrial working class: 'Terraced housing that dominates significant neighbourhoods in Newheartlands was built pre-1919 to house this industrial population' (Nevin 2006a, paragraph 3.3).
- Time has moved on and there is no longer an industrial working class: industrial decline has resulted in a massive 'population loss experienced in the conurbation's inner core . . . [and has been] most acute' (Nevin 2006a, paragraph 3.5).
- There are increasing numbers of affluent households with 'rising aspirations': this problem has been exacerbated by economic and income growth, which 'is generating a demand for "higher value homes" but this growth in demand for housing is focused on traditional suburban housing markets' (Nevin 2006a, paragraph 3.11).
- These households want 'modern' and 'contemporary' homes: the result of economic and income growth is therefore a large number of inner-urban terraced dwellings which have been rejected by consumers with 'rising aspirations': 'The extent of this flight from Inner Liverpool is evident in the large amount of vacancies in inner city Liverpool. Concentration

of vacancies in Edwardian and Victorian ring of terraced properties . . .'
(Nevin 2006a, paragraph 3.19).
• Terraced housing is therefore 'obsolete': although Liverpool is now enjoying
  a substantial period of economic growth with projected population growth,
  'the market has "failed" to provide a balance between supply and demand
  in inner-city Liverpool for terraced housing for at least a decade' (Nevin
  2006a, paragraph 5.6).

Furthermore, the consultants have been remarkably successful in mobilising this 'end of history' narrative amongst policy makers, whose penchant for
being seduced by simple ideas that negate the complexity of the social world is
well known (Allen *et al.* 1999; Kemeny 1992). This is nowhere more apparent
than in the way in which agents in key positions within housing market renewal
in Liverpool articulated 'first order' impressions of the housing market renewal
area 'in the thick of general conversation' as a diverse space with potential in its
existing form before, paradoxically, iterating an 'end of history narrative' to justify the proposed demolition of working-class houses when they were subjected
to specific questions about HMR in the context of the social science interview.
For example, an NDC officer and a Neighbourhood Inspector both described
the housing market renewal area as 'incredibly diverse' in terms of its housing
and physical landscape in the course of a general conversation about the area:

> In physical terms [the HMR area is] incredibly diverse because the five neighbour-
> hoods are so different, however at least three of the neighbourhoods I'd characterise
> by terraced houses built before 1919, a lot of which are suffering now with the stock
> condition. [Q: So this would be?] Head Lane, Holte Road and Kensington Fields,
> there's some terraced housing in Fairfield of the same sort of character but both
> Holly Road and Fairfield are actually quite mixed. [Q: How would you describe this
> Fairfield then?] Fairfield, probably mixed is the word, it's mixed both in terms of
> tenure, housing type. [Q: There's some quite big houses there isn't there?] That's
> it yeah, there's only one part in the area which is the usual sort of mostly packed
> terrace streets, otherwise there's a lot of large semi-detached homes, a lot of infill
> developments of various qualities and properties there are quite expensive as well
> . . . . There's a lot of listed properties and there's a lot of properties that have got
> really nice architectural features as well but intermingled with the houses in Holly
> Road are places such as Kensington Market.
>
> (NDC Physical and Environmental Regeneration Manager)

It's a lot of large properties around, the main thoroughfare of Edge Lane, Beech

Street, Dean Road, a lot of really big houses in part of the area. They're too big for a single occupancy.

(Neighbourhood Inspector)

These perceptions are reflected by small developers, who refer to the 'absolutely wonderful' dwellingscape of Kensington and the 'renovation potential' of its housing stock.

The local council gave grants to restore these Victorian houses. All the outside brickwork was cleaned up and brand new double glazing was put in. New tiled roofs were put on, and the street really does look absolutely wonderful. They resurfaced the street. I think they put in new street lamps, and it is quite incredible, those houses. I know when I made my first trip up to Liverpool in March the next street up, which hadn't been refurbished, houses were selling on there for £45,000. At an auction about three months ago, or less than three months ago, a property on Jubilee Drive with the inside requiring work done to it sold at auction for £107,000 . . . . Those houses are definitely the future in my opinion. I think they are going to soar in value because they are in Kensington, very close to the city centre . . . . This money has to be spent on restoring them and maintaining some local architecture within the Kensington area because Kensington otherwise is going to become like the city centre, where you have these monstrous glass buildings, high-rise flats with these penthouses that sell, you know, for £800,000. I think it's very sad that a lot of these terraced houses, a lot of the architecture is just being demolished for all this high-rise glass stuff really.

(Small property developer)

Despite offering these 'first order' impressions of Kensington and surrounding areas as a physically diverse space with good architecture and large houses that offer opportunities for conversion to multi-dwelling buildings, the same two respondents quoted above, as well as other housing market institutions, invoke the 'end of history' narrative that has so successfully been mobilised vis-à-vis terraced houses when questioned about the proposals to demolish working-class homes in the context of the social science interview.

Two or three bedroomed terraced houses, they're not what families particularly look for these days, so it's family housing really, gardens and a mixture. It's a total mix really, with apartments and bungalows. It's basically providing a whole variety of houses whereas now there is just one housing type.

(NDC Physical and Environmental Regeneration Manager)

The kind of houses young people want to live in nowadays, they don't want to live in terraced houses do they, everyone wants a detached house on a nice estate, people are concerned about their children's upbringing at schools and all that.

(Neighbourhood Inspector)

And:

Some of these old terraces, they're long past their sell by date, in a lot of areas it's not economically viable to renovate.[6] Renovation to a good standard is a very expensive business. It's much easier to do new build . . . . I guess young professionals would look at the housing market here.

(Director, development and property management company)

The vision for Kensington is about transformational regeneration. It's about keeping Kensington, not bulldozing it. *It's about taking out redundant terraced houses*, many of which include the stairs arriving in a bedroom not on a landing, you know, properties like that that. We've got in Kensington, there are properties with toilets at the back of the downstairs kitchen consuming what should have been a yard and so there's effectively no yard. There are properties that we could not, with confidence, invest money in for a 30-year life here, you know. There are two up, two down, three up and three down terrace houses that don't have that kind of future . . . So big issues are stock condition, *removing obsolete stock*, providing new appropriate accommodation as opposed to chance developments that people just put up what they think they can sell or whatever. Or housing associations or public bodies, for instance, just build anything they can get a grant for to increase the portfolio.

(Director, registered social landlord)

The research, you know, that has been done over the last five years is saying that, people, they want the change to happen. They recognise that some of *these houses have reached the end of their lifetime and they need to go* . . . The issues are the same, you know, *there's still too many terraced houses and I think that's where there needs to be something done.*[7]

(HMR senior manager)

The end of history narrative does not simply stand in contradistinction to these institutional agents' first order impressions of Kensington as a diverse urban space. They also stand in contradistinction to their observations that 'the same houses in other areas' were very popular (see also Townshend 2006), which, of course, undermines their 'official' definition of the housing problematic in self-referential terms, i.e. terraced houses are unpopular *because* terraced housing is unpopular.

If you look down any typical road in, say, I don't know, Liverpool 16, where you've got the same sort of terraced houses, except they go for about £200,000. Houses which are built in 1849, they're all sold, there's none of them let or if they are let they're very high-level lets. If you did a profile of all the people in that road, some of them will have been there forever, some will have moved in last year, some will have moved in 10 years ago and so on, so you've got this whole different range. Some are professionals and some of them are struggling to pay a mortgage; some could probably afford much better but they think 'well I've got a lot of equity anyway'; and some of them are empty nesters that probably sold a much more expensive house to buy this so they own it outright, fabulous lifestyle, holiday when they like and whatever . . . . And then mirror that to a road where the only people there are the people who have to be there but don't want to be there, a completely different lifestyle, totally different lifestyle. And then it's like everything else, the catalyst rolls, once one thing goes wrong, it all goes wrong. The bin men don't come as often, or if they do they invariably don't empty all the bins.

(Estate agent)

'Sociology text books' and the end of terraced housing

The official view of the housing market renewal area is that the 'area as a whole is characterised by a preponderance of low value terraced and otherwise monolithic housing – typically with limited space and sometimes failing to meet decency standards' (Elvin and Litton 2006: para. 17). The corollary of this is the policy view that:

> We need to ensure that homes are fit for modern living standards . . . . Where the housing has reached the end of its useful life *there is no alternative* but to demolish the outdated stock to make way for well designed modern new homes.
>
> (Elvin and Litton 2006: para. 35, emphasis added)

This official view is, of course, 'evidence based' because it has emerged out of the findings of eight consultancy reports that analyse the Liverpool housing market from the standpoint of the dominant housing market doxa, that is, as a space of positions. The nature of the policy problematic is that Kensington has become disconnected from the space of positions in the Liverpool housing market because its 'outdated' housing stock is 'unpopular' with 'modern' housing consumers, who prefer 'modern contemporary homes'. Yet evidence of an apparent consumer preference for 'modern contemporary homes' is highly questionable. For example, work undertaken on the HMR research programme in Manchester–Salford found that 'emerging households' (that is, younger households that tend to commence their 'housing careers' in places such as Kensington) 'would not consider purchasing a newly built home unless it was the only option in the neighbourhood. They claimed that new housing lacked individuality, were not strongly built and that the walls were so thin you could hear the neighbours talking' (Cole *et al.*, 2005: 29). A study of housing consumer preferences in Newcastle and Gateshead by Townshend (2006) similarly found that

> people did not necessarily see the demolition of low demand areas as achieving anything positive. The argument that these areas need to be demolished to develop more standardized modern housing in order to attract house purchasers does not seem to be supported by the research. Most, mass-produced, contemporary housing was criticized by participants in the study. People bought these houses, it seemed, not because they met their aspirations, but because they were the only way of living in particular locations.
>
> (Townshend 2006: 617)

That said, what are we to make of the housing market surveys that indicate a 'consumer preference' for 'modern contemporary homes'? A key problem with housing market surveys that indicate an apparent consumer preference for 'modern contemporary homes' is that they tend to be undertaken by housing consultants who, apparently unacquainted with perspectives in the philosophy of knowledge and thus lacking understanding of the epistemological status of the data they are collecting, fail to acknowledge the social and epistemological separation between the questions asked and the responses given and, therefore, the epistemological status of consumers' responses to their questions. For example, key questions that support the case for HMR are asked from the 'policy view', which provides respondents with a list of possible changes to the urban landscape that might prompt them to move into Liverpool ('which two or three of the improvements on this list, if any, would make you more likely to consider moving into Liverpool?'). The presumption here is that responses to identified changes (11 per cent of all respondents identified 'better quality housing' as a change that would make them more likely to consider moving into Liverpool) translate into possibilities. Yet this could be based on misrecognition, by the researcher and respondent, of the interview conditions in which an answer is articulated, which are, quite clearly, different from those of practice (Allen 2005, 2007a). This apparent misrecognition occurs when consultants assume that speculative answers to speculative questions provide an accurate insight into possibilities ('would you consider living in Liverpool at any time in the next 6 years?'; 10 per cent provided a 'yes' answer) leading to the conclusion that:

> This research has provided clear evidence that the likelihood of a household liv-
> ing outside the city of Liverpool is directly linked to its income. Within the city
> boundary there is also a strong correlation between place of residence and income.
> This finding suggests that employment, economic and income growth in Liverpool
> may exacerbate resident turnover and population loss in areas where the housing
> market is already weak . . . . The survey data suggests that up to 10% of people that
> currently work in the city could be persuaded to purchase a property in Liverpool
> if an appropriate environment could be created . . . . This would be a long term
> project underpinned by niche marketing . . . . The importance of the 'suburban'
> concept to house purchasers will need to be reflected in the size of sites provided
> to developers.
>
> (Nevin *et al.* 2001: 43–4)

Such conclusions make no sense at all from a phenomenological point of view, which suggests that perception and action within social space is pre-reflexive, that is, the product of a form of being-toward the social world that provides particular ways of grasping the possibilities that exist in the world. The imposition of rational choice forms of questioning (i.e. given this, what would you do?) upon survey respondents violates the fact that perception and prac-tice emerge from particular forms of being-in-the-world that circumscribe the range of possibilities that are considered to be open *in practical house moving situations.*[8] In other words, the consultants have collected a range of answers to a series of questions rather than an indication of real possibilities.

Herein lies a larger problem with the 'evidence base' that sustains the claims that justify the HMR programme to demolish working-class houses. The claim that the provision of 'modern' and 'contemporary' houses will bring suburbanites back into the city is directly at odds with the insights provided by the sociology and geography literature on gentrification, which demonstrates that inner-urban revival happens not as a result of people moving into the city but, on the contrary, as a result of people staying within the city (Ley 1996; Smith 1989, 1996). This is something that housing research consultants partly acknowledge but, unfortunately, their understanding of this trend lacks a grounding in the contemporary social science literature. For example, their analysis follows the logic of their economism, which is that 'the likelihood of a household living outside the city of Liverpool is directly linked to its income' (Nevin *et al.* 2001). That is to say, rising affluence amongst housing consumers has resulted in an increased demand for 'modern' and 'contemporary' new build homes in suburban areas and rejection of 'outdated' terraced housing that is 'unsuitable for modern living'. Consultants provide support for this argument by analysing the location of middle income employees in Liverpool which apparently shows 'a clear correlation between occupational grade and the residential location of employees such that as occupational grade increases the greater the likelihood that an employee will live outside the city and inner core boundaries' (Nevin *et al.* 2001: 6). This is further substantiated by the observation that:

> Clinical staff living within the Inner Core, for example, are paid less than two-thirds the salary of clinical staff living outside Liverpool, whilst technical staff within the Inner Core receive slightly more than three quarters of the salary of their colleagues living outside the city . . . . [A]ll employees living within the Liverpool housing zones are on lower salaries than their peers outside the city . . . . Those with higher incomes tend to live outside Liverpool.
>
> (Nevin *et al.* 2001: 7–8)

Although consultants present this as a robust analysis of market trends it is, in fact, based on the type of linear theorisation of social change that has no credibility in the contemporary social sciences (see Giddens 1990; Foucault 1994). This can be seen if we look again at the 'end of history' narrative that represents 'housing market change' as a linear process of suburbanisation.

- Terraced housing in neighbourhoods such as Kensington was built for an industrial working class.
- Time has moved on and there is no longer an industrial working class.
- There are increasing numbers of affluent households with 'rising aspirations'.
- These households desire 'modern' and 'contemporary' homes which are currently available only in suburban locations.
- This has resulted in a process of suburbanisation that will inevitably continue unless 'modern' and 'contemporary' homes are built in the inner city in place of 'life expired' terraced houses, which need to be demolished.

The key claim that is generated by a linear interpretation of urban history is that terraced housing has 'had its day' and that, therefore, there is 'no going back'. In the words of one of the principal architects of the HMR programme, Brendan Nevin, areas containing 'monolithic' provision of terraced housing will suffer 'complete market failure' if 'left to their own devices' (Nevin 2006a).

The logic of this linear view of urban history is that inner-urban areas composed of terraced houses will 'die' unless a housing product is provided that meets 'rising aspirations'. Yet there is an abundance of academic research that suggests that the products of urban history, such as terraced housing, constantly undergo a process of revaluation that results in their reappropriation as valued commodities. The difference between this academic research and the research undertaken by the consultants who have informed the HMR programme in Liverpool is that the academic research accomplishes what the Audit Commission accuses the consultants of neglecting:

> The data which is presented [by the consultants] provides only a partial picture of how people make decisions where to live. Whilst it may be acceptable to conclude that the areas that perform worst in socio-economic terms also do so in housing market terms there is little evidence presented to support a direct correlation based on cause and effect. In simple terms the fact that characteristics exist side by side or that through community consultation there may be evidence of 'neighbourhood dissatisfaction' is not in itself clear evidence of the inter-relationship between drivers. It merely confirms the co-existence of them. This point is related to the earlier conclusion for more 'people-related' data to clarify this link.
>
> (Audit Commission 2004: 24)

The Audit Commission's criticism here is directed at the linear economism that underpins Nevin *et al.*'s modelling of urban futures. Specifically, the Audit Commission critique suggests that increasing affluence does not necessarily or automatically translate into a rejection of terraced housing and concomitant preference for 'modern' and 'contemporary' homes. Such analysis reduces housing choices to a function of the economic capital possessed by households, i.e. rising levels of economic capital produce 'rising aspirations' for 'modern' and 'contemporary' houses.

> Staff living within inner parts of Liverpool and employed in the public sector are disproportionately at the beginning of their income cycle. As salary increases there is a tendency to drift out of the inner parts of Liverpool into suburban zones and potentially out of the city.
>
> (Nevin *et al.* 2001: 10)

> In areas where there are large concentrations of pre 1919 terraces, there is an absence of *higher paid* public sector professionals.
>
> (Nevin *et al.* 2001: 8)

But a large body of work in the social sciences has convincingly demonstrated that housing choices are a product of the way different combinations of capitals (economic, cultural, social etc.) produce particular housing preferences. Many households do not 'drift out' to suburban areas as their income rises. Such 'drift' tends to occur for households with rising levels of economic capital and low or modest levels of cultural capital (Savage *et al.* 2005). Households with rising levels of economic capital *and* high levels of cultural capital tend to value – rather than abandon – the existing housing fabric of the city, which they 'gentrify' (Butler 1997; Savage *et al.* 2005). For example, sociologists and geographers have shown that houses making up the historical urban fabric (such as terraced dwellings) have become valued commodities and that, furthermore, it is exactly the groups that Nevin *et al.* claim to want new build homes in suburbia (health workers, education workers etc.) that are leading the way in reimposing value on abandoned parts of the historical urban fabric (Zukin 1982; Butler 1997; Butler with Robson 2003a; Ley 2003; see also Chapter 2 of this book). This is evident in the current trend to rehabilitate and restore Edwardian and Victorian terraced properties in inner-urban areas, with large increases in the amount of money being devoted to such activities (Ley 1996; Butler 1997; Butler with Robson 2003a; Savage *et al.* 2005). Indeed Nevin even alludes to this himself in a recent paper that points out that 'during one week in 2006 UK terrestrial TV transmitted 20 programmes focused on the purchase and renovation of residential property' (Sprigings *et al.* 2006).

Thus many previously abandoned inner-urban areas are now much sought after, which shows that urban history ebbs and flows rather than moves in linear directions. Who would have thought, only 10 or 15 years ago, that city centres with virtually no residential population would now be thriving housing markets (Allen 2007b)? This is why some urban geographers refer to the phenomenon of 'uneven development', which is the process through which urban areas periodically attain and lose value in a cyclical manner (Smith 1996). The irony here is that the Audit Commission critique of linear conceptions of 'housing market change' implies that academic research (which has used the notion of 'bundles of capitals' to develop a broader understanding of housing market 'drivers' and their interplay) has something to contribute to the debate about HMR. Yet this is exactly the type of research that Nevin describes as 'sociology text books, many of which are dated . . . few of which will have any data relating to the Liverpool housing market' (Nevin 2006b: para. 4), as if sociological and geographical research were at worst irrelevant, or at best valid *only* in the spatial context of its production. The Audit Commission rightly points out, then, that Nevin *et al.*'s neglect to consider the interplay of this broader range of 'drivers' results in a failure to consider housing market trajectories other than those predicted by their linear model.

> The prospectus would have benefited from a trend analysis which showed whether drivers were getting stronger or weaker. Taken further this would have been useful in creating a projected picture of what would happen if there was no intervention.[9]
>
> (Audit Commission 2004: 25)

The other irony here is that Nevin and his team of consultants did have a base of information from which to make predictions based on alternative sets of assumptions. For example, they could have used the 'bundles of capitals' approach to develop a non-linear understanding of the 'housing careers' of the large number of health and teaching staff that they, themselves, identified as living within the inner core of Liverpool. This would have required a focused piece of research that examined the housing trajectories of those households at the lower end of the income spectrum. Suffice it to say that institutional members of the housing market renewal partnership in Liverpool had already identified early signs of gentrification activity in Kensington that was being driven by these very professionals.[10] The professionals who were said to be moving into Kensington included the type of households that have been repopulating and revalorising the inner core of other cities because it is cheap, in the context of an otherwise expensive market, and also because it possesses the aesthetic qualities that gentrifiers look for, that is, older terraced houses that can be renovated.

> I would like to think that, because it's fairly well known as a regeneration area, that would make most people automatically think that things are likely to improve and that's the case . . . . It's been, certainly, the student population. It wasn't so popular a few years ago but I think it's probably become more popular because it's situated towards the city.
>
> (Director, development and property management company)

> The other thing we're finding is that people who traditionally not have looked at areas like Kensington are now having to because of the affordability which . . . [Q: You mean young people?] Yes, young people, first time buyers, so they are having to look at areas like Kensington where they probably wouldn't have done in the past.[11]
>
> (HMR senior manager)

Q   Could you see, for example, young professionals moving into Kensington?

Estate agent   I can see them moving into Kensington Fields now because it has started to establish this identity. It's a little bohemian and it does need to do something about its environment, particularly the shops and the frontage. And get the trams running. At the end of the day, it's still very close to the city centre, you know, it's a short hop, so students love it. I've already sold houses, I can recall one, to a professional.

Q   Recently?

Estate agent   Yeah.

Q   What are they going for at the moment?

Estate agent   £110,000 that one went for, a fronted terraced, which is now on three floors 'cause they've gone into the loft and put Velux windows up there. But a big house, two big receptions, big kitchen diner, generous size bedrooms upstairs.

Q   Good value for money that isn't it?

Estate agent   He loved it. He was actually brought up in Kensington and in a house like that.[12]

Estate agent   Notably we also were selling large houses. I can think of one in particular. I can't remember its address. I can remember the house, a big Victorian house which a couple had bought. It was very big. It was far too big for them really. But they just fell in love with it and they bought it a number of years ago, so they got it relatively cheaply. And they did a house doctor job on it, you know, these style programmes.

Q   Stripped it down to the bare?

Estate agent   Absolutely, every floor board was exposed and sanded. They'd managed to find an old range from somewhere which they put in the kitchen. It didn't work but it really suited the big kitchen. It really looked the part. They had this big old table which looked like, you know, a huge slab of oak on big square legs and it really looked the part. And they put that on the market and we literally had a fight over it. We put it on with a guide price of, I think, about £80,000, which doesn't sound a lot but that then was a huge leap from what they paid for it. And we got well in excess of £100,000 and could have gone on. It was amazing.

Indeed estate agents described a market for housing in the existing dwelling-scape of Kensington from the very groups that the consultants identified as potential leavers, that is, those who work at the hospitals and universities in the city centre:

Q   How would you pitch it, what's the sales pitch for Kensington?

Estate agent   It would be a property suitable for owner occupation or investment and the key phrases would be 'city centre', 'universities', 'Royal Hospital'. And we use those key phrases because that's in the body of the description and search engines pick it up.

This should not be greeted with surprise, because middle-class graduates involved in professions such as teaching, research, social work and health services as well as industries such as architecture, art, music, media and culture are well known for their key role in the gentrification of inner-urban areas (Ley 1996). Furthermore these are exactly the type of workers that Liverpool City Council accepts are feeding the city's economic growth and presumably, therefore, providing its future stream of inner-urban housing consumers. For example, Liverpool City Council's opening submission to the public enquiry into the compulsory purchase of working-class houses in the city points to strengths such as:

*   an outstanding critical mass of culture, sporting, heritage and leisure assets including the programme for delivering Liverpool's European Capital of Culture 2008;
*   an internationally significant knowledge economy through the city's three universities, health related research, Liverpool Science Park and the national bio-manufacturing centre;
*   internationally and nationally significant clusters such as life sciences, tourism and creative cultural industries (Elvin and Litton 2006).

The economic situation in Liverpool is such, then, that its inner-urban neighbourhoods are arguably 'ripe' for gentrification yet this potential is completely overlooked within a linear model of urban change, which claims that terraced houses are 'holding back' its economic growth and that curiously, therefore, urban economic growth and terraced housing are mutually incompatible! Yet studies of gentrification from cities in the UK, Europe and America suggest that, on the contrary, terraced housing and economic growth are bedfellows rather than enemies. Furthermore housing market indicators in the UK point to a *likely* intensification of gentrification activity in the inner-urban areas of cities such as Liverpool. This is because in general house prices have risen faster than incomes, which has prompted some middle-class groups (especially 'emerging households' such as first time buyers) to become more pragmatic about *where* they purchase their first home (Cole *et al.* 2005). Nevin acknowledges the existence of these housing market conditions in a recent paper, which notes that:

Change in house prices has often been related to the ratio of house prices to average earnings. Hamnet (1996) tracks this from 1956 to 1996 and the ratio runs, for 30 years of this 40 year period, at 3:1 to 4:1 with minor fluctuations. There are short periods where the cycle of inflation rapidly increases prices and the ratio jumps to up to 5:1 before returning to the modal value. The return to the norm usually involves a collapse of prices where annual percentage change falls rapidly to negative figures around half of the peak of the upward surge. Clearly this ratio is only meaningful if it is households spending from income on housing that drives the market. Once investment income on the scale [of recent years] intervenes in this market the established relationship collapses. The ratio is currently quoted as being 7:1 hence anxiety about the desirability of a 'soft landing' for the current price surge. It seems likely that the extra 2 points in the ratio without a crash so far is due to the continued faith of investors in the rising housing market.[13]

(Sprigings *et al.* 2006)

It is instructive to note that this widening ratio creates a situation in which many middle-class people are forced to rely on their *cultural capital* rather than *economic capital* to secure their position within the market for houses. This is evident in the examples that housing market institutions gave, above, of early signs of gentrification in Kensington, which, if consistent with trends in other cities, could lead to a process of 'staged gentrification'. This happens when 'urban pioneers' are followed into housing markets such as Kensington by other urban professionals and developers, who become more confident in them as a consequence of the valorising efforts of pioneers (Ley 1996). Nevertheless, despite these early signs of gentrification activity[14] and the emergence of an economic and cultural context sympathetic to gentrification, the institutions of housing market renewal in Liverpool were apparently deterring such activity.

What they were saying to Southern Investors was just get lost, that was the way you had to interpret this, because I said I've got people who want to come and buy in here and improve the housing stock, which I assumed would be one of their primary objectives, but their response was you know, almost meaningless.

(Regional property investment and property management association)

Extracting super-profits: Kensington in the space of positions in the city of Liverpool

Institutional denial of the chance for the market for terraced houses in Kensington to revive through gentrification activity (notwithstanding the undesirable side-effects that this has on working-class people) is not without reason. But to understand the reasons for this denial we need to understand the 'new' market logic that underpins urban regeneration initiatives such as housing market renewal: the 'official' articulation of the housing market renewal problematic from the point of view of unequal housing wealth (e.g. Lee and Nevin 2002) and therefore 'in the name of the poor' obscures the fact that housing market institutions (housing developers, estate agents etc.) structure the market for houses as a space of positions on the urban landscape for specific reasons. Notably, the constitution of the market for houses as a space of positions creates an impetus for households to engage in position-taking and therefore in struggles for position upon the urban landscape, which, in turn, generates economic benefits to the house sales industry, which profits from housing market activity, as well as researchers and consultants who are asked to study the 'volatility' of the market or the 'dynamics' of niche segments of it. A key purpose of constituting the market for houses as a space of positions, then, might be to facilitate the institutional accrual of economic profits rather than to equalise housing wealth.

The work of Neil Smith is helpful here. Smith (1989) argues that the strategic importance of positions on the urban landscape emerges at a point when a 'rent gap' opens up between the current rental values of land and the potential values that such land possesses. Now, following the revitalisation of city centre housing markets in the early 1990s and, as a consequence, declining stocks of land available for development within the city centre, the urban living phenomenon has undergone a process of inner-urbanisation, with developers now seeking profit-making opportunities in the urban ring (Allen 2007b). Kensington has attained a position of value on the urban landscape of Liverpool because it is situated adjacent to the city centre, where the market for houses has been growing since the end of the twentieth century, whilst, at the same time, possessing super profit-making opportunities as a 'low-value' market that has been in a period of relative decline since the housing market collapse in the early 1990s. In other words, Kensington possesses a large 'rent gap'. It is for this reason that the institutions that constitute the HMR partnership in Liverpool refer to Kensington as a 'prime position' in terms of its location adjacent to the booming city centre and therefore as a 'massive opportunity'.

> Kensington is in a prime position for, you know, its access into the city and out of the city as well but it's on that major route of Edge Lane. I think, from my point of view, Kensington is a *massive opportunity* if you can get it right and phase it right, so, and *quite desirable if you are looking for that kind of not quite into city living* but you know there's a certain potential there.
>
> (HMR senior manager)

I think probably the best way to describe it would be it was an area that has potential, significant potential in terms of its location. I think the Kensington frontage is a massively important factor for the scheme. It's an area that, unless you knew the area very well, you wouldn't know the site was there because it's not really a road that people cut through. You've obviously got Edge Lane here and Kensington there so I think that is a key part of the scheme. And the creation of a successful market in the area is getting the frontage right. I think the relationship between the site and the city centre was another key benefit for the area in that it had obviously, in terms of trying to attract people to come and buy in the area, be it nurses, be it teachers, be it other sorts of key worker. Although we are not necessarily targeting it as a key worker type development.

(Developer)

Institutional members of the housing market renewal partnership, for whom Kensington represents a valuable position within the space of positions within the market for houses in Liverpool, even make explicit reference to the 'massive potential' for super-profit making given its position on the urban landscape and currently depressed land values. In their first report on Liverpool, then, Nevin *et al.* (1999) make reference to how

> the [housing market renewal] strategy should be developed using an entrepreneurial approach which maximizes the value of land, developer contributions and the rising confidence of individual consumers.
>
> (Nevin *et al.* 1999: 120)

These institutions are not referring to the 'massive potential' that exists for working-class people. The language of 'potential' makes no sense to working-class people, who do not perceive their dwellings as a source of wealth accumulation and who experience Kensington as a lived space rather than one that is positioned within the field of possibilities in the market for houses (see Chapters 4 and 5). Indeed working-class people actually resent references to the investment potential of housing as a source of wealth accumulation (see Chapter 4). The institutions of housing market renewal are actually referring to the 'massive potential' that exists in terms of the 'young professionals' who can be attracted into Kensington. The strategic importance of Kensington therefore emanates from the size of its rent gap, which means that land values are so low that 'renewal' can take place in a way that allows super-profits to be made whilst also allowing prices to remain lower than those in the city centre and therefore attractive to 'young professionals'.

As people push out from the city centre, they will be looking round the inner core area . . . . Location, location, location. It's close to the city centre, within easy walking distance, so there is an emerging market from young professionals . . . [Q: Do you think there is?] Yes these are people who, if you like, aspire to city centre living but can't afford it . . . . If they purchase a property in Kensington Fields with a small amount of investment then it's a very attractive property . . . . If you are into café life and the clubs and pubs and restaurants in the city centre then it's just as easy to live in Kensington Fields as anywhere in the city centre.

(Director of regeneration)

In contradistinction to the 'official' claims made by the housing market renewal partnership, which were that renewal of Kensington would attract households *into* Liverpool from the suburbs, this was not mentioned by any of the 16 institutional 'stakeholders' who were interviewed.

We would always see a lot of what we sell in areas like this as being the first time buyer market. I think because there is quite a mix in terms of the variety of the units, from a small amount of one bedroomed apartments, there is then two bedroomed apartments, there are then small three bedroomed houses up to fairly large three bedroomed three storey town houses. So I think for the variety of houses there will be quite a mix, so we don't see it being all first time buyers, obviously, but I think we will see a tidy market of first time buyers of like former students that have started to work at the hospital, be it in the city centre, that want to be near to the city centre but perhaps can't afford an apartment right in the city centre . . . . *We wouldn't see our main target market as being people from 20, 30, 40, 50 miles away. We would see it as being a fairly tight radius of purchasers.*

(Property developer)

The broadest conception of the potential market for houses in Kensington is therefore articulated as 'key workers' such as teachers and nurses. For the developers who seek to attract these buyers into Kensington, the availability of public subsidy in their pursuit of super-profits is a key motivator of involvement:

There certainly are factors in the immediate environment or the immediate locality as well as the city centre location that gave us a lot of confidence that it would be a market in which we could sell in. Then if you go on top of that, the fact that you've got funding coming into the scheme from English partnerships, from Kensington Regen to help with site acquisition [compulsory purchase orders etc.] and then Kensington Regen money being spent on the wider sort of public realm area. They were all factors that gave us confidence that there would be a fairly thriving market, we think, in terms of potential sales.

(Property developer)

Kensington in the space of positions of the City of Culture

Practitioners of the policy view that constructs Kensington as a position within the space of positions within the Liverpool housing market have sought to justify the demolition of working-class neighbourhoods on the grounds that they have become disconnected from the market as a result of changing aspirations. When they articulate this point 'in the name of the poor' they point to the inequalities in housing wealth that have emerged as Kensington has apparently become disconnected from the wider housing market, even though working-class households that are wedded to the 'reality principle' do not regard Kensington as a position within the space of positions or, therefore, a source of wealth accumulation. However, the 'official' rationale for the committal of symbolic and physical violence upon working-class neighbourhoods is not simply that Kensington has suffered 'housing market failure'. For practitioners of the official view, Kensington exists as more than simply a position within the space of positions within the Liverpool housing market. They also regard it as occupying a key position within the space of positions on the urban landscape. The key consideration in this regard is the award of the status of 'European City of Culture 2008' to Liverpool, which, so the claim goes, will deliver a range of cultural, social and economic benefits to the city.

'European City of Culture' status provides cities such as Liverpool with an opportunity to 'place market' themselves as successful post-industrial economies built on leisure and cultural tourism. The key to success in this regard is to present the city as a 'dynamic' place that is worth investment (Mooney 2004). The problem in this respect is that Kensington sits on the main arterial route into the city and, in the eyes of urban elites in the city, currently provides the 'wrong image' of Liverpool as an industrial working-class city. This was clearly a consideration for the HMR partnership, who articulated the view that the demolition of Edge Lane was necessary because it contained the wrong (working-class) imagery of 'terraced houses' and 'washing on the line':

You can make a neighbourhood fantastic and it's important that it does by 2008 because it's the main thoroughfare into the city. I think that, to be perfectly honest, is what's driving regeneration in Edge Lane more than anything else. So it's like, it's going to be incredibly important, and it will hopefully give people a sense of pride and they'll like what they see . . . . People driving into the city must have a more pleasant outlook than is currently there, . . . so it is important that physical regeneration is done.

(HMR senior manager)

Kensington is the main gateway into Liverpool and it's a disgrace. Once you get onto Edge Lane, just over here, and start your way through the university down to the city, you've got a couple of miles of total degradation on the way in, so that's what they should do first.

(Director, development and property management company)

[The] idea was, was well if we can take a further four to five houses down behind [Edge Lane as well as those fronting Edge Lane] we could build three to four storey apartment blocks, because the view for the people coming into and leaving Liverpool wouldn't be very nice because they'd be able to see the backs of houses, and that was the explanation that they gave us. So they would want to take down a further five houses. [Q: So that they wouldn't spoil the view?] Exactly. Top of Jubilee Drive, Leopold Road, Adelaide, and I think it was about two houses down, basically it was to make the plot sellable to a developer, that's what was behind it. Very early on all the residents of Kensington Fields voted for no demolition in the area, that so far has put paid to the Royal Hospital's plans to expand onto the area known as the Triangle . . . . The Liverpool Land and Development Company, they have on the 8th October issued a public notice for the 'Demolition and/or Reconfiguration of the following houses', and in that they included more or less the whole of Edge Hill, a lot of the Gilliard Street Property, but they also included number 1 to number 43 Jubilee Drive.

(Ward councillor)

[The official] said 'well you wouldn't want people driving past Edge Lane and seeing washing on your line would you?', and I said 'why not?' They're perfectly good houses, decent sized houses, what they propose to build now are tiny little rabbit hutches, most of the properties that are getting built now, all mainly apartments.

(Chair, residents association)

The official view that situates Kensington as a position within the space of positions in the housing market and, more importantly, as a *key position* within the space of positions on the urban landscape of the 'City of Culture' (situated on the main arterial route that tourists will use when travelling by car or coach into the 'City of Culture') impelled representatives of the official view to problematise working-class imagery on the urban landscape, which appears to have no rightful place in the City of Culture. From the official point of view, there also appears to be a perforce necessity to inscribe 'statements' on the urban landscape that visitors to the city will interpret in the 'correct' way, that is, that Liverpool is a successful post-industrial city worth investing in and not a post-industrial city whose struggle to succeed in a post-industrial economy is exemplified by a landscape scarred by the ruins of urban industrialisation.

> We need a significant improvement in the public realm and the quality of frontage onto Kensington. So not only are we redoing the frontage here, there are proposals to redo a lot of the retail frontage along the full length of Kensington. It's about really making a statement to people that this isn't just about more social housing, more low-quality social housing and a lot of the stuff that was done in the Eighties and Nineties. It's about a new and exciting scheme with contemporary sort of architecture and high-quality use of materials, and very much making a statement to people that this is an area that people are going to invest big in with the confidence that people will come and spend serious money to actually live there.
>
> (Property developer)

There is a paradox at work here. City of Culture status is ostensibly awarded to urban centres that possess 'culture' *and* require regeneration yet, once awarded, the impetus to regenerate the City of Culture (the success of which is measured in terms of future patterns of investment that flow into the city) necessitates an institutional denial of key elements of its own historical past. This has resulted in the use of the 'housing market renewal' programme to wipe working-class imagery from strategically important parts of the urban landscape. This denial of *any* sense of the urban past is also exemplified in the way that institutional members of the Newheartlands pathfinder only articulated a future oriented view of Kensington which involved 'going on a journey'.

> It's based on the future and it's getting better and this is the time to get in on the ground floor.
>
> (NDC officer)

> I also think with the level of investment that's going into the inner core area generally and the HMR areas generally that that perception will change and people will see that there is potential to get in at the beginning of a journey . . . . They probably need to look at it on much more a medium- to long-term view and see that this will be an area that has massive potential.
>
> (Property developer)

The symbolic domination of the policy view of Kensington, which involves a denial of its history to which working-class respondents were oriented, violates the working-class view of Kensington as a lived space that possesses a history to be appropriated rather than denied ('I want to see it go back to the way it used to be'). It also violates the working-class relation to housing as a 'thing' that is 'ready to hand' because the primary consideration governing the reconstruction of the dwellingscape is the necessity to inscribe 'contemporary' and 'exciting' statements on the urban landscape that will apparently enable 'local people' to 'be proud of being in Kensington'.

> One of the things that can give this a slight edge is the fact that it has frontage on Kensington. We think it's really important in terms of trying to make people aware that there is something new. There is something exciting and certainly, in terms of the designs that we've developed for the site, not a Brookside Close type suburban development. It's very much an urban scheme. Quite a contemporary approach to house type design and choice of materials. We thought that was important in Kensington because we don't see this as being suburbia. We see it as a city centre, well, not another city centre apartment style development but it's within the boundaries of the city centre and we certainly reflect that with the design.
>
> (Property developer)

> The Edge Lane improvement will make a really physical statement, you know. You come into the city centre. You're coming in, the first real contact with the city centre is Kensington. What we're trying to do is say to people here 'be proud of being in Kensington'. For people coming into the area, this is a good place to come. Like, people with company cars and all that kind of thing, that's quite important.
>
> (NDC officer)

Building a brave new Kensington

The 'official view' of HMR has sought to justify it in terms of the need to reposition Kensington within the space of positions in the Liverpool housing market, yet 'unofficial views' articulated within the context of the social science interview suggest that the repositioning of Kensington is also inextricably linked to the 'needs' of the City of Culture. The extent to which housing market renewal has been subsumed to the 'needs' of the City of Culture is nowhere more apparent than in the strategic priority that the housing market renewal programme gives to Edge Lane. This is the main arterial route that runs through Kensington into the city centre and that, apparently, needs to make a 'statement' on behalf of the City of Culture. The strategic importance of Edge Lane was such that 'nothing else could happen' with HMR until that priority had been realised in planning and permission terms.

> [Name of officer] thinks we're all tin pot idiots. At the planning group our main concern was, like, 'what is going to happen?' and he always kept saying 'well we can't reach proper decisions until we know what's happening with Edge Lane', 'cause it was always on the cards that any demolition would be paid for by, like, as it turns out, Liverpool Land Development Company and, as I say, they always fobbed us off with 'well we can't really make decisions about what's going to happen, not until we get the plans for the Edge Lane' . . . . Most of the planning group meetings were, you know, everyone was concerned about what was going to happen to our houses? Where are we all going to go? What is going to happen? As I say, we were basically always fobbed off with 'well, until we get the, you know . . .' Them words are the words I'm sick of hearing. 'When we get the Edge Lane plans.' Now we went to meetings in the Devonshire with, oh, who were they? The consultants that drew up the plans for Edge Lane, and they were supposed to listen to us, and again, we feel they didn't listen either because we've stipulated at every meeting about these properties staying up and at every meeting we've basically been ignored.
>
> (Chair, residents association)

The necessity to create a dwellingscape on Edge Lane that makes a 'statement' about the 'exciting' nature of Liverpool as a 'City of Culture' not only implies that the current dwelling landscape is deficient but, more importantly, that it is possible to communicate a sense of 'excitement' through the physical landscape. This is exemplified in the way estate agents market new apartment dwellings via reference to lifestyle, which is indicative of the extent to which housing has been extracted from the logic of its basic economy ('dwelling space') and integrated into symbolic economies of cultural and lifestyle goods (Lash and Urry 1994; Featherstone 1991). For institutions involved in the repositioning of Kensington, this has created an impetus to eradicate working-class urban imagery from Edge Lane so that it can be replaced with apartments and other 'frontage'.

> The apartments are all concentrated in the frontage. The Kensington frontage was always going to be, by the very nature of a main street like Kensington, was always going to be a high development and much denser. So all of the apartments are concentrated in that area.
>
> (Property developer)

The proposals I've seen from the regeneration people amount to improving the sort of corridors into the city and I can just imagine, you know, the Deputy Prime Minister being taken down Wavertree Road in a few years' time and saying 'look at all this, it's terribly improved you know'. Taken into Kensington Fields and shown a few choice streets that they've tarted up, and not being allowed anywhere near Holte Road, which has been basically untouched. So I mean they're going to do, as I understand it, they're going to improve this road into the city, they're going to improve Edge Lane, which is a terrific bottleneck, improve Kensington itself, the three main arteries into the city and you know, improve a few specimen roads.

(Regional property investment and property management association)

There appears to be a fundamental contradiction, then, between the official and unofficial views articulated by the HMR partnership in Liverpool. On the one hand the official view articulates the need to reposition Kensington within the space of positions in the Liverpool housing market by attracting those who have conventionally chosen to live in the suburbs:

the importance of the 'suburban' concept of house purchase will need to be reflected in the size of sites provided to developers. Part of the success of developments on the fringe of Liverpool and in Knowsley can be attributed to the fact that they were on a sufficiently large scale to create their own environment and be marketed as suburbs . . . . [This requires] an emphasis on changing neighbourhoods and [creating] *new suburban locations within the city.*

(Nevin and Lee 2001: 43–4, emphasis added)

Yet this sits uneasily with the unofficial view, articulated by institutional stakeholders within the context of the social science interview, that there is a 'need' to create 'something exciting and certainly, in terms of the designs that we've developed for the site, not a Brookside Close type suburban development. It's very much an urban scheme.'

Another contradiction is that 'City of Culture' status actually necessitates the denigration of elements of urban cultural history (working-class terraced housing) because they are thought to illustrate urban economic decline. What we are witnessing here, then, is the emergence of an urban regeneration ideology that provides a justification for any 'intervention' that eradicates 'economic ruins' (terraced housing etc.) from the urban landscape – no matter how culturally significant. Moreover, this regeneration ideology does not simply denigrate 'economic ruins' such as terraced houses (e.g. by attaching an 'end of history' narrative to them). It deploys the same language of 'failure' and 'viability' to denigrate *operative* urban *stores* (such as '50 pence shops') that are integral to working-class life but are thought to be 'out of place' in the 'City of Culture'.

> Most of these shops, if you look at them, are unviable. They're either business which probably last just a few months, like second hand furniture stuff, you know. There aren't many businesses, like this, which are properly viable and have been here for a long time. I mean, there's the chip shop, the chemist and, you know, one or two others up and down the road. But a lot of the shops are closed or just open temporarily now and then. You can see it if you walk up and down, so it is true. They need to do something with the shops in this road.
>
> (Regional property investment and property management association)

The language of 'viability' used here is intended to denote a simple economic relation between supply and demand. The contention is that there is not enough demand to sustain the businesses that occupy Kensington High Street, so that 'something needs to be done with the shops in the area'. That said, the representation of these 'second hand' shops as 'unviable' should not be taken at 'face value', since this would neglect to consider the social position from which the language of 'viability' is articulated. The language of viability and associated prescription that 'something needs to be done with the shops' is born of the same semiotic logic that has resulted in the production of the 'end of history' narrative that has been so successfully attached to terraced houses ('outdated', 'no longer suitable for modern living') in order to provide a self-evident justification for their demolition. Far from providing an objective assessment of the 'viability' of 'second hand' shops, then, the language of viability is articulated by social agents (regeneration agencies, housing developers etc.) that occupy social spaces that compel them to situate Kensington within the space of positions in the Liverpool housing market. This necessitates the imposition of comparative judgments ('low-quality shops') that justify reconfiguring the retail landscape so that it 'competes' with other neighbourhoods that service the middle class, but which violates the working-class relation to consumption, which seeks nothing from shops other than the 'things' that are necessary to 'getting by'.

> It is very much an ageing population with currently very few local amenities. They are generally low-quality convenience stores. We talked about some of it. We find that the attraction of the site is its proximity to the city centre and good transport links. *We're after first time buyers and need to cater for their lifestyle needs.*
>
> (Property developer)

> We're trying to reverse the image of Kensington and an awful lot of money is for the main corridors in Kensington, *rationalising the shopping* off there and putting money into the units that are left to make them a lot better. So *we are not messing around anymore with piffling little improvements like in the past, like, shop fronts have*

just been done up, you know, with grants. We're looking to take out blocks and stuff . . . so we're hoping anyone passing through Kensington will actually see it as an area that is going to *make a change. So what will attract people is they see quality shopping aspects and that's starting to work 'cause a lot of new retailers are coming in. Actually seeing quality houses instead of rows and rows of terraced properties the way they are now.*

(NDC physical and environmental regeneration manager)

Conclusion

This chapter has examined how institutions involved in HMR are seeking to reconstitute the market for houses in Kensington. This programme involves the imposition of the dominant view of the market for houses, as a space of positions, on working-class people in Kensington who view the market for houses in quite different terms. The violation of this whole way of being-toward the market for houses symbolises how the market for houses has become yet another site in which the dominant are able to exercise their domination over the dominated. The City of Culture programme has simply heightened the urgency for institutions involved in housing market renewal to forge this 'class remake of the urban landscape' (Smith 1989). This is because the City of Culture award is about *selling Liverpool* as a successful post-industrial city. The key constituency in this respect is international investors. The need to sell the city in this way (for example, by eradicating the 'wrong type' of working-class imagery from the urban landscape, and inscribing it with 'new' and 'exciting' statements) has produced institutional hostility to the working class, whom the imperative is to remove from view. We should not be surprised at this because something similar happened in 'Glasgow 1990'.

> The year of culture has more to do with power politics than culture . . . . More to do with millionaire developers than art . . . . 1990 makes an unequivocal statement on behalf of corporate wealth . . . . It is more a question of art sponsoring big business . . . to a shallow ethos of yuppie greed. And for all of this, of course, the people of Glasgow will be made to foot the bill.
>
> (McLay 1990: 87)

This is why the Liverpool MP Jane Kennedy has described HMR as 'municipal vandalism', 'social cleansing' and a 'gross waste of public funds'. It is also why the Liverpool Labour Party has stated that institutions involved in HMR have long claimed to be on the side of the community but it seems that they are more on the side of big business . . . . Kensington people, it seems, and their long standing communities are merely in the way of . . . plans to change the city from one that was for the people to one that sees the people as being in the way.[15]

Chapter 7

Working-class experiences of the brave new housing market

Introduction

Chapter 6 argued that the official rationale for 'restructuring' the Kensington housing market, to reposition it within the space of positions in the Liverpool housing market, sits alongside an unofficial rationale for 'restructuring', which is to ensure that Kensington makes a 'statement' about Liverpool as a 'City of Culture'. The ostensible aim of 'City of Culture' status is to produce social and economic (as well as cultural) benefits to the city and its residents. However, as working-class houses are demolished so that they no longer dominate the urban landscape of the 'City of Culture', the question of whether working-class people will actually reap any benefits from demolition remains unanswered. There are two dimensions to this problematic. The first concerns the working-class relation to the City of Culture. This chapter shows that working-class people, whose lives are characterised by their proximity to necessity and distance from symbolic economies, are simply unable to 'grasp' the City of Culture as something 'for the likes of them'. So the City of Culture programme that is partly driving HMR in Kensington means nothing to the people that live there.

The second concern of this chapter is to understand the manner in which working-class people experience the 'brave new housing market' of Kensington as it is repositioned within the space of positions of the metropolitan housing market. Working-class people, whose lives are wedded to the 'reality principle', and who relate to the market for houses in terms of the practical possibilities it presents to them to dwell, are simply unable to 'see the point' of HMR, for example, the objective to demolish 'perfectly good houses' so that they can be replaced with a dwellingscape inscribed with 'exciting statements'. Although working-class people are being presented with 'affordable' housing options, as well as 'loan products' to help them to afford to buy in the new Kensington, the chapter shows that such initiatives cannot simply be understood in the terms they are presented, that is, as 'help'. The imposition of a dwellingscape of 'high-value products' that represent 'investment opportunities' violates an entire (practical) way of being-toward the market for houses. This is because it imposes a requirement on working-class people to assume higher levels of 'mortgage debt' when they are terrorised by the insecurity of their economic position, as well as consumed by the necessities of getting by from day to day.

Apparently 'helpful' initiatives, such as 'special loan products', exemplify the manner in which the dominant view of the market for houses (i.e. housing as a vehicle for capital investment) has been imposed on working-class people, who are now required to 'play the game' according to the rules established by the dominant if they want to remain in Kensington, which is where they say they feel 'comfortable'.

Being working-class in the City of Culture

Working-class people living in Kensington articulate a sense of pride in 'belonging' to Liverpool ('I certainly feel I belong to Liverpool, Liverpool is my home') and resistance towards its spoiled identity ('I'm not embarrassed to say I'm a Scouser, I was born and bred'; 'I'm from Liverpool and I'm proud of it to be honest'). This strong sense of identification with Liverpool is essentially a product of a form of we-being that leaves working-class people with no way of articulating themselves other than through recourse to a collective form of biography ('I don't know [what I am], I am just a Scouser, I'm just proud of that, you know what I mean') and results in their valorisation of the collective ('I think we're one of the friendliest cities, alright everybody's got their fair share of crime and everything but'). Yet, although working-class respondents identified with Liverpool in stronger terms than other social groups,[1] they are, paradoxically, the furthest removed from the 'Liverpool City of Culture' that is seeking to reposition itself on the global economic landscape. This is because the idea of 'City of Culture' makes sense only to those whose existential actuality enables them to relate to the city as a site of cultural production and consumption, which, Bourdieu argues, does not include working-class people.

> The low interest which working-class people show in the works of legitimate culture to which they could have access . . . is not solely the effect of a lack of competence and familiarity . . . . [Culture is] excluded, *de facto* and *de jure*, from working-class conversation . . . . Perhaps the most ruthless call to order, which in itself no doubt explains the extraordinary *realism* of the working-classes, stems from the closure effect of the homogeneity of the directly experienced social world . . . . The universe of possibles is closed.
>
> (Bourdieu 1984: 381)

For working-class people, whose everyday lives are characterised by the imminence of their proximity to necessity, and thus distance from culture, the 'City of Culture' is therefore articulated as something that is 'not for the likes of us'.

Q   Can I just ask you briefly about the Capital of Culture? Does that mean anything to you?

DH26   I'm made up they got it like yeah.

Q   Are you?

DH26   Yeah.

Q   Is it anything to do with you personally or do you think it is?

DH26   Nothing to do with me, is it? We just live here, don't we? They're going to do what they do anyway, so. But I'm made up they got it, deserve it.

As something that was 'not for the likes of us' working-class people articulate a distance between themselves and the City of Culture that is exemplified in their perception that its benefits will be concentrated on particular places that also have nothing to do with them (e.g. the city centre) or social groups that are already occupying privileged social positions (middle-class people, businesses) (see also McLay 1990; Mooney 2004).

Q   What about the City of Culture. Does that mean anything to you?

MP47   Not particularly. I know what it is, obviously, but no, I don't think it's going to make my life any different, no . . .

I think myself, personally, I don't know, I mean they call it City of Culture. They haven't been like to some of the places round here, I don't think, and some of the other places. It's all just a city centre thing for me. I don't think the actual areas like this will see any benefit of it. Millions will just get spent on the city centre, building this hotel and that statue and that's all you'll see of it. It'll come and go I think.

RM32

Q   The City of Culture 2008, does that mean anything to you?

JC54   No.

Q   What do you think about it?

JC54:   I think it's a big farce, I think it's just a good excuse for the councils and other people to spend money on things to make all these bits nice in the city centre and the lead-in to the city centre. It's a good excuse for them to use all kinds of money.

Q   And do you think it'll bring more people into Liverpool?

JC54   I think it will do. I think it will do. But I can't see how that's going to benefit me or anyone living in Liverpool.

Q   Or the wider area, yeah?

JC54   Yeah. It won't benefit anybody at all. Maybe business, shops and that will get more business but that's about all. No, I'm just really totally disillusioned with all of it.

Q   You know the City of Culture thing. What kind of impact does that, what does it mean to people that grew up here?

MB70   It means nothing to me whatsoever. I don't even think about it . . . . I think they spend too much time on the city centre than on the outskirts of the city. The city centre's getting all done up and the outskirts, to me, is getting left and I think it's a shame.

Q   Do a lot of people feel like that about the City of Culture?

MB70   I don't know. I don't speak to anyone about it . . . .. I never talk to my friends 'Oh, what do you think of the City of Culture?' It's like all this money supposed to be coming to Kensington. Nothing's been done.

These working-class people are not simply articulating a 'lack of interest' in the City of Culture. They are articulating a point of view on the City of Culture that is the product of a form of being so wedded to the reality principle (and distant from culture) that it cannot comprehend its relevance in terms other than those that are generated by the reality principle. This is exemplified by the way working-class people make references to the City of Culture that are almost always articulated in terms of its direct *impact* on their everyday lives (road works, travel disruption, local tax increases) rather than in 'cultural' terms.

Q   What about the City of Culture, what does that mean to you?

RH65   It's an honour I suppose. But culture, see what they're doing to town? Mother of God! It took me an hour nearly this morning to get the bus into town. I'd have been quicker walking to get into town because of all the road works that's going on in Renshaw Street. And that Liverpool Hospital car park, that's always stopping the traffic up. I think there might have been something going on in London Road because we waited from Wavertree Road. We must have waited about 20 minutes before we could actually turn the corner.

I mean there's been massive road works. They've been doing the water mains all the way down Edge Lane, which has caused havoc, you know. So that caused a major headache in terms of just general travel but, initially, there was a concern as to how we were going to be affected by the change and what's going to be dug up, what's going to be replaced, what's going to be knocked down. And again, you've got all the sort of the noise, the pollution and all the rest of it. There are a lot of issues to take into account.

MY45

If it means they can carry on improving Liverpool the way they are doing, it'll be a good thing. You know, there's an awful lot of work going on in Liverpool. I mean it's going to look better, but we haven't got long till 2008, have they? There are some big jobs going on. I mean Edge Lane. They've tried to improve Edge Lane for a long time because it comes off the M62. There will be all these people coming into Liverpool and they want to make it look better. So as people are coming into Liverpool that way, and going into the city centre, whether it will ever get there to make it as good as what the plans are, I don't know. As long as they don't put the council tax up too much to pay for all this.

FS62

Being working-class in the brave new housing market

The imposition of the housing market doxa that positions Kensington within the space of positions in the Liverpool housing market, and on the urban land-scape of the City of Culture, violates the working-class being-toward housing as a 'thing' that is 'ready to hand' (just being) as well as 'for me with others' (we-being). For working-class respondents who articulate a view of housing that is consistent with the reality principle that governs working-class lives ('bricks and mortar', 'it's four walls', 'a roof over your head'), and that provides them with their legitimate criteria of judgment, this form of housing market restructuring makes no 'common sense' because it is based on sense that is common only to social agents that view houses as situated within a space of positions. The extent of the social distance between working-class respondents and the social agents that are imposing their plans on Kensington is exemplified by the way working-class respondents are simply unable to 'see the point' of why anybody would want to live in an apartment, which, to them, represents the triumph of status over utility.

Q   You know where the large Victorian houses are now? The plan is to demolish them to build apartments.
TP26   I fail to see the point really. If you asked anyone would they rather live in a flat or a house, for the most part people would say they'd live in a house. I don't really see the point.

The working-class relation to the restructuring of Kensington cannot simply be reduced to an inability to 'see the point' that is born of a form of being oriented to housing as a 'thing' rather than an 'exciting statement'. The primordial relation of working-class people to housing as a 'thing' that is ready to hand 'to me' (and not a 'statement') is exemplified by the way that working-class people, who take an 'interested disinterest' in the market for houses (i.e. *looking* at house prices, occasionally *watching* TV programmes on houses), actually spend little or no time *talking* to each other about houses as a general topic of conversation.

Q	Do you ever talk about housing with your parents?
SP26	Not really no. It's not really something that, you know, its not a conversation piece really. I mean occasionally I'd say 'Well, you know . . .', basically discussing the possibilities of how to finance moving but other than that no.
Q	Is housing ever a topic of conversation for you or your husband or anybody in your house? Do you ever talk about housing?
JE42	No, not really.
Q	Do you ever talk to your family about housing or anything like that?
JC40	Well, not really.

Working-class people, whose being is conditioned by, and immersed in, a social world that devours them with its urgent demands ('you just live from day to day, I can't see beyond that really'), primarily relate to housing in terms of their struggle for existence rather than a struggle for position. They primarily encounter houses as 'things' that are 'there' and 'ready to hand' for them on an average-everyday basis, and therefore only really understand them from within the parameters of the 'reality principle' ('four walls', 'bricks and mortar', 'comfortable'). Like Heidegger's (1962) broken hammer, then, houses only become 'present at hand' objects of reflexivity that announce themselves to working-class people when they are no longer 'just there' and 'ready to hand' on an average-everyday basis. Housing announced itself as a topic of conversation in this way to working-class people (who had never previously talked about housing) when the HMR programme targeted their homes for demolition.

> Until all this started, regeneration, I would never have thought I would have a conversation about housing, other than saying 'I'd like to live in a house like that' or 'I'd like to live there'. You know, just casual comments, but not as a piece of information, I don't think so, no.
>
> MB70

Q	Is housing ever a topic of conversation for you?
LR55	Always. Constantly. Wherever I go, it comes up.
Q	Why do you talk about it?
LR55	Why? Because they're trying to knock my house down and I'm not having it. Plus, as I say, I've spent the last five, six years going to meeting after meeting on the regeneration of this area to be totally ignored. Not just myself but all the other residents.
Q	Do you talk about housing as a topic of conversation with anybody?
CS47	Just the few friends in the bingo whose houses seem to be getting knocked down like but. . .

The manner in which housing announces itself in conversation is, of course, contingent on the form of being-toward housing that these interlocutors possess, since this determines the way in which they will 'grasp' the issues at stake. The 'official view' that housing market restructuring provides an 'opportunity' for working-class people (to secure a position within the housing field, accumulate housing wealth, live in a 'contemporary' home) can only make sense if they possess the form of being that enables them to relate to housing in terms of this range of possibilities, that is, as a position within the space of positions in the housing market, a form of investment and a signifier. But these rationales for housing market restructuring are anathema to working-class people, who articulate a primordial point of view on housing that is a product of a form of being literally unable to comprehend the idea that their houses are anything other than 'somewhere to live' (just being), which, for the woman below, translates into a need for 'somewhere decent' or 'comfortable'.

> Oh, I think it's very important, you know, if you've got somewhere decent to live, I mean it's everything.
>
> JR77

Working-class people, who also articulate a primordial view of housing as something 'for me with others' (we-being), are also unable to comprehend a rationale for housing market restructuring that involves working-class people making way for middle-class incomers who are displacing a 'community' (we, us) in their pursuit of social position and economic profits. Thus working-class people articulate the housing issues that have announced themselves to them (as a consequence of the way HMR is engendering a class remake of the urban landscape) in terms of the need to ensure 'housing for all':

Q   So when I say housing, I mean it can mean a lot of things to a lot of people, but
         for you it's not just your house?
NL67   No, no, no.
Q   You see it as being more?
NL67   Wider, oh it's wider than that. It's the heart of a community. Affordable and
         decent homes for people.
Q   How important is housing to you?
LR55   Oh very important because it's housing. Well, decent homes for everybody
         should be a right. It should be automatic. And these are built properties and
         they're good family properties.

What is significant here is that working-class people in Kensington had not hitherto articulated a political opinion about the market for houses, which was something in which they had simply taken an 'interested disinterest'. Yet the mobilisation of official 'truths' about the market for houses in Kensington by social agents with an economic interest in the repositioning of Kensington within the space of positions within the housing market in Liverpool has produced a field of discourse through which working-class people have 'found' their own form of political truth about housing. Thus the imposition of official 'truths' that highlight the need to inscribe the dwellingscape of Kensington with 'exciting statements' does not impress working-class people who, wedded to the reality principle ('it's somewhere to live'), now opine that they are simply unable to comprehend the type of housing market restructuring that involves the demolition of 'good family properties'. Apartments and 'Barratt boxes' were not for the likes of these working-class people, whose criteria of legitimacy concerned the practicality of dwelling space ('we don't want to live in rabbit hutches') and who felt that the new dwellingscape symbolised the 'social cleansing' of Kensington of working-class people.

NL67   Now they're knocking houses down on Edge Lane and we've seen the plans.

Q   To make way for?

NL67   For the motorway. But it's not for the motorway really. They're knocking those houses down to build apartments.

Q   And I mean what do you think of that idea?

NL67   I think it's absolutely disgusting.

Q   Why?

NL67   Well, they're knocking people's homes down not for the road. It's not for the road at all. It's to build apartments on. Who's going to buy apartments? Not local community people. And there's not enough space for them to build houses for people whose house they're knocking down. And people don't want, I don't want to move house. I don't like new houses. If I had a million pound now I wouldn't go and buy a new house. A lot of people's houses are coming down . . . . It's rubbish. They've totally, totally ignored the community.

How are you going to sustain this community with apartments which are basically for, nothing against students, nothing against graduates, you know, there's lots of them, well let them, you know, let them buy a small house. They are building some houses but too many apartments . . . . They're not thinking for families. Apartments are not, well, for a start off, we don't need them. What they do build is rabbit hutches anyway.[2]

LR55

Q   So I mean do you support the council with the regeneration of the area?

JC54   No, I don't support them whatsoever. I've got no faith and interest in them or anything.

Q   And what about, say, the housing, the CPO and all that. Do you think that's going to make any difference?

JC54   No. All they're doing is taking the people from Kensington out.

Q   What do you think of that?

JC54   It's like social cleansing.

RM32   I don't agree with putting apartments in.

Q   Why don't you agree with that?

RM32   It's just wrong. It's like sort of driving off the local community. We've got no chance of purchasing something like that because it will just be too dear, won't it? So who do you end up with in the apartment? I mean they built apartments there at the back, I don't know if you've seen them? They're nice and that but they've gone down the nick already, do you know what I mean, half the windows are smashed in and all that. They'll be charging a hundred grand for that . . . . People in the area can't afford to buy them . . . . I don't see the point in replacing [terraced houses] with apartments.

The contrast between the middle and working-class relation to housing is never more apparent than in what these people say above. We have already seen that the middle classes have successfully imposed the principles of their own relation to the market for houses to such an extent that they are accorded recognition by working-class people in Kensington who judge the 'failures' of their own housing practices with reference to the successes of middle-class housing practices ('I was a lunatic not to move'). Yet these are not 'real' working-class perceptions of housing. They are merely a consequence of the way working-class people misrecognise the legitimacy of the middle-class relation to the market for houses, as a space of positions, which produces their tendency to 'regret' aspects of their own housing practices. The symbolic violence that this implies (that is, when the middle-class relation to the market for houses is regarded as legitimate by working-class people who communicate it back to social scientists in the form of 'regret') produces what Merleau-Ponty (1962) refers to as 'second order thought'. This is a 'representational' form of thought that presents our experience to us through the concepts supplied by others – in this case the middle class – rather than through 'first order' perceptions that emerge from within our own form of being-in-the-world:

> What I communicate with primarily is not 'representations' or thought, but a speaking subject, with a certain style of being and with the 'world' at which he directs

his aim . . . . My process of taking up this intention is not a process of thinking on my part, but a synchronizing change of my own existence . . . . We possess within ourselves ready-made meanings . . . . Second order thoughts . . . are translated into other words.

(Merleau-Ponty 1962: 213)

This suggests that the 'real' working-class orientation to housing can be picked up only in their primordial 'first order' perceptions of housing that emerge 'in the thick of it' (that is, as housing 'happens' to working-class people on an average-everyday basis) and not through 'second order' forms of articulation that arise as a consequence of their symbolic domination. Heidegger (1962) refers to this form of being-toward houses, which is immersed 'in the thick of it' on an average-everyday basis, as the 'ready-to-hand' relation to houses. Yet Heidegger also warns us that

the things which are closest to us are 'in themselves'; and they are encountered as 'in themselves' in the concern which makes use of them without noticing them explicitly . . . . When the [thing] cannot be used, this implies that the constitutive assignment of the 'in-order-to-'and a 'towards-this' has been disturbed. The assignments themselves are not observed; they are rather 'there' when we concernfully submit ourselves to them. But *when an assignment has been disturbed* – when something is unusable for some purpose – then the assignment becomes explicit . . . . When an assignment to some particular 'towards-this' has been thus circumspectively aroused, we catch sight of the 'towards-this' itself, and along with it everything connected with [it] . . . . Within this totality, however, the world announces itself. Similarly, when something ready-to-hand is found missing, though its everyday presence has been so obvious that we have never taken any notice of it, this makes a *break* in those referential contexts which circumspection discovers. Our circumspection comes up against emptiness, and now sees for the first time *what* the missing article was ready-to-hand with and *what* it was ready to hand for. The environment announces itself afresh.

(Heidegger 1962: 105, emphasis added)

Heidegger is basically impelling us to pick up on how the 'first order' perception of houses that working-class people in Kensington possess on an average-everyday basis has been 'disturbed' by the way the HMR programme to 'reconnect' Kensington to the metropolitan market for houses is rupturing their primary relation to their houses as simply 'there' for them. This is because the programme to demolish their homes, in order to create a 'new' and 'high-value' dwellingscape, has announced the market for houses afresh to them.

Specifically, the political goal of housing renewal, which is a vehicle for class domination, has invoked in working-class people a political attitude towards housing, as 'present-at-hand', that was not evident in the way they discussed housing on an average-everyday basis, that is, as something that is ready to hand. Thus working-class people who never previously conversed about 'housing' now make references to how they take more interest when 'housing issues' appear in television programmes, since this provides them with a means of informing themselves so that they can resist HMR.

Q   So what kind of things do you talk about when you talk about housing?
JC40   Well, if there was a news item, for instance, about Cumbria, I mean the local people can't even get housed. The property crisis there!
Q   Do you ever look at property programmes on the TV?
LR55   Yeah, Janet, she lives in X Street and she's got both [programmes about saving a run-down street on video] because it was done in two parts and she's taped it all as one, I think, and she's going to lend it me when I ask her for it. She said 'Just ask me when you're ready for it' and, in all honesty, I just haven't had time at the moment. But I want to see that because Welsh Street's been saved, bar four roads, and they're still fighting for the four roads.

If you don't mind me saying though, what is happening now is that the house prices are going up 'cause of the City of Culture. The only thing is you're getting a lot of people from outside Liverpool, who are coming in buying property . . . . The big block that's been built, now there's people who've bought about 10 flats in that block and then sold them on, bought them for like, say, £250,000 and they're not moving into them, . . . They've sold them for £350,000. So they get a £100,000 profit, you know what I mean. So it's with the people who've got the money, it's not the likes of us, ordinary Joe public on the street.

MB70

The tyranny of 'affordability'

The notion that houses are situated within a space of positions within a market for houses is so taken for granted in societies such as Britain that it is taken to be a definitional matter rather than a point of view that is articulated from a particular position in social space and that is, therefore, potentially controversial. That is to say, the conceptual notion that houses are situated within a space of positions within a market for houses constitutes a *housing market doxa*, that is, something that is so pervasive that it is beyond the capacity of most people to question it. The doxic nature of this point of view on the market for houses is exemplified by the complete lack of controversy about a key contention of HMR. This is the proposition that some urban areas have become 'disconnected' from their wider markets, thereby suffering 'housing market failure', that is to say, some areas have lost their position within the space of positions in the market for houses, thus necessitating a programme of restructuring that can reconnect them to the space of positions. Thus controversy about HMR has been limited to the 'rights' and 'wrongs' of the demolition programme that has been proposed as the solution to this 'woe' and *not* the basic assumptions that underpin the dominant perception of the market that 'necessitates' housing demolition. Thus Cole and Flint (2006) suggest that the controversy surrounding HMR has been more or less limited to arguments about 'saving heritage'.

Yet the notion that houses in urban areas such as Kensington are situated within the space of positions in the Liverpool housing market is an entirely arbitrary view articulated by housing research consultants that occupy social spaces (universities, research organisations etc.) that provide them with the means (institutional privileges, contractual rights) to access the type of data (house price statistics, empty properties etc.) that enables them to objectify the market for houses as a space of positions. The problem here is that these housing consultants misrecognise the epistemological status of the point of view that the market for houses consists of a space of positions and, therefore, treat it as a definition (rather than point of view) of the 'market for houses' that they use to conduct research: '[E]ach scientific universe has its specific *doxa*, a set of inseparably cognitive and evaluative propositions whose acceptance is implied in membership itself' (Bourdieu 2000: 100). We saw how this happened in Chapter 6 when we examined the housing market studies that have informed the HMR programme in Liverpool (Nevin *et al.* 1999), where the idea of the market for houses as a space of positions was taken for granted (doxa) and therefore simply operationalised in research. We also saw how the result has been a theory of 'housing market failure' that represents the dominant point of view of the market for houses in Kensington ('disconnected') but *not* the views of the working-class people living there, who do not see Kensington in such terms. But that is not all.

Housing research consultants' neglect to consider the particularity of the 'official' point of view from which theories of 'housing market failure' are produced (which is separate in social and economic terms from the 'lived view' of the market for houses) results in theories of housing market failure that, although particular, are never recognised as such. The corollary of this is apparent in the statement of the legal team acting on behalf of Liverpool City Council at a public enquiry that 'it might be asked whether, if the CPOs [compulsory purchase orders] are not confirmed, the market will step in and regenerate the areas within a reasonable time. The answer is *clearly* not so' (Elvin and Litton 2006:

para. 84). But that, also, is not all. The reification of this discourse of 'housing market failure' is facilitated by collective misrecognition of its epistemological status by social agents (government departments, local authorities etc.) that occupy the same social spaces as the research producers (the policy network), which obliges the viewing of the market for houses from the same objectifying distance, i.e. through statistics that 'reveal' the 'dynamics' of housing market change. It is this collective misrecognition that facilitates the domination of the dominant (institutional predators seeking to exploit 'rent gaps' as they emerge in urban spaces that 'need' to be 'reconnected' to the market for houses) over the dominated, that is, working-class people whose homes will now make way for a dwellingscape that makes the correct 'statements' to the 'right kind of people'.

Now, since the process of forcibly removing working-class people from their homes (through the issue of compulsory purchase orders) is ostensibly being undertaken 'in the name of the poor' (to tackle housing wealth inequalities), the HMR partnership in Liverpool has been obliged to ensure that 'affordable housing' and 'loan products' are provided to enable working-class people to buy within the brave new dwellingscape of Kensington. It is important to understand that the notion of 'affordability' that applies here can be understood only within the context of the rationalities that govern the HMR programme. It is imperative, therefore, to understand what these rationalities are before moving on to understand what 'affordability' means to both the housing market renewal partnership in Liverpool and working-class people living in Kensington. The housing market renewal rationale (to 'connect' Kensington to the space of positions in the market for houses) has produced an institutional compulsion to replace 'low-value' properties with 'high-value products' that attract the highest possible prices:

> The intention is to widen [Edge Lane] and put in a boulevard [aesthetic] . . . . But you must have noticed on your way down, the properties on Edge Lane are quite big and go far back. So we said we want family housing, family homes. So, now 99 per cent of the new build are going to be apartments. Not flats, apartments. When I asked the question 'What is the difference between an apartment and a flat?' the advisor said 'Oh, about £20,000 on the price.'
>
> (Chair, residents association)

Working-class people simply cannot afford to purchase 'high-value' products in the new dwellingscape that is being developed in housing market renewal areas because 'many owner occupiers affected by demolition have encountered a substantial affordability gap between the compensation they receive [through CPO] and the cost of buying a new property. The size of the gap varies but on average is around £35,000 . . . . but may be as much as £50–90,000 for new build developments' (Cole and Flint 2006: 7, 26).

> City of Culture! Look what they're doing to us. There was a fellow on the radio before saying he's got this three bedroom house *with garden back and front* and they've offered him £65,000 for it. Now that man's obviously put a lot of work into his house and he sounded as though he was proud of it, you know, saying he was, you know, decorating outside and inside . . . . And he said and they're building these flats and they're £130,000 for an apartment. You can see how that man feels. Well £65,000 is no good to him 'cos even if he put all of that on one of these apartments. I really do think they'd be better modernising these houses. But no they want to demolish and they want a new build and then all these people who can afford them will buy them and where will we be? Shoved somewhere where we don't want to go probably. . . . And then you're stuffed aren't you.
>
> RH65

These 'high-value' apartments do not, of course, constitute the 'affordable housing' that will also be offered to working-class people in Kensington. The 'affordable' houses that will be offered to working-class people in Kensington are those that a member of the HMR partnership referred to as the 'minimum' number of houses that the partnership needed to 'set aside' to satisfy existing residents who would then 'no longer care what happened to the area'.

> We've got to work with the developer, in this case it's going to Bellway, to say develop some houses that are affordable cost to local people. These are figures I'm speculating about now because we haven't got to this yet, but we need 100 houses, so many three beds, so many two beds, so many four beds, and so many bungalows or whatever for the local community that we've spoken to. And they can't be more than 80 grand . . . . But the community are going to be less interested in what you develop on the rest of the site once they've got their assurances of what they are getting. Then you can go and sell them. And if you can get £200,000 in private, just get on with it. Who cares? You have seen to the needs of the local people. In fact, after that [affordable housing], the more higher value properties you can get into Kensington the better for it as a place. That message is a very difficult one for the local people to swallow . . . . It's anathema to them to even think about most high-value properties. So the project has been to say to the developer 'We're working with local people to find out what they need, to see how many there are, and to tell you that you've got to build so many houses at this level, and then go and make your profit on the others.'
>
> (Director, registered social landlord)

Now, although the prices of 'affordable' houses have been set below the 'market value', they have still remained 'out of reach' of working-class people because of the aforementioned 'affordability gap' between the compensation received from CPO and the price of 'affordable housing'. This has compelled local authorities to provide 'equity loan products' that should enable working-class people to buy a share in an 'affordable' house.

> The price level has got to be affordable. What affordable means is that some people have got a market value for their [demolished] house of, say, 50 grand, which is the current market value. The developer has indicated they can build a two bedroom house, town house, for 80 grand. So there's a 30 grand gap. So the equity gap has got to be made up with an equity loan from the council. So if that 30 grand loan from the council represents 40 per cent of value of the property, the city have got 40 per cent stake in that house, which grows all the time. The equity loan product has now been launched. But there's a 25 grand ceiling on it because the city have had to take a view that says 'Look, we've only got so much money and we're trying to quantify the demand so we've got a brief idea of the supply here and we're trying to get more money off government but it's not a bottomless pit so we're going to pitch this at 25 grand.' That's the product.
>
> (Director, registered social landlord)

Thus institutional members of the Newheartlands HMR partnership accept that 'affordable housing' within the new dwellingscape of Kensington remains unaffordable to many working-class people, even with the 'equity loan products' that are available to them (see also Cole and Flint 2006: 47).

Q   So even with the equity loan products people can't afford to buy?
NDC officer They're forced into renting or maybe forced into buying in another marginal area, so it's an ongoing cycle isn't it, to be honest . . . . If you look at the ethos of it, it is supposed to be about assisting the residents of the area, so if investment in housing is not going to assist existing residents you've got to question this.

The irony of this is that HMR is creating space for an influx of investors and middle-class households, but at the cost of forcing some working-class households out of owner occupation and into social renting, which has generated considerable anger (Cole and Flint 2006: 26).

> I've had the council out asking me where I want to live but it'll be quite hilarious because I still owe the mortgage £20,000. So I owe the mortgage company about

£20,000 and if they [the council] compensate me [for demolition] I'll have to pay the mortgage company back and whatever's left I don't think they'll let me have a mortgage, so I'll have to go into rented accommodation. But I will not live in a flat . . . . The family come on Boxing Day, they're all here, 12 grandchildren and all their mums and dads. Imagine if I lived in a flat. So they asked me where I'd like to live so I said 'Well, I'd like to live in a house with a garden' and I started laughing. He said 'It's not beyond the realms of possibility' . . . . I don't know what choice we'll have but, as I say, I'll have to rent a house.

RH65

Such testimonies exemplify the discriminatory nature of HMR, which even members of the HMR partnership in Liverpool themselves admit is tantamount to a programme of 'social engineering':

It's about, well, trying to keep that economically active population, increase the population who are economically active, not less economically active people, change the balance of the area. So I think that's not displacing people, it's just, *it's social engineering really isn't it. Well it appears to be.*

(HMR senior manager)

Nevertheless, the problematic here is not simply that the price of houses within the new dwellingscape of Kensington might be out of the reach of working-class people. Another *key* issue is that the housing market renewal partnership has defined the 'affordability' problematic in terms of a need to provide working-class people with loan products. This is because their definition of the problematic in these terms is emblematic of the 'official view' that houses represents a 'high-value' investment and that, through position-taking within the market for houses, working-class households will be able to 'grow' their investment.

Yet the notion that houses represent an 'investment' makes sense only to those whose existential actuality enables them to relate to housing in such terms, that is, those who have 'economic capital' to invest. The idea of 'housing investment' is existentially foreign to working-class people who live their lives in close proximity to economic necessity, and whose being-toward houses as 'things' that are 'there' means that they are literally unable to comprehend the idea that houses are anything other than somewhere to live. That said, the provision of 'loan products' to enable working-class people to purchase within the new dwellingscape of Kensington cannot be understood in the terms in which they are presented, that is, as help. On the contrary, the whole idea of a 'loan product' exemplifies the dominance of the dominant point of view on the market for houses as a 'high-value investment' and, worse still, the manner in which it has been imposed on the dominated who are now forced to 'invest' such 'loans' in the housing market in order to remain home owners in Kensington.

> They want to demolish all the houses, and build from new, which, well people like me won't be able to afford it. Even if, if, if the mortgage – say they paid my mortgage – 58, say 60 thousand, I'd have to pay the mortgage company back, plus, because of the interest they would have had over the years, the mortgage, remortgaged, I'd be left with about 15 or 20 thousand pounds. And even if I put that as a deposit, I'd be 99 before I finished paying for that, wouldn't I? So I'm stuck really.
>
> RH65

These working-class residents are not simply articulating a point of view against the demolition of their *own* home, then. They are suggesting that HMR constitutes a violation of an entire way of being-toward houses, which does not relate to them as 'investments' and, as such, simply prefers to spend 'what is necessary' to secure 'somewhere to live' that is comfortable etc.[3] Moreover this enforced positioning of working-class people within the space of positions in the market for houses has, as Heidegger (1962) warned us earlier, compelled them into a 'fresh' awareness of the market for houses, which is generating considerable anxieties for those who remain within owner occupation.

JJ37   Looking at what they're building now, in fact the prices are frightening.
SJ35   They're frightening, aren't they, absolutely frightening.

> We would only get a house half this size probably in somewhere that we didn't want to live for £110,000 . . . . It's just not enough. So that's, you know, that's because of the property boom, ridiculous prices for ridiculous places. So if someone knocked on my door tomorrow and said Jackie, here's £90,000. What am I going to do with that? Nothing. I'd be lucky if I got a flat, a one bedroom flat for that.
>
> JC54

Thus working-class people who have conventionally treated their houses for what they were to them on an average-everyday basis (just being) now feel compelled, by HMR discourse, to objectify their relation to the field of housing, which is creating considerable anxieties ('prices are frightening'). Violation of the working-class being-toward houses through the imposition of a dominant point of view over a dominated point of view – as in this case – constitutes yet another form of symbolic violence.

Conclusion

This chapter has explored the ways in which working-class people experience the 'brave new housing market' of Kensington, as a position within the space of positions of the metropolitan housing market. Working-class people, whose lives are wedded to the 'reality principle', and who relate to the market for houses in terms of the practical possibilities it presents to them to dwell, are simply unable to 'see the point' of demolishing 'perfectly good houses' so that they can be replaced with a dwellingscape inscribed with 'exciting statements'. Moreover, although working-class people are being presented with 'affordable' housing options, as well as 'loan products' to help them to afford these 'options', many still cannot afford to purchase within the new dwellingscape of Kensington. This is why Cameron (2006) has argued that:

> It is often argued that housing market renewal will provide greater housing choice and meet rising aspirations. The choice will not in reality be available to many of the mainly low-income existing residents of these areas. Housing market renewal will, rather, increase the range of choices for the more affluent who already have significant choice . . . . at the cost of reducing choice for those who need low-cost housing, whose aspirations will not be met by the market.
>
> (Cameron 2006: 13)

The problems that HMR imposes on working-class people do not finish there. This chapter has shown that initiatives to provide 'affordable housing' and 'loan products', to assist working-class people to purchase within the new dwellingscape, do not straightforwardly constitute 'help', even though this is the way in which they are presented by practitioners of HMR. This is because even 'affordable housing' imposes a requirement on working-class people to assume higher levels of 'mortgage debt'. Yet these people are terrorised by the insecurity of their economic position, which, as we saw in Chapter 4, is manifest in the 'first order' way they talk about housing in terms of its matter-of-fact practicalities ('it's where I live') and not as an investment opportunity. Initiatives such as 'affordable housing' and 'equity loan products' do not straightforwardly constitute 'help', then. On the contrary, they actually exemplify the manner in which the dominant view of the market for houses has been imposed on working-class people, who are now required to 'play the market' according to the rules established by the dominant if they want to remain in Kensington.

Chapter 8

Housing market renewal and the politics of middle-class domination

Introduction

Chapters 6 and 7 have discussed the politics of HMR. Housing market renewal is constituted on dominant views of the market for houses, as a space of positions. Working-class people who do not relate to the market for houses in these terms tend to oppose it. This suggests that there is nothing inevitable about its implementation, which many working-class people resist. This is evident in the public enquiries that have taken place to (ostensibly) examine the concerns of working-class residents who are being subjected to HMR. This chapter now examines the politics of implementing HMR in Kensington. The chapter further develops themes that have run through previous chapters by discussing the rationale for working-class resistance to HMR. It then moves on to examine institutional responses to this working-class resistance. Institutions that are wedded to the dominant doxa, that the market for houses consists of a space of positions, and meta-doxa, that terraced housing has reached the 'end of history', cannot grasp HMR other than in terms of its self-evident benefits. It will inevitably produce 'something better'.

Although the view that HMR will produce 'something better' is represented in terms of the Kantian 'disinterested aesthetic', this obscures the manner in which such aesthetic judgements are perceptions that are particular to the social conditions in which they are formed, that is, at a social and economic distance from Kensington. It therefore obscures the power that these institutions have to shape the space of appearances in the market for houses in Kensington. Moreover, as doxa, the perception that HMR will inevitably produce 'something better' results in a chronic lack of institutional reflexivity about HMR implementation. This is because doxa compels these institutions to interpret working-class resistance to HMR in terms of a communication problematic; the objectives of HMR need to be communicated more efficiently and effectively. The task, then, is to 'sell' the programme of change to people. This is achieved by shaping the conditions of communicative transmission and reception so that the dominant view prevails within Kensington. Such is the nature of institutional arrogance that is produced by adherence to the dominant housing market doxa that, even when confronted with resistance, this is understood as a problem of communication rather than a problem born of a conflict of interests.

Housing market renewal doxa and working-class resistance

Previous chapters have shown that institutional misrecognition of the 'policy view' (that the market for houses consists of a space of positions) as self-evident has resulted in the reification of this view, which, in turn, has obscured its arbitrary nature as well as the particular conditions of its production and articulation. This is why previous chapters have referred to 'housing market doxa'. The doxic nature of this official view of the housing market has, in turn, obscured the arbitrary nature of the meta-views that have been produced within its parameters. For example it has buttressed meta-doxa, such as the notion that Kensington has become 'disconnected' from the space of positions within the wider metropolitan market for houses, as well as meta-narratives such as 'the end of terraced housing' and its corollary, the myth that 'contemporary' housing consumers desire 'modern' and 'contemporary' homes.

Although the housing market doxa promulgated by social agents occupying the institutional space that enables them to view the market for houses as a space of positions also finds expression in the practices of middle-class households that possess the requisite levels of economic and cultural capital enabling them to view the housing field likewise, previous chapters have shown that this does not apply to working-class people who live in Kensington. Working-class people who are wedded to the reality principle possess a form of being-toward houses as 'things' that are ready-to-hand on an average-everyday basis (just being) as well as emotionally meaningful spaces that are 'for-me-with-others' (we-being). Since this form of comportment toward houses ('just being', 'we-being') means that working-class people *experience* rather than *contemplate* houses, they seldom talk about 'housing' in conversation.[1]

Now the silence towards housing that has hitherto reigned among working-class people in Kensington speaks of the lack of any *direct* or *physical* interference in their relation to their own houses hitherto. The declaration of HMR programmes has, of course, changed this because it threatens to remove the homes of working-class people from the dwellingscape of Kensington. From the official point of view, HMR represents an 'opportunity' for working-class people to purchase a 'product' that occupies a position within the space of positions. Yet working-class people possess 'just' and 'we' forms of being-toward houses, which means that they do not *ordinarily* objectify the position of their houses within the space of positions but, on the contrary, relate to them as a 'lived space' whose meaning ('I've always loved my house') derives from the brute fact that it is simply 'there' for-me-with-others on an average-everyday basis.

Q Was there ever any point in time when you thought of moving from this house?

RH65 Never wanted to, but I do now.

Q Do you? Why do you want to move now?

RH65 I've got no choice. We're being demolished. We're being bought out, aren't we?

Q If that wasn't happening?

RH65 No, I'd stay.

Q Would you?

RH65 Oh yeah. I've always loved my house and I always loved my street.

Although the HMR programme has sought to provide local people with 'opportunities' ('affordable housing options' etc.) to 'remain within the community', then, working-class people do not see 'the community' in the Euclidian terms that characterise the 'policy view' of community. Specifically, the policy point of view is that the 'community' is a geographical space, which means that the displacement caused by demolition can be resolved by providing working-class people with 'opportunities' to remain within that geographical space. Yet the woman above indicates that working-class people *experience* 'community' as a 'lived space' ('I've always loved my street') rather than a geographical space. And because working-class people *experience* the community as a 'lived space', they articulate resistance to the 'opportunities' that housing market renewal has presented to them to 'move over the road'.

NL67 Well, I'm in Edge Hill, now I wouldn't move to the north side of Edge Lane.

Q You mean cross over Edge Lane?

NL67 To a new accommodation? There are a lot more I think like me in Edge Hill . . . . Now the answer to that I couldn't tell you, it's just the territory that they live in.

Q There's Cotswolds?

NL67 Yeah, Cotswolds, that's in Kensington Field.

Q Yeah, which isn't a million miles away from you?

NL67 It's only over the road, but what I was saying before it's on the north side. I have no inclination of living on the north side. I've got relatives and family who live over there, but it's not where I want to be.

Q   So if you won the lottery and you had an unlimited amount of money to buy a house anywhere, what would you do?

NL67   I wouldn't be in any rush . . .

> Well because this just was our patch. . . . I'm not going to change my opinion 'cause now I'm parochial, I like my patch, this is my patch here and, you know, although I'm part of the wider picture with the NDC projects, this is my patch. I've no desire to live in Holly Road or Fairfield. This is where I'll be. They'll pull this house down around us but, at the end of the day, I'll still be here 'cause I'm not moving anywhere.
>
> JR43

Nevertheless, resistance to the HMR programme is not simply a consequence of the working-class relation to houses and 'community' as a lived space. It also emanates from the criteria of judgment that working-class people impose on houses in order to evaluate their worth. Working-class people who are wedded to the 'reality principle' valorise houses as 'things' ('bricks and mortar', 'somewhere to live') rather than 'signs' to be read, interpreted and speculated upon within the field of possibilities. For working-class people, then, houses are experienced as 'equipment' and thus judged in terms of qualities such as solidity ('materials they use nowadays are rubbish') and functionality ('new houses are like rabbit hutches'). And as 'equipment' that is simply 'there' and ready to hand they seldom have reason to talk about it unless, of course, it 'breaks' (cf. Heidegger 1962). That said, the production and circulation of discourses about the 'obsolescence' of terraced houses in places such as Kensington has had productive effects because it has enabled working-class people to 'find their voice' and thereby *articulate a critical resistance* towards HMR that is expressive of their particular form of being-toward housing.

> We were a vibrant community. But now. We're just living in, I don't know what we're living in. We're waiting to be told that our houses are going, and they're building these new places, and really, they build rubbish, don't they? These houses are solid. Why don't they use the money to modernise it? Let us live in the same environment, but no, they want the land so they can build all these fantastic houses for people who can afford them.
>
> RH65

That's the housing programme, in March, I don't know how many houses, and they're saying that they're going to build new houses and so on. One of my pet

arguments is that the houses that they build today do not last as the houses of yester-
year . . . . The materials they put in new houses aren't as good as the old materials.

JC40

I just wish they'd say 'No. We're not going to demolish now 'cause they're solid
houses' and modernise it, you know, 'cause they're breaking communities up. But
then they build these estates . . . . They're horrible.

JE42

LR55   Oh yeah, it's still my home, they're not going to knock it down . . . . Well, you
        don't put up with it. You fight it and try and do the best we can.
Q   So do you still feel some attachment?
LR55   Oh yeah, it's my house. The more they want to knock it down, the more
        attached I get to it.

This critical resistance towards HMR is significant because working-class
people in Kensington had not articulated any opinions about the market for
houses *in their community* prior to the imposition of HMR. However, working-
class people have not simply 'found voices' that *expressed critical resistance* to
the demolition of 'good solid houses' and enforced removal of working-class
people from their own 'little patch'. The mobilisation and imposition of 'official
truths' about the 'end of terraced houses' in Kensington, by social agents with
an economic interest in the repositioning of Kensington within the space of
positions within the housing market in Liverpool, has created a field of discourse through which working-class respondents have also been able to 'find'
their *own political truths* about housing. Thus the imposition of 'official' HMR
truths that violate the working-class form of being-toward houses and, as such,
make that form of being explicit to working-class people, have had productive effects because they have enabled working-class people to 'find' their own
political language to express their relation to the market for houses.

This can be seen if we examine the productive effects of the imposition
of HMR truths that 'necessitate' the eradication of working-class housing from
strategic points on the urban landscape in favour of a dwellingscape of 'high-
value' 'products' that constitute 'investments'. We have already seen that the
idea that houses are an investment opportunity is alien to working-class people
who, existentially wedded to the reality principle, are literally unable to comprehend houses as anything other than 'somewhere to live'. For working-class
people who exist in close proximity to necessity and refer to mortgage costs as
a 'burden' that they seek to rid themselves of at the earliest opportunity (the
corollary of which is a distaste for the superfluous luxury of treating houses

as an investment), the imposition of 'high-value' 'products' necessitates their self-elimination from the market for houses in the 'new' Kensington ('no good to me that'). And since the mobilisation of truths about houses as a field of investment opportunities has resulted in the self-elimination of working-class people from the market for houses in Kensington, so that other social groups can take their place, it has compelled those working-class people to find and articulate their own political discourse about housing as a field of investment. This is exemplified in the way the respondents below (who did not previously possess any political views about housing) articulated a working-class point of view about housing market renewal as 'land grabbing' for the purposes of extracting economic profits from Kensington.

> We again have made it quite plain that our objection to the demolition of these properties is that it is land grabbing. It's just the way of big business to make more money at our expense. They've got nowhere ready to move us to, I know. Those who want to leave, by all means. I've got nothing against anyone selling up and going if that's what they want, nothing against that whatsoever. But this, you know, considering we are supposed to be a regeneration area which is supposed to be community led, we keep emphasising this is community led, so why are you not listening to the community?
>
> JR43

> To me they're all the same, exactly the same, no matter who's in power, you know. No benefit to me ever, and it's the same thing, if anything because we're working class.
>
> SJ35

The emergence of a class politics of resistance through forms of articulation such as 'land grabbing' and 'it's because we're working class' is interesting in a political context that has apparently moved 'beyond left and right' (Giddens 1994) and a social context in which people are apparently more likely to disidentify with their working-class identity rather than articulate a class politics (Savage 2000).

Truth and the necessity for communicative efficiency

Practitioners of the official doxa that the market for houses constitutes a space of positions, and who are wedded to the meta-doxa that terraced houses have reached the end of history and need to be replaced with 'modern' and 'contemporary' homes, articulate the restructuring of the market for houses in Kensington through a language of 'progress' ('they'll get something better').

And as the progressive programme of restructuring is opposed by those upon whom it is imposed, institutional adherents to the HMR meta-doxa can do little more than assert that its self-evident 'benefits' will become apparent to working-class people 'when they can see the results'.

> When they're threatened they'll come out fighting unless there's been a recognition that they'll get something better at the end of it.
>
> (HMR senior manager)

> The visual impact, which, of course, is what most people would see and, you know, they would see the results and then make a judgment.
>
> (Director, development and property management company)

The representation of the policy view in terms of the Kantian disinterested aesthetic (articulated here in terms that emphasise how 'people will make a judgment' that restructuring produced 'something better' when they 'see the results') obscures the manner in which perception of 'modern' and 'contemporary' houses as 'something better' is actually a product of a socially positioned form of perception and not 'pure' judgment. The language of the pure and disinterested aesthetic that is being used by the HMR partnership in Liverpool (which has an economic interest in producing such representations) also obscures from view their power to shape the space of appearances, which, in this case, represents HMR as a programme that will self-evidently produce 'something better'. This is not entirely intentional, of course. It is a consequence of the power of doxa that exists as doxa only because its adherents misrecognise it as 'pure' and 'disinterested' rather than particular to the circumstances in which it is produced. By obscuring the power of the aesthetic judgment in this way, from themselves as well as others, institutions involved in the restructuring of the market for houses in Kensington have therefore reduced the problem of resistance to a 'communication' issue rather than what it actually is, that is, a problem of different modes of being-toward the market for houses. And, as a problem of communication, practitioners of the policy view define their communicative task in terms of a need to complete more 'projects' that can be used to 'demonstrate' that what is proposed *really is* 'something better'.

> We can get there but we just want more photographs like that, you know what I mean. A few more projects to come off and we'll be alright . . . . You need to get in and to come on board and to see the vision for the place and to buy into the vision.
>
> (Director, registered social landlord)

For the practitioners of housing market renewal, then, the communicative task is framed in terms of a need to draw on examples of 'projects' to 'explain to people' and 'sell to people' the programme of activity that will result in a 'better' market of houses in Kensington.

> It's productive if you actually spend the time with people in actually explaining to them the process involved and where they can and can't influence the process. It takes a lot. You've got to be prepared to spend time sitting down with a lot of the community leaders on a one to one basis . . . . The people don't understand what they're going through, what's happening to them. They actually think that things are happening to them instead of happening with them. [Q: So you're hoping that they get on board voluntarily?] That's right, so we've got to sell the scheme to them.
>
> (NDC physical and environmental regeneration manager)

As adherents to housing market renewal doxa, and the network of meta-truths that sustain it, practitioners of the policy view therefore have no way of deciphering problematics that arise other than in terms of a breakdown of communication *from practitioners to residents*.

> I think the communication is the thing that kills it all at the end of day, isn't it? I mean there are a number of things that we are putting into place to support people to enable them to bridge the gap between what they've got now and the range of products in [the new Kensington] . . . . It feels like all those things are in place but I am not totally convinced about how that is being communicated to local people yet, and it doesn't help that C7 and the city council weren't at the community meeting because there was an opportunity lost there. [Q: You mean the meeting you were at?] Yes, the one that I went to. There was an opportunity lost there for communicating with people and trying to allay some of those fears. Those two people who were very vocal at that meeting, it wouldn't have mattered what you said because they had their personal agenda so whatever you said wouldn't have been right . . . . So, it's little things like that that cause people to get all steamed up and so the communication concept is going to be so important in the next few months about the proposed plans and what they mean to people.
>
> (HMR senior manager)

The 'democracy' of efficient communication

When the particularity of the privileged circumstances in which housing market discourse is produced goes unrecognised (as privileged) by the discourse producers, the discourses that they produce become reified (doxa), resulting in the unwitting imposition of the truths that it speaks. Although the imposition of these truths is unwitting, which is exemplified in the way the problematic of resistance is articulated as a 'communication issue' ('we need to sell housing market renewal to them'), it nevertheless results in a level of institutional arrogance that is the corollary of the lack of institutional reflexivity exhibited by the discourse producers in the face of working-class resistance to their schemes. This institutional arrogance is exemplified by the way in which institutions, which articulate the 'solution' to the resistance problematic in terms of a need for 'communicative efficiency', have configured 'decision making' forums in such a way as to enhance their ability to communicate, thereby providing the conditions for their symbolic domination of those who resist. Symbolic domination of working-class people who resist HMR in Kensington has been achieved through the abolition of 'neighbourhood planning groups' that were 'resident controlled' and concomitant creation of 'neighbourhood assemblies' which are chaired by an institutional member of the housing market renewal partnership.

> We came from a community consultation structure about a year ago. We moved from neighbourhood planning groups, with people planning their own neighbourhoods, to neighbourhood assemblies. The neighbourhood assemblies have to be chaired by a Kensington board member or a Kensington senior officer, and some of the community leaders in Kensington Fields object to that because they want to be able to chair the neighbourhood assemblies using their own people. We still hold assemblies in Kensington Fields.
>
> (NDC physical and environmental regeneration manager)

> The neighbourhood assemblies are a farce. They've done away with our neighbourhood planning group without asking us and put these neighbourhood assemblies where they actually stand and talk at us. They don't discuss things with us. [Q: When you say 'they', who's 'they'?] Kensington Regen, because they insist that they chair it or a member of the Regen board chairs it. We weren't allowed to even pick our own chair. And our chair person has never ever attended [our resident] planning group meeting so how the hell does he know what we're talking about? And he just sits there looking gormless, and the other one sits there nodding her head and giggling, like a pair of idiots.
>
> (Chair, residents association)

The purpose of this procurement of the chair, and control of the agenda of meetings, is to facilitate control of discussion, thereby enabling the institutions that make up the HMR partnership to 'talk at' residents:

The chair and vice chair would be a [Regeneration] board member or NDC officer. So therefore you've got the situation whereby whoever's the chair and the vice chair, they dictate the agenda, they dictate who can talk on the agenda, how long the agenda's talked for and they can, you know, virtually vote it through themselves.

(Ward councillor)

Nevertheless, symbolic domination cannot be achieved by simply exerting control over the right to speak and the content of discussion. Since the efficacy of communication is contingent on the efficiency of its reception, the HMR partnership has also sought to exert control over the reception of communication. This has been achieved in Kensington through the 'hand picking' of resident representatives that other residents described as 'yes men'.

There were no residents [on the neighbourhood assembly]. There was a couple of hand picked ones, I think, but there were no residents at first. Then there were five, but the Regen [board] picked them themselves. They are what I call the five 'yes men'. But then we, as I say the independent forum we got together, we fought for at least 10 members. We wanted it the way it was originally. The residents were out-voted every time. There was no chance that a resident's proposal would go through if they didn't agree with it because we were so outnumbered. I think originally there was five [residents] and then we fought for 10 and that is still not enough with the way the board's gone again now, because like C7 never used to be on the board for Kensington Regen but [C7 senior officer name] was seconded onto that last year and councillors have got on. There's more councillors on it now than there used to be. [Q: So even though they've increased the number of residents from five to 10 it's been balanced by the fact that they've also increased officer numbers?] Well now they have, yes, so we're now outvoted again . . . . I think Liverpool Land Development Company are on the board, I'm not sure to that, I'm not sure about that, but I do know that the board's getting bigger and bigger all the time and we're not getting consulted on it. It's just getting done unilaterally again. They're not taking our views into account . . . . Everything's got to go through the [Kensington Regeneration] board. And each area has two reps. And our two reps are a total waste of space. When Kensington Regen say do this, they do it, you know, or jump, they go 'how high?' [The resident representative] actually voted for the demolition of these houses and every one of our residents was against it. I wouldn't say everyone but the majority were against it. And she voted against us.

(Chair, residents association)

Maximising the efficiency of institutional communication by configuring the conditions of its reception, that is, by hand picking 'yes men', effectively constitutes what Bourdieu and Passeron (1977: 4) define as symbolic violence, which, as we saw earlier, is the power 'to impose meanings and to impose them as legitimate by concealing the power relations which are the basis of its force'. These power relations are concealed by the articulatory strategy that invokes the Kantian disinterested aesthetic in order to legitimise the official view of HMR. We saw earlier, for example, how this was achieved through the institutional mobilisation of statements such as 'people will make a judgment' that HMR has produced 'something better' when they 'see the results'. The extent to which this strategy 'worked' on hand picked residents is exemplified by the way such statements are received by resident representatives, who, as intermediaries between the institutions that constitute the HMR partnership and 'the community', transmit them within their own community. For example, one resident representative who had absorbed the discourse of the HMR partnership was said to be transmitting to 'the community' the official view that working-class imagery had no place on the urban landscape of the 'new' Kensington, which, of course, must make an 'exciting statement'.

> She's just a yes person. When Kensington Regen say jump she says 'how high?' She's the one that said to me 'we've got to knock your house down. We can't have people seeing washing on the line.' This is the one that's done the 'anybody who's against demolition we will back you 100%'. No chance! She just didn't turn up for meetings, or she sits there giggling. She hasn't got a clue what's going on. She hasn't got a clue. I'm alright Jack, sod you. But at least [resident representative 1 name] had been to the Planning Group meetings. [Resident representative 2 name] has never, ever attended one. He's our other board member for this area . . . . I know a lot of people who I believe have not gone, and a lot of people walked out when I walked out as well and I'm not one usually to walk out, but I just thought 'this is a waste of my time and energy'. I can do more at the independent forum or through our own residents' group.
>
> (Chair, residents association)

There are two things to note about this. First, the use of 'hand picked' residents (who are able to operate as intermediaries by efficiently receiving and transmitting 'official communication') is an explicit element of the strategy employed by the HMR partnership. This, of course, exemplifies the manner in which they define the resistance problematic in terms of the need for greater communicative efficiency and efficacy.

> If a lot of proposals are to be sold to the community . . . and sold in the right way, you actually want the community leaders to be working alongside you so that they're actually able to bring other residents in. If the community leaders feel as

though they're not part of the process it can be quite destructive, mainly because of misinformation going round . . . . We rely quite a lot on the community network to keep sort of lifting the spirit of these other people and helping them through the process that they're going through . . . . We are spending a lot of time getting them to understand the issues so that they can go out and help other members of the community . . . . [Resident representative name] chairs the group so she doesn't allow residents to become too negative. She keeps people on board, so it's good.

(NDC physical and environmental regeneration manager)

Second, the above quotations not only reveal the efficiency of the communicative strategy employed by the HMR partnership, which is a product of the extent to which intermediaries 'properly' receive and transmit communications ('we can't have people seeing washing on the line'). They also reveal substantial resistance to, and non-compliance with, the 'decision making' forums that have been established by the HMR partnership. This is exemplified by resident 'walk outs' and non-attendance at 'decision making forums', which residents describe as undemocratic because the HMR partnership has used them as an opportunity to achieve communicative efficacy ('they sit there telling you how good we've done') rather than as opportunities for democratic discussion ('never enough time for our items to be put on the agenda').

[Q: You've stopped going to the neighbourhood assemblies?] Yes. [Q: Why?] Because one, they're undemocratic. With the planning groups we voted in our own chair and vice-chair. We had an input into the agenda. We could ask for things to be put on the agenda. They tell you here [at neighbourhood assemblies] you can [have items on the agenda] but there's never enough time at the end for your items to be discussed. All it is, they sit there telling you how good we've done. We've only had like three or four [meetings] and I went to the first one where I basically just observed to see how it went and get a rough idea and then come back and talk to people who were away on holiday at the time and what have you. We were informed that, no, there wouldn't be a chair. [Q: Nobody would chair the meeting?] No, it would be sort of led by [senior NDC officer] . . . . They [residents] all walked out . . . . They were told categorically 'This is how it's going to be, this is what you're going to do' and they just stood up and went 'no'.

(Chair, residents association)

My friend goes to all these meetings, and it's the same old hogwash time after time. It's a waste of time. . . . These meetings, it's all hogwash, it really is.

RH65

Symbolic domination and 'communicative inefficiency'

The symbolic domination of residents is achieved primarily through the achievement of communicative efficiency, which has necessitated the configuration of communication systems so that they facilitate the transmission and reception of 'official' communication. We have already seen how this has occurred through the control of agendas, 'hand picking' of residents and the explicit use of 'hand picked' residents as intermediaries. But symbolic domination of residents is not achieved through communicative efficiency alone. Apparently paradoxically, it is also achieved through the explicit pursuit of communicative inefficiency. This occurs in a number of ways. First, the articulation of the 'official' view in a professional language that presents HMR plans in *such a fine level of detail* undermines the possibility that plans will invite resident interest.

> You've basically got an archived box full of lever arch files and random scraps of paper and large drawings and then about a three foot square table to lean them on. So it was a case of, right, start with one, then you flick through the lever arch file. A lot of them are not really relevant to the ordinary bloke on the street. Some of them are architectural sketches so, you know, it went down to what kind of paving slab was going to be put down, what sort of kerb stone was going to be used, what sort of light was going to be put into what place and what trees were going to be where.
>
> TP26

Second, the provision of 'telephone directories' to residents to read prior to meetings undermines their ability to digest information and therefore their ability to 'speak with clarity'.

> They put, you know, a telephone directory in front of you the day before the meeting. You've got no chance whatsoever to speak with any sort of clarity. You'd more or less be blinkered as regards to which decision you can make.
>
> (Ward councillor)

The strategy that involves presenting residents that are opposed to housing market renewal with a 'telephone directory' to read 'the day before the meeting' clearly does not seek to achieve communicative efficiency by shaping the conditions that facilitate the reception of communication. On the contrary it constitutes a deliberate strategy to undermine the conditions of communicative reception, so that specific proposals that might invite controversy can 'sneak through' unnoticed by residents that are opposed to HMR.

You might have to go to six or seven meetings and you might glean one relevant fact from that. I mean we had six meetings alone on discussing the style of the new street lamps, and the style was already decided because the council did one particular style that would match Victorian buildings. But what we found out from the meeting, we were looking at the map and there was a dotted line that went across the bottom of the map. . . . . We asked 'Excuse me, what's the dotted line for?' And the lady who was there [to answer questions was] more or less just as a clerk. But there was a lot of suits milling round from the council with their name badges hidden. So she said 'Oh, that's the underpass that's going to lead from the University Hospital to its car park and housing estate.' I said 'Well, has anybody informed the people in the area that, you know, that they're going to make way for a car park and housing estate?' 'Oh, I'm sorry, we don't deal with that.' But as soon as she mentioned that, she was more or less surrounded by the suits, and that more or less confirmed all what we'd heard by the rumour that there was a demolition or proposed demolition of the area. And it also revealed the player who was involved, because the Royal University Hospital needs to expand or it needs to move [somewhere else].

(Ward councillor)

A consequence of this strategy of communicative inefficiency, which involved withholding information about regeneration plans from potential investors, has been to undermine the possibility that an organic process of renewal would take place (see Chapter 5). Communicative inefficiency has also ensured that resistance to HMR has been negated, for example, through the concealment of controversial proposals within a 'telephone directory' that is circulated only one day in advance of a meeting. It is only when such strategies of concealment become apparent that the potential for resident opposition to housing market renewal plans emerges. When this happened in Liverpool, the HMR partnership sought to blunt resident opposition by articulating their plans as 'proposals' that were 'not definite' or by articulating plans in terms of a range of possibilities that had yet to be decided upon. The institutional purpose of this 'planned uncertainty' was to immobilise resistance to housing market renewal by obscuring the object of its source.

They're always saying 'proposals' and 'nothing is definite'. One scheme is in the next streets up, Corn Street, Wedgwood, not Wedgwood, Corn and Whimpell. They are going to be car parks for the new builds and for Sure Start and the school. Now that is what we're told on one hand. Then we're told, on the other hand, 'No, no, no, no, no, there is no plans for that'. It is definitely new properties, apartments. Now everyone has stipulated they don't want apartments, they want housing.

(Chair, residents association)

Everyone wonders what's going on. No one seems to know what's happening. They tell us it's going to be apartments, it's going to be houses, but we don't know. And yet the bricks have been delivered. You'd think that someone would know.

TP26

Yeah, they know it all anyway, but no one still seems to know what's going to happen.

JS63

Nevertheless the institutional configuration of decision making forums, so that communicative efficiency and inefficiency can be coterminously achieved, was not a total success because opposition to HMR remained strong and widespread in Kensington. For the majority of residents who articulated opposition to HMR, an inevitable consequence was the frustration and anger that emanated from 'being talked at' but 'not being listened to'.

SJ35	They are telling us what to do.
JJ37	Are telling us what's to be done.
SJ35	Instead of listening to what the people want.
JJ37	They're not listening to the people, they're not listening to the plans of the people, and . . .
SJ35	And you know, you've only got to look at the . . .
JJ37	The Caledonian Village, the people regenerated that, not some high-flying executive coming in from elsewhere, and telling us what's good for us.
SJ35	You know, why do you need these people?
JJ37	And that's where the anger comes from.

This whole thing is supposed to be community instigated and community led but, as I said, the community is not being listened to whatsoever with anything. Absolutely nothing . . . . We were the token resident board members and it literally was token . . . . You weren't listened to. It was pretended that you were listened to, but you weren't listened to. When you went to a board meeting or the other meetings that involved housing, health and safety, police, they were all in the daytime. So, if you worked, you couldn't go to any of those meetings.

JC54

Yeah, well, we've actually gone to all the committee meetings and all that, the regeneration, I mean . . . . I've been phoning up about it to find out what is happening because we went to one of those meetings and they did have plans of what they were going to do. . . . They show you plans and you never hear anything else.

MP47

Well they didn't give people what they wanted because they were never consulted. When you're dealing with people's lives, you can't assume anything, you must get things right.

AR39

Although frustration and anger is a consequence of 'being talked at' and 'not being listened to', the latter problematic ('they don't listen to us') is a consequence of a lack of knowledge of how to 'play the game'. The problem here is not that the points of view articulated by residents are not received by an HMR partnership that simply will not listen. The problem here is that residents wrongly assume that the rules of political discourse necessitate an open dialogue that is 'based on the facts' as they stand at a point in time. If this were the case, then the articulation of a point of view that was buttressed with 'facts' would ensue in open dialogue. Indeed this is what residents expected when they articulated 'good views' that were supported by 'facts'. The problem with this is that the articulation of a point of view cannot take place outwith considerations about the conditions of its reception. Now, since the conditions of reception are framed by the housing market doxa that governs the production of legitimate truths about housing market renewal ('end of terraced housing' etc.), the articulation of 'good views' that emerge from a working-class form of being-toward housing ('these are good solid houses'), but are alien to the perceptions of those who dominate the field, can only invoke responses that denigrate these 'good views' as possessing little or no validity and therefore legitimacy.

I get disappointed at the city council not listening half the time when you try to put good views over. I get disappointed in regeneration officers if they don't take on board what you say or try to react on it. Sometimes you feel as though you're wasting your time, but I'd never give up. I'd carry it through to the end to make sure things came out for the people of the community I live in.

NL67

'Good views' that are articulated from a form of being-toward houses that is alien to the dominant form of being-toward the market for houses are not simply ignored, then. They are aggressively denigrated as lacking validity and therefore legitimacy. Indeed social agents who have a doxic relation to the dominant point of view on HMR, and who legislate on the legitimacy of all viewpoints about housing market renewal, have no way of relating to the alternative viewpoints of working-class people other than as attempts at 'mischief making' and 'spreading misinformation'.

> It can be quite destructive mainly because of misinformation going round. . . . Every time they hold an assembly there's literature going round or the assemblies are picketed by a group who object to the assemblies to try and prevent other residents from going in. So there is quite a lot of mischief making, there's a lot of misinformation being spread round that isn't particularly true . . . . I think you'd have to meet some of the characters involved there to really understand what exactly their motives are.
>
> (NDC physical and environmental regeneration manager)

This problem is exacerbated when the 'mischief makers' that generate 'misinformation' articulate themselves through a vernacular form of language that exhibits a proximity to the issues at stake ('you can stick your fucking apartments') rather than through a legitimate form of discourse that denotes a level of objectivity ('surveys suggest that . . .'). This is because it enables practitioners of the dominant (sanitised) form of discourse to dismiss the alternative views of residents as 'inappropriately aggressive' or 'miserably expressed', thus legitimising the practitioner view that 'we do not have to listen to this abuse', which is a wholly undemocratic state of affairs that results from the dominance of the 'professional' form of being.

> There is such a lot of anger . . . . Sometimes it's unfair. Often it's poorly and miserably expressed because it hates hard luck on the professionals, but that's their life, their daily life. It is more unusually negative and nasty than another job might be. So Kensington has seen, in all my experience of 20 years in this business, a remarkably high turnover of professionals moving out into other jobs. 'Oh, I'm getting away from this. Why do I need to go to four night meetings a week to get slaughtered?' You know what I mean. 'Why do I need to turn up and face these people?' however understandable. . . . 'I've got me kids and me family so why should I take these headaches home of a night?' So they move off to other jobs and that's been real.
>
> (Director, registered social landlord)

This notion that alternative points of view constitute 'mischief making' also justifies the practitioner view that the 'mischief makers' who 'miserably express' marginal views are 'lone voices'. Indeed, the researchers involved in the 'National Evaluation' of HMR have similarly dismissed resident opposition to the programme as a 'vocal minority' on the grounds that this is what regeneration officers told them, but without undertaking any research into resident opposition to housing market renewal themselves (Leather *et al.* 2007). Yet this denial that a collective voice exists in opposition to housing market renewal fails to acknowledge that the 'vocal minority' receive 'mumbling agreement' from the body of residents, which *is* indicative of the existence of a collective view born of a common form of being-toward the market for houses and against HMR.

> Well there is an agenda . . . . But what happens is that you get someone who is vocal, is opinionated, is able to hold an audience. They are probably able to stand before an audience and ramble on and on and on about some issue which is not even on the agenda but which sufficiently strikes a chord with a mass audience, you know, to get mumbling agreement. So much of the meeting then will be spent on a topic which is just really a talking point. No decision's going to be made on it. No action will be taken on it. No result can come from it. You know, it won't result in anything other than he's had a gripe. And voting just becomes difficult. It's got a long way to go. They've got a very tired housing stock with a dreadful façade of shops with flats above that virtually nobody wants.
>
> (Estate agent)

Thus there is no such thing as 'lone voices' that are opposed to HMR in Kensington. Insofar as 'lone voices' appear to exist this is a consequence of the symbolic domination that practitioners of HMR exert over working-class people, which intimidates all but a handful of them into silence. The symbolic domination of residents by those who possess legitimate views of HMR, as well as forms of language that enable them to articulate those views in a legitimate manner, results in the intimidation of residents whose historical disinterest in the market for houses has meant that they do not possess the linguistic instruments that could enable them to articulate their point of view on HMR in a legitimate way. The absence of large-scale vocal opposition to HMR does not indicate the lack of a collective voice, then. On the contrary, the resident below describes how the collective voice is sought and then articulated through those who retain the confidence (if not the instruments of language) to speak, yet who are denigrated as 'lone voices' that are 'over opinionated' by the practitioners of HMR, who regard their views as lacking validity and therefore lacking legitimacy.

> Not everybody in the community can stand up and put their opinions forward so they contact people within the community who can do that for them, who can take their fears and get some answers for them. But most importantly, and this is very important, report back to them.
>
> NL67

The problem here is that the institutional denial of any legitimate or collective opposition to HMR (which is a product of adherence to HMR doxa that leaves adherents unable to comprehend opposition as constituted on anything other than 'misinformation' generated by 'mischief makers') buttresses the perception that initially defined the solution to the resistance problematic in terms of a need for communicative efficiency. At the point when communicative efficiency is no longer effective, because opposition to HMR persists, institutional denial of the legitimacy of opposition to HMR becomes manifest in a rigid adherence to HMR 'no matter what'. This is exemplified in the way the HMR partnership issued CPOs on the homes of working-class people who oppose their plans. It is also exemplified by the way the partnership signalled its intention to win a public enquiry into the issue of CPOs no matter how many times it needed to attend court in order to secure the 'necessary' CPOs.

> I forget what they call it – it's a planning group like for the area. At our first meeting, me being me, I asked, because C7 are there, Kensington Regen are there and we actually had some people from Liverpool City Council there, so I asked 'All the boarded properties, that you've managed to acquire on this side at the moment, what is going to happen to them should we win the public enquiry?' And they went 'Uh, well, you're not going to win so we've got no plans.'
>
> (Chair, residents association)

Conclusion

This chapter has explored the politics of HMR implementation. Housing market institutions that are wedded to the dominant doxa, that the market for houses consists of a space of positions, and meta-doxa, that terraced housing has reached the 'end of history', were shown to be unable to grasp HMR other than in terms of its self-evident benefits. It will inevitably produce 'something better'. Now although these institutions represent their view that HMR will produce 'something better' in terms of the Kantian disinterested aesthetic, this simply obscures the manner in which their aesthetic judgements are actually perceptions that are particular to the social conditions in which they are formed, that is, at a social and economic distance from Kensington. It therefore obscures the power that these institutions have to shape the space of appearances. Moreover, as doxa, the perception that HMR will inevitably produce 'something better' has produced a level of institutional arrogance that is quite literally breathtaking. This is because doxa compels these institutions to interpret working-class resistance in terms of a communication problematic; the objectives of HMR need to be communicated more efficiently and effectively. This has compelled them to define a key implementation task in terms of a need to 'sell' HMR to working-class people. We saw how this resulted in attempts to shape the conditions of communicative transmission and reception so that the dominant view prevailed within Kensington. Yet resistance persists. And, wedded to the dominant doxa, so does the institutional perception that the problem they face is essentially communicative. For this reason, institutions respond to questions about 'what will happen if we win the public enquiry?' by suggesting that 'you won't'. Indeed, despite losing a high court hearing into CPOs in Liverpool brought by the resident Elizabeth Pascoe, English Partnerships responded by stating that they would overturn the court judgment so that the CPOs happened. What we can decipher from this, then, is that HMR is being imposed on working-class people in Kensington whether they like it or not.

Chapter 9
The rich get richer
Profiteering from working-class suffering

This book has provided a phenomenology of the relation between social class and the market for houses that differs, in key respects, from analyses of class formation in the housing market that have previously been undertaken. The purpose of Part I of the book was to examine approaches to contemporary class analysis, which, I argued, are constituted on 'resource epistemology' and a focus on consumption. My own view is that this work has provided invaluable insights into processes of class formation in the context of the housing market. However, it has also provided a limiting view. The development of class analysis within the parameters of the sociology of consumption has meant that the focus of recent class analysis has been on those who have a devotion to consumption (of houses etc.), in other words the middle class. Part I of the book therefore focused on literatures that have explored the issue of middle-class formation in the market for houses. Working-class people are largely missing from these literatures. Insofar as working-class people do appear in these literatures they do so in negative terms, that is, as 'failed consumers' or as 'displaced' by middle-class gentrifiers. Working-class formation is therefore theorised in relational terms whereas 'the working class' is seen to be constituted vis-à-vis the middle class (Sayer 2005; Lawler 2005a). Of course, there are good reasons for going down this route. The working class is a dominated and denigrated class that is dominated and denigrated by the middle class. This book has shown this too. However, this book has also shown that this is only part of the story.

Part II of the book argued that we need to understand working-class housing consumption on its own terms and not simply in relational terms. I also argued that 'resource epistemology' provides a limited way of understanding working-class housing consumption in its own terms. The reason for this is obvious. A defining characteristic of working-class people is their comparative lack of resources. For this reason I theorised the working class in existential terms, that is, in terms of a form of 'being-in-the-world' that is constituted at close proximity to economic necessity and insecurity. This enabled me to provide an insight into the 'internal economy' of working-class housing consumption. Working-class people who are devoured by the demands of an economic world that urgently demands to be dealt with ('bills to be paid', 'keep the wolf from the door', 'you just survive from day to day') are oriented to the practicalities (rather than social significance) of housing consumption. That is to say, working-class people who are *primarily* involved in a struggle for existence (rather than a struggle for recognition) engage in *the basic essentials* of housing consumption (rather than its symbolic significance). This is exemplified in the matter-of-fact way that working-class people refer to their houses as 'bricks and mortar' or a 'place to live' rather than in terms of its position within the space of positions in the market for houses.

Understanding these points is crucial to understanding the working-class relation to the market for houses. Working-class people who view their houses in these ways were shown to happily occupy 'failed' inner-urban areas such as Kensington. They constitute themselves as a particular fragment of the working class, an inner-urban working class. Thus, even though they take an 'interested disinterest' in the 'tyranny of suburbia' (which exemplifies the manner in which working-class people are complicit in their own domination), this is not because they are seeking to disidentify with their own social class or Kensington. It simply exemplifies the nature of their domination (symbolic violence). But that represents only part of the story for an inner-urban working class that, despite its domination, is generally satisfied with its current housing and neighbourhood circumstances.

If Part II provided an insight into the constitution of the inner-urban working class, then Part III examined how HMR is erasing this element of the working class from strategic positions on the urban landscape. Part III of the book therefore sought to develop a critical view of HMR by showing that dominant representations of HMR (which represent it as an urban renewal programme 'in the interests of the poor') ought to be challenged. This exercise has been perforce necessary because such critique has not been forthcoming from within the academy, notwithstanding a limited number of honourable interventions (for example, Cameron 2006). Unfortunately most members of the academy have been too busy providing 'research and intelligence' for HMR partnerships to have given any critical thought to it. Emphatically, HMR is not simply a technocratic 'fix' that is designed to 'reinvigorate' what Nevin *et al.* (1999) refer to as 'failing housing markets'. Neither is such a programme being practised in the interests of the urban poor. Such suggestions are based on the contestable notion that HMR simply seeks to ensure that the market for houses works properly, that is, more efficiently and effectively in providing and allocating housing resources so that some sort of match between supply and demand can be achieved.

It is a strange situation, indeed, to find so many 'social scientists' peddling the view that HMR is a technical matter that will succeed only if we develop 'better understanding' of how housing markets work (for example, Cole and Nevin 2004; Hickman *et al.* 2007). How utterly absurd for social scientists, of all people, to deny outright (at worst) or downplay (at best) the conflict of interests upon which HMR is constituted. And how unforgivable that all but one or two social scientists involved in housing research have completely neglected to address issues of power, class and social stratification in analyses of HMR. These critical oversights, and the academy's embrace of the technocratic discourse of HMR, commit the cardinal sin of obscuring what HMR is really doing, thereby facilitating the domination of the dominant over the dominated. As Bourdieu (1993b) would say, and Foucualt (1994) would concur, this constitutes a dereliction of duty for a social scientific profession whose key purpose should be to 'make trouble' for urban elites who would otherwise do as they wanted, unchallenged. It constitutes an unforgivable failure (the dire consequences of which are becoming apparent as working-class people lose their *homes*) to perform the critical task that social science is there to do.

If HMR says anything to us at all, this book has shown that it tells us that class analysis is as important as it ever was. The argument in the book therefore reinforces what sociologists such as Skeggs have been saying about the working class for a long time. It is important to remind ourselves, though, that Skeggs and I are, to some extent, dealing with different fragments of the working class and therefore different dynamics of class reproduction. We already know that some working-class people have achieved social mobility *of sorts* and have therefore moved out of the inner-urban areas of major cities (Smith 1996). Skeggs (1997, 2004) and Lawler (2005b) have already shown us that this relatively mobile fragment of the working class seeks 'respectability' and therefore to appropriate, in some ways, the consumption patterns of middle-class people (also Watt 2006). The purpose of this consumption strategy is to disidentify with the working class, largely because it is increasingly being constituted as an underclass. But, since the middle class possesses the cultural power to constitute the 'correct' forms of consumption (what to consume, where to consume, how to consume etc.), working-class people who are lacking in cultural capital, and therefore lacking the conceptual instruments that would enable them to 'correctly' decipher the consumption patterns of the middle class, find that their consumption practices are doomed to failure. This is why Nancy Fraser (1995) refers to a 'politics of recognition', because class positions are constituted on the ability to achieve recognition for consumption practices.

This is important stuff but it addresses a particular fragment of the working class that is engaged in a *struggle for recognition* (i.e. those that have 'made good': Wynne 1998) and that seeks to disidentify with its own (working-class) position. But, as I have indicated, this book has been concerned with a different, less mobile fragment of the working class. This is the fragment of the working class that has not 'made good' and abandoned the inner city. This is the fragment of the working class whose level of proximity to economic necessity and insecurity is such that it is primarily involved in a *struggle for existence* rather than a *struggle for recognition*. Whereas Fraser, Skeggs, Lawler and a series of other class analysts have devoted their energies to understanding the *politics of recognition* (which, as I have suggested, is a political struggle that concerns a particular, relatively mobile fragment of the suburbanising working class), this book has been centrally concerned to understand the *economics of being*, which, as I have suggested, reflects the concerns of a different, less mobile fragment of the inner-urban working class.

Now Skeggs and her colleagues have already shown us how painful it is for working-class people to engage in the politics of recognition. Not only do working-class consumption strategies end in failure, but the working class is denigrated for its failures. As Sayer (2002, 2005) points out, these are essentially issues of 'worth' where working-class people are positioned, by those who possess worth ('the judges of worthiness'), according to their lack of worth. This book has shown how similar injuries are being inflicted on the inner-urban working class, whose primary involvement in the world is constituted on its struggle for existence. These injuries are to a form of being that is wedded to the reality principle, and relates to houses in terms of their being 'ready-to-hand' (practical economy) rather than their position in the space of positions (symbolic economy), but is being violated by an urban renewal programme that is extracting housing from its basic economy (a space to dwell) and into the symbolic economy of consumption (a space of positions). The manner in which this violates the working class form of being-toward housing, which grasps houses in terms of their basic essentials, is exemplified in the speech forms that working-class people employ to describe the symbolic economy of houses as a space of positions ('no good to me that'). It is also evident in the terror that the idea of mortgage debt, the assumption of which is necessary to obtain a position in the brave new market for houses, strikes into working-class people.

The book has not only shown the violation of a whole form of being-toward the market for houses. It has also shown that this violation of the inner-urban working class being-toward houses has not simply been a mistake born of benevolent intent. This violation is the consequence of an institutional strategy to reposition 'failed housing markets' within the space of positions in the metropolitan market for houses. There are specific reasons for wanting to do this. These are to 'reconnect' places such as Kensington in the space of positions, partly because this generates market activity and therefore economic profits for those institutions that create that market activity, e.g. local authorities, developers, estate agents. These institutions are not only violating a form of being-toward the market for houses but also destroying working-class houses and the lives of people that live in them while extracting super-profits from places such as Kensington.

But why Kensington? Neil Smith (1989, 1996) would argue that inner-urban areas, such as Kensington, have been ripe for exploitation in the current phase of urban restructuring because they possess large rent gaps. The rent gap consists of the distance between the rent that can be extracted from land in its current usage and the potential rent extract that can be achieved if land is redeveloped. The existence of the rent gap in Kensington (which is located on the edge of Liverpool city centre) is a product of, among other things, the gentrification of the city centre (which has resulted in rising apartment prices) and the potential that exists for this to spread into inner-urban areas. Understanding this point helps us to understand why institutions involved in the housing market renewal of Kensington do not want, and therefore sought to frustrate, an organic process of gentrification.[1] This point was made by the BBC2 programme *How to Rescue an Empty House* (5 October 2005). This programme showed that Liverpool City Council and local housing companies were keeping properties empty and boarded up, despite admitting to increasing levels of interest in the purchase of such properties *by households that wanted to live in them*. This contradicts Nevin's (2006a) claim that such interest has been confined to investors seeking to make a 'quick buck' out of HMR. Suffice it to say that this is not an argument for organic gentrification, which, at worst, displaces working-class people from their homes (Slater *et al.* 2004; Slater 2006) or, at best, changes the character and feel of working-class neighbourhoods so that indigenous residents feel they no longer belong in their own neighbourhood (Savage *et al.* 2005).[2] I am simply highlighting the potential for organic gentrification to occur in inner-urban Liverpool as an alternative to HMR.

With such a large rent gap in Kensington, organic gentrification is the last thing that some institutions (notably developers) wish to see. Fortunately for these institutions, arguments about organic gentrification presented at a public enquiry in Liverpool were dismissed for being taken from 'sociology text books, some of which are dated and which contain no data on Liverpool'. The consequence of dismissing the argument for organic gentrification was to secure land in Kensington for *institutions* with an economic interest in the *redevelopment* of the market for houses therein. The 'end of history' narrative that has been created and mobilised against terraced housing has had the same effect, since this has also enabled institutions to dismiss the potential for organic gentrification, thereby justifying a demolition and redevelopment programme that enables them to secure the profits. Developers' motives in this regard were nowhere more apparent than in what they said about Kensington as a 'prime position' with 'significant development potential' and therefore as a 'massive opportunity'. It should be said that this is entirely consistent with the original idea, that HMR constitutes 'an entrepreneurial approach which maximizes the value of land [and] developer contributions' (Nevin *et al.* 1999: 120).

The impetus to institutionalise profit-making that the HMR programme encourages has, if anything, been further encouraged by the conferment of City of Culture status on Liverpool. Specifically, I have already argued that the mobilisation of an 'end of history' narrative has been used to justify the demolition of working-class houses, thereby producing the 'necessity' for the institutional redevelopment, rather than organic gentrification, of the urban landscape. However the City of Culture (whose purpose is to represent Liverpool as a successful post-industrial economy so that it can attract inward investment) has created a parallel impetus to denigrate any form of urban imagery that is representative of the industrial working class. So, not only are terraced houses denigrated but also imagery such as 'washing on the line', 'fifty pence shops' and so on, which must now make way for a brave new dwellingscape that makes 'exciting statements'. Although Liverpool City Council rejected the claim that City of Culture status was a key factor driving HMR (which they claim was being driven by 'consumer preferences') during the public enquiry into the CPOs on working-class houses in 2006, members of the institutional partnership quoted in this book suggest that it is being driven by the City of Culture. Official denials of the importance of the City of Culture were, therefore, contradicted by unofficial acknowledgements that its relevance to HMR is axiomatic.

As social scientists we should not be surprised by this. Housing market renewal is a regeneration programme that seeks to reposition Kensington within the space of positions on the urban landscape of Liverpool 'City of Culture', thereby enabling institutions (developers, estate agents, local authorities) to extract super-profits. The tragedy of this programme is that it necessarily involves the compulsory purchase of working-class houses with all the suffering that this has caused to working-class people. That this programme of institutional profiteering is inevitable (supported, as it is, by a lawyer who is a 'leading specialist' in the compulsory purchase of property along with a huge team of legal support and housing research consultants) is galling to say the least. That it is justified 'in the name of the poor' leaves one speechless.

The obvious retort to this is 'what would you do?' Cole and Flint (2006: 63) pose this question to critics of HMR: 'There is also a need for those critical of demolition programmes to set out what alternative mechanisms should be utilized to achieve the longer term goals of bringing about housing market recovery.' Indeed, I was presented with a very similar demand during a public enquiry into the compulsory purchase of working-class houses, where I was accused of presenting no alternative plan. Now academics may be under pressure to be 'relevant' (Imrie 2004) but this does not mean that academic work should assume the same level of instrumentality as that of policy makers. Relevance can mean many things. Moreover there are good reasons why academics should avoid the level of instrumentalism that policy makers embrace. For example Giddens (1990) would warn us that the notion that social scientists or anyone else understands society enough to be able to impose a grand plan on it is naïve, at best. But this is not simply about the approach to HMR in Liverpool. A broader issue about the future of critique is at stake.

Foucault (1994) pointed out, as quoted at the very beginning of this book, that those who work in the sphere of thought should not be obliged to come up with 'practical alternatives'. This is because such obligations serve to blunt the force of scholarly critique (by restricting critical thought to the context of its applicability and to problems defined by, of all people, policy makers), which is what the establishment that demands academic 'relevance' wants. That is to say, thought, to be critical, requires the freedom to think. The lack of critical thought about HMR emanating from the British academy shows what happens when academic thought is shaped according to the principle of applicability and to 'real world' problems defined by policy makers. Put differently, academics who study HMR have been so blind to supposedly abstract *academic issues* of power, class and conflict that they have found themselves supporting a programme that they believe to be concerned with increasing the 'efficiency' of housing markets yet that is actually designed (at least in Liverpool) in a way that is enabling rich institutions to profit from working-class suffering. If this book has achieved anything, it will have forced readers to think critically about HMR and without undue restriction. Only by deconstructing programmes such as HMR, and understanding them critically (for example, through the lens of class analysis), can we make constructive contributions to debates about urban renewal. This book is intended as a constructive contribution. But, in the same way that the institutional partnership driving HMR has ridden roughshod over the lives and feelings of working-class people, the constructive contribution in this book has been equally confrontational. Housing market renewal is, after all, constituted on a conflict of class and other interests and *not* necessarily a desire to 'fix' or enhance the efficiency of housing markets: 'A reform is never anything but the outcome of a process in which there is conflict, confrontation, struggle, resistance' (Foucault 1994: 457). In 1968 E. P. Thompson wrote about the 'Making of the English Working Class'. At this point in the early twenty-first century, it is pertinent to note that HMR represents a 'Breaking of the English Working Class' living in the inner city, in terms of both its being-toward the market for houses and its visibility on the urban landscape.

Appendix I
Summary characteristics of working-class respondents

1 Age profile of working-class respondents (*N* = 30)

Age	Number	% of sample
18–25	2	7
26–35	8	27
36–45	6	20
46–60	5	17
61 or over	9	30

2 Gender profile of working-class respondents (*N* = 30)

Gender	Number	% of sample
Men	10	33
Women	20	67

3 Tenure profile of working-class respondents (*N* = 30)

Tenure	Number	% of sample
Owner occupiers	24	80
Private renters	2	7
Social housing	3	10
Living with parents	1	3

4 Length of residence at current address for working-class respondents (*N* = 30)

Length of residence (years)	Numbers
0–1	0
2–5	5
6–15	4
16 or more	17
Missing data	4

Appendix II
Individual characteristics of working-class respondents

The sample of working-class households was drawn from 25 households and included 30 interview respondents. The characteristics of these respondents were as follows:

Household 1	
ID	KB55
Age	55 years
Gender	Female
Tenure	Owner
Employment	Auxiliary nurse
Qualifications	None
Marital status	Widowed
Ethnic origin	White British
Number of children	2
Length of residence	Since 1958

Household 2	
ID	MB70
Age	70 years
Gender	Female
Tenure	Owner
Employment	Full-time career
Qualifications	None
Marital status	Single
Ethnic origin	White British
Number of children	None
Length of residence	62 years in Kensington, 32 years in this house

Household 3

ID	JR43	ID	AR39
Age	43	Age	39
Gender	Female	Gender	Male
Tenure	Renting from housing association	Tenure	Owner
Employment	Care support worker	Employment	Security worker
Qualifications	None	Qualifications	None
Marital status	Single	Marital status	Single
Ethnic origin	White British	Ethnic origin	White British
Number of children	2	Number of children	Unknown
Length of residence	17 years	Length of residence	Not resident in this household

Household 4

ID	JS63	ID	FS62
Age	63	Age	62
Gender	Female	Gender	Male
Tenure	Owner	Tenure	Owner
Employment	Retired	Employment	Retired
Qualifications	None	Qualifications	School leaving qualification
Marital status	Married	Marital status	Married
Ethnic origin	White British	Ethnic origin	White British
Number of children	2	Number of children	2
Length of residence	35 years	Length of residence	35 years

Household 5

ID	RM32
Age	32
Gender	Male
Tenure	Owner
Employment	Postman
Qualifications	GCSEs
Marital status	Married
Ethnic origin	White British
Number of children	1
Length of residence	7 years at this house

Household 6

ID	RH65
Age	65
Gender	Female
Tenure	Owner
Employment	None
Qualifications	None
Marital status	Married, living on own
Ethnic origin	White British
Number of children	5
Length of residence	42 years

Household 7

ID	JJ37	ID	SJ35
Age	37	Age	35
Gender	Male	Gender	Female
Tenure	Owner	Tenure	Owner
Employment	Fruit market labourer	Employment	Call centre operator
Qualifications	Unknown	Qualifications	Unknown
Marital status	Married	Marital status	Married
Ethnic origin	White British	Ethnic origin	White British
Number of children	3	Number of children	3
Length of residence	7 years	Length of residence	7 years

Household 8

ID	TP26
Age	26
Gender	Male
Tenure	Living with parents
Employment	Clerical officer
Qualifications	Degree level
Marital status	Living with partner
Ethnic origin	White British
Number of children	None
Length of residence	Since two months old

Household 9

ID	JA35	ID	SA33
Age	35	Age	33
Gender	Female	Gender	Male
Tenure	Owner	Tenure	Owner
Employment	Full-time mother	Employment	Chef
Qualifications	None	Qualifications	None
Marital status	Married	Marital status	Married
Ethnic origin	White British	Ethnic origin	Not available
Number of children	3	Number of children	3
Length of residence	Not available	Length of residence	Not available

Household 10

ID	SH78
Age	78
Gender	Female
Tenure	Owner
Employment	Voluntary work
Qualifications	None
Marital status	Married
Ethnic origin	White British
Number of children	1
Length of residence	52 years in this house

Household 11

ID	JC54
Age	54
Gender	Female
Tenure	Owner
Employment	Sales assistant
Qualifications	None
Marital status	Married
Ethnic origin	White British
Number of children	2
Length of residence	Lifetime

Household 12

ID	JR77
Age	77
Gender	Female
Tenure	Owner
Employment	Retired
Qualifications	Unknown
Marital status	Widowed
Ethnic origin	White British
Number of children	1
Length of residence	Since 1961

Household 13

ID	JS67	ID	AC63
Age	67	Age	63
Gender	Male	Gender	Female
Tenure	Owner	Tenure	Owner
Employment	Delivery van driver	Employment	Doctor's receptionist
Qualifications	None	Qualifications	None
Marital status	Married	Marital status	Married
Ethnic origin	White British	Ethnic origin	White British
Number of children	3	Number of children	3
Length of residence	43 years	Length of residence	43 years

Household 14

ID	DH26
Age	26
Gender	Male
Tenure	Renting from social landlord
Employment	Full-time factory worker (part-time bar worker)
Qualifications	None
Marital status	Single
Ethnic origin	White British
Number of children	None
Length of residence	25 years in this house

Household 15

ID	CS47
Age	47
Gender	Female
Tenure	Renting from private landlord
Employment	Full-time carer
Qualifications	None
Marital status	Single
Ethnic origin	White British
Number of children	2
Length of residence	2.5 years

Household 16

ID	JE42
Age	42
Gender	Female
Tenure	Renting from social landlord
Employment	Full-time mother (husband – bin man)
Qualifications	None
Marital status	Married
Ethnic origin	White British
Number of children	5
Length of residence	3 years

Household 17

ID	AC19
Age	19
Gender	Female
Tenure	Owner
Employment	Call centre operator
Qualifications	GCSEs
Marital status	Married
Ethnic origin	White British
Number of children	None
Length of residence	2 years

Household 18	
ID	SN24
Age	24
Gender	Female
Tenure	Owner
Employment	Training scheme
Qualifications	Part-time mature student
Marital status	Single
Ethnic origin	White British
Number of children	None
Length of residence	16 years

Household 19	
ID	LR55
Age	55
Gender	Female
Tenure	Owner
Employment	Chef
Qualifications	Computing diploma
Marital status	Married
Ethnic origin	White British
Number of children	3
Length of residence	10 years

Household 20	
ID	MP47
Age	47
Gender	Female
Tenure	Owner
Employment	Bank clerk
Qualifications	None
Marital status	Married
Ethnic origin	White British
Number of children	4
Length of residence	23 years

Household 21

ID	MY45
Age	45
Gender	Female
Tenure	Owner
Employment	Telesales
Qualifications	O levels, BTEC
Marital status	Married
Ethnic origin	White British
Number of children	Not available
Length of residence	24 years

Household 22

ID	JC40
Age	40
Gender	Male
Tenure	Owner
Employment	Supervisor
Qualifications	Degree
Marital status	Divorced
Ethnic origin	European
Number of children	Unknown
Length of residence	Not available

Household 23

ID	DH31
Age	31
Gender	Female
Tenure	Renting from private landlord
Employment	Unemployed
Qualifications	Undertaking business management qualification
Marital status	Single
Ethnic origin	White British
Number of children	2
Length of residence	2 years

Household 24	
ID	SP26
Age	26
Gender	Male
Tenure	Owner
Employment	Delivery manager Royal Mail
Qualifications	GCSEs, City & Guilds, NVQs, CAD
Marital status	Single
Ethnic origin	White
Number of children	None
Length of residence	3 years

Household 25	
ID	NL67
Age	67
Gender	Female
Tenure	Owner
Employment	Retired
Qualifications	None
Marital status	Widow
Ethnic origin	Not available
Number of children	3
Length of residence	45 years

Notes

Introduction

1 It should be said that Kemeny, whose interest is in labour movement influence rather than class analysis, would no doubt agree with this.
2 This is to say nothing about how the education system, which is an instrument for class domination and reproduction (Bourdieu and Passeron 1977; Reay 2001a; Reay *et al.* 2001), institutionalises and inscribes failure into the subjectivities of working-class people.

1 The death and resurrection of class in sociology

1 A key exception to this general trend is London, where significant numbers of middle-class people can be found to reside in council housing (Watt 2005).
2 A study by Gershuny (1994) is also relevant here. Gershuny studied the career histories of men and women between the ages of 40 and 60 and found evidence of a largely immobile working class composed of various categories of manual workers. The overriding pattern was one of continued manual employment, punctuated by periods of unemployment, with manual workers often spending over 90 per cent of their working lives in manual employment. These individuals tended to move between different types of manual employment rather than between different classes of employment.
3 A partial exception to this rule might be London.
4 There is a stark contrast between Fraser's (1995) 'politics of recognition', which highlights the power of the middle class to impose moral judgments about lifestyle that maintain working-class people in their place, and Giddens's (1991) concept of 'lifestyle politics', which frames the same process in emancipatory terms, that is, as a positive thing for everyone.

2 Theorising social class

1 It should be noted that ambiguity surrounds the notion of 'relative autonomy' (How much autonomy? From what? Or whom? And in relation to what issues?) and 'the last instance' (What is 'the last instance'? How do we know when we are 'in the last instance'?), which means that empirical analysis runs the risk of collapsing into confusion.
2 Marxism is confusing here. This is because some Marxists argue that classes develop their own collective consciousness as a result of the collective experience of exploitation; but others argue that a dominant ideology can obscure their understanding of their 'objective' interests and ensure that they develop views that are contrary to their objective interests.
3 Weber himself was fully aware of the infinite variability of market situations and therefore of the difficulties involved in identifying social classes without under-

taking empirical work into the conditions in which they emerge. Indeed he identifies over 20 social classes in *Economy and Society*, which places him on a level with Marx's *Eighteenth Brumaire of Louis Bonaparte*.
4 Quoted in Morris and Winn (1990).
5 This contrasts with the highly educated middle-class households studied by Savage *et al.* (2005), in which traditional gender roles had broken down.
6 Lash and Urry (1987) argue that the service class of senior white collar workers have a central role in breaking down previously fixed divisions between high and low culture because they are less awestruck with certain lifestyles and can easily engage with ballet, opera, rock music and Californian sports, treating none as *the* legitimate culture.

3 Social class and the question of 'being'

1 The reproduction of the working-class habitus that results from this quasi-perfect fit between objective structures and the internalised structures (that is, through realisation of the socially structured dispositions of the working class habitus in the fields of education and labour that result in the occupation of a social position conductive to the reproduction of the schemes of perception of the working-class habitus) is not simply a consequence of working-class respondents' 'inadequacies' in the field of education, even though working-class respondents frequently imply this to be the case by referring to themselves as 'stupid', 'thick' or 'lazy' ('I did the computer course, it's just me again being lazy, I just started it and then got about six months into it and just stopped it'). Bourdieu and Passeron (1977) argue that such rhetoric is indicative of the 'symbolic violence' that the cultural arbitrary that constitutes the education system commits on those working-class people who misrecognise it as an objective judge of intellectual worthiness (thereby compelling them to objectify themselves as 'thick', 'lazy' or whatever) rather than for the cultural arbitrary that it is. Yet what is clear from talking to working-class people is that they are not 'thick', 'stupid' and 'lazy' – which means, therefore, that the symbolic violence committed by the judges of intellectual worthiness only works its effects on *some* rather than *all* working-class people. This is obvious in the periodic scandals that erupt as 'bright' working-class children find themselves excluded from prestigious educational institutions by admissions decisions as well as through other, more subtle, mechanisms that make entrance to such institutions an economic impossibility even if they do 'accept' working-class children:

> There was a proper uniform and you'd have to wear a boater and everything in summer, and winter uniform and indoor and outdoor shoes and everything.
> And did you have to pay for that yourself?
> Yeah.
> So that sounds like it was quite . . .
> It wasn't though, then it was 'cos you had to have indoor shoes and outdoor shoes, all your uniform, PE kit, hockey sticks, tennis racquets, you know, which now you've said that I never even thought about that, that was a lot then.

However, exclusion from such places is not simply a consequence of institutional discrimination but also a form of self-exclusion from institutional environments that results when working-class people do not have the intentionality to 'grasp' what they are about and, therefore, regard as 'not for the likes of them'. This had happened to some working-class people in Kensington who had been judged as possessing sufficient 'intellectual worth' to justify their sitting an entrance exam at the Bluecoat Grammar School but opted out of even sitting the exam on confronting the institution.

> I don't know, it was very . . . I know you don't go to school to look at like . . . but it was something like out of, I don't know, like it was like a film, everything was so, just bare, nothing on the wall. I just couldn't . . . you could imagine like in the winter, you know, the windows seemed to be high up from the floors that you couldn't look. Oh it was just like something out of . . . and I was thinking oh, it was just . . . And they wore big gowns, you know, the teachers and that with the big gowns and the big hats and all that. And I thought God you know if your child was like of a nervous disposition even though they were clever. Ah I don't know it was very . . .

Evident here is a form of working-class complicity with the discriminatory dynamics of the educational field, which is realised in decisions to self-exclude from parts of the educational field to which working-class people 'do not belong' (cf. Reay 2001a,b; Reay *et al.* 2001). This is not to say that decisions to self-exclude from grammar schools, and in one case Oxbridge, were made reluctantly or even lamented. On the contrary, they were constituted upon misrecognition of the field of education that was contained in the perception that some parts of the field were 'better' than others ('it would be nice to get into Bluecoat') but that, ultimately, 'if you are clever, you will do well wherever you go to school'.

> I don't know where she gets it from, I mean her dad's clever but she is really, she's a bright child, she really is and I just want to do, she'll do well I think wherever she goes.

> [Going to comprehensive school X is] not a better start but as my mum says, if he's clever enough he'll do well wherever he goes, no matter where he goes and I said that. I wouldn't say he's gifted or, you know, he's super clever, but he isn't a thick child, there are certain things like, you know, he does like. I mean we got a letter sent home from school, excellent work this week, history, he loves history.

So exclusion from strategic positions within the field of education is a consequence of doxic complicity with the socially structured position of working-class people within the educational field ('I could not imagine him being there') as well as misrecognition of the logic of the field ('he is bright so he will do well wherever he goes').

2   However, it is important to note that the association of strong social bonds with working-class communities has been disputed (Forrest and Kearns 2001).

4 Being in the market for housing

1   From the point of view of these working-class people, the housing ladder consists of 'only mega money houses. Not houses like these. No way, not houses like these.'

2   The other key reason is that the practical economy of working-class housing consumption makes sense in its own terms, even though it does not make sense to the middle-class judges of legitimate housing consumption who would denigrate working-class people as failed housing consumers.

5 Being in a 'depressed' market for houses

1 I am extremely grateful to Rionach Casey, who compiled this 'profile' of Kensington using official sources. This is my edited version of the profile that she wrote for me.
2 Residents have accused Liverpool City Council and Housing Associations of deliberately 'running down' the market for houses in Kensington. They claim that Liverpool City Council and Housing Associations have done this by populating the area with asylum seekers as well as by boarding up other properties in order to keep them empty.

6 HMR and the 'new' market logic of urban renewal

1 http://news.bbc.co.uk/1/hi/programmes/file_on_4/4327431.stm (accessed 26 July 2007).
2 See www.persona.uk.com/newheartlands (accessed 5 October 2007). Readers can contact Graham Groom at the above organisation in order to obtain the documents if they cannot find them on the website.
3 This goes some way to explaining why the controversy surrounding HMR concerns *the activity of demolition* rather than the *ideology on which it is constituted.*
4 It is instructive to note that academics and other experts have accused Liverpool City Council of deliberately 'running down' the market for houses in Kensington, prior to issuing the CPOs, in order to minimise the price of houses in the area, thereby maximising the 'rent gap'. Critics claim that Liverpool City Council has 'run down' Kensington by keeping properties empty and boarding up the same empty properties (see Chapter 9). Fifty-one per cent of respondents to an NDC survey of Kensington mentioned boarded-up properties as a 'serious problem'.
5 The 'lead developer', Bellway Homes, presented its credentials for leading the redevelopment of Kensington to a public enquiry in the following way:

> [Our] most notable achievement [is] the redevelopment at Hulme, Manchester. Bellway has led the private sector regeneration and redevelopment of one of the most notorious 1960s deck access council estates, creating a high-density, mixed use development comprising 649 new homes ranging from 2 bedroom apartments to 4 bedroom houses, along with shops . . . . Following on from the success at Hulme, Bellway could see significant regeneration opportunities emerging on Merseyside. As a consequence, the former Urban Regeneration Division was purposely relocated to Liverpool in order to champion the massive housing regeneration needed.
>
> Yet the Centre for Sustainable Urban and Regional Futures recently published a research report, *Hulme, Ten Years On,* which found that 'there is dissatisfaction with the design, quality and space standards of some of the private stock' (SURF 2002: 17–18). The rationale for housing market renewal starts to fall apart when we understand that a key justification for renewal is the need for 'bigger and better' houses, yet the dwellings that Bellway proposes to build in Kensington are actually 'smaller than the properties they replace' (Ord 2006: 7).

6 And yet the Assistant Executive Director for Housing and Neighbourhoods within Liverpool City Council has stated that 'the most economic option was option 3 (traditional improvement) [but] it was least likely to respond to the Vision for the area' (Green 2006: 38).
7 A key claim that is used to justify housing market renewal is that 'there are too

many terraced houses' and not enough family housing. Yet this is contradicted by research evidence that:

> the problems of first-time property buyers are compounded by the surprisingly limited supply . . . . Two-thirds of housing is 'family' homes of three or more bedrooms with three bedroom properties accounting for just under half of all stock . . . . Though the plight of first time buyers is well documented, the debate is based on the assumption that there is a ready supply of property making up the 'first rung' of the housing ladder . . . . The lack of smaller-sized homes, combined with a strong demand from investors and first time buyers, has led to a constant upward pressure on prices at the bottom of the ladder . . . . This in turn has led to the value of one and two bed homes being compressed up towards the price of three bed properties.
>
> (Seager 2007)

8 The consultants in this case even acknowledge that their survey respondents hold deeply entrenched anti-urban attitudes that, one would presume, are not going to be changed by the construction of new build houses with gardens in the centre of the city.
9 In other words, it would have been useful to have considered – and examined – the possibilities for organic gentrification.
10 This probably accounts for the coterminous increase in house prices noted by the team undertaking the National Evaluation of the HMR programme (Leather *et al.* 2007).
11 This corresponds with findings of the HMR research programme in Manchester–Salford. This found that young people (such as ex-students) were 'widening' their house search criteria. They were now considering the purchase of houses in 'unpopular' neighbourhoods in Salford (Cole *et al.* 2005).
12 'He was actually brought up in Kensington'. Research suggests that neighbourhoods such as Kensington are likely to be gentrified by indigenous urbanites who originate within the inner city rather than suburbanites, who tend to be anti-urban (Ley 1996). The presumption that the future of Kensington is in the hands of suburbanites, who need to be attracted in, represents a key flaw in the HMR programme in Liverpool. It flies in the face of everything that scholarly research has told us about who is likely to gentrify inner-urban neighbourhoods. The task for the proponents of HMR in Liverpool, then, is to demonstrate what makes Liverpool so unique that its housing market dynamics are different from those in every other city that has undergone a process of gentrification.
13 The authors suggest elsewhere in this paper that these trends 'may undermine HMR'.
14 The research on which this book is based also picked up signs of gentrification activity. Interviews were achieved with hospital and education staff who were buying in the area because it was cheap and because they liked its urban location and 'feel'.
15 www.liverpool-labour.org.uk/Liverpool.htm (accessed 14 February 2007).

7 Working-class experiences of the brave new housing market

1 Middle-class interviewees tended to dis identify with the city of Liverpool whilst identifying with the City of Culture.
2 It is instructive to note that the proposed new build properties in Kensington 'are 2 and 3 bedrooms – and smaller than the properties they replace' (Ord 2006: 7). The same author also notes that 'the use of "smaller" Victorian properties as

a description [of existing terraced houses] is strange. These properties are very large 2 and 3 bedroom homes when compared to modern equivalents' (Ord 2006: 2).

3 This was exemplified by working-class people who referred to perceiving 'extra income' (for example, as a consequence of children leaving home) as an opportunity to spend on 'little luxuries' rather than as an opportunity to engage in position-taking in the market for houses for the purposes of 'growing' their investment (see Chapter 4).

8 Housing market renewal and the politics of middle-class domination

1 That this has received scant attention in the social science literature is indicative of the dominance of the doxic view of the market for houses in the academy (see Chapter 6), which has meant that academic research only ever seems to examine the market for houses as a space of positions (see Hickman *et al.* 2007 for a classic example of this tendency).

9 The rich get richer

1 By this I mean a gradual process of gentrification that occurs as middle-class people move into the area in an orchestrated fashion but that, on the surface, appears to be a chaotic and sporadic process.

2 Nevertheless it is important to note that there are key differences between different forms of gentrification. The winners in an organic process of gentrification are those *households* that take the risk to purchase in a 'fragile' market as well as indigenous working-class households. Although working-class households may eventually be displaced by gentrification, then, they at least receive the significantly higher 'market value' for their home, which is produced by gentrification activity, when they decide to sell. That is to say, the profits that can be extracted from the gentrifying market accrue to the 'new' middle-class households that buy and sell in that market and working-class households that sell up and move on as prices rise.

Bibliography

Abercrombie, N. and Urry, J. 1983. *Capital, Labour and the Middle Classes*. London, Allen and Unwin.

Aglietta, M. 1987. *A Theory of Capitalist Regulation*. London, Verso.

Allen, C. 2001. On the social consequences (and social conscience) of the foyer 'industry': a critical ethnography, *Journal of Youth Studies*, 4(4), 473–96.

Allen, C. 2005. On the epistemological limits of the 'area effects' debate: towards a phenomenology of urban deprivation, *Housing, Theory and Society*, 22(4), 196–212.

Allen, C. 2007a. *Crime, Drugs and Social Theory: A Phenomenological Approach*. Aldershot, Ashgate.

Allen, C. 2007b. Of urban entrepreneurs or 24 hour party people? City centre living in Manchester, England, *Environment and Planning A*, 39(3), 666–83.

Allen, C., Gallent, N. and Tewdwr-Jones, M. 1999. The limits of policy diffusion: comparative experiences of second home ownership in Britain and Sweden, *Environment and Planning C: Government and Policy*, 17(2), 227–44.

Althusser, L. 1969. *For Marx*. London, Verso.

Atkinson, R. and Flint, J. 2004. Fortress UK? Gated communities, the spatial revolt of the elites and time–space trajectories of segregation, *Housing Studies*, 19(6), 875–92.

Audit Commission. 2004. *Market Renewal: Newheartlands Pathfinder Scrutiny Report*. London, Audit Commission.

Ball, M. 1983. *Housing Policy and Economic Power: The Political Economy of Owner Occupation*. London, Methuen.

Ball, M. and Harloe, M. 1992. Rhetorical barriers to understanding what the provision thesis is and is not, *Housing Studies*, 7(1), 3–15.

Bauman, Z. 1988. *Work, Consumerism and the New Poor*. Philadelphia, PA, Open University Press.

Beck, U. 1992. *The Risk Society: Towards a New Modernity*. London, Sage.

Beck, U. 2000. *What is Globalization?* Cambridge, Polity.

Bell, D. 1960. *The End of Ideology*. Glencoe, IL, Free Press.

Berger, P. L. and Luckmann, T. 1966. *The Social Construction of Reality*. London, Penguin.

Binnie, J. 2004. *The Globalization of Sexuality*. London, Sage.

Bourdieu, P. 1977. *Outline of a Theory of Practice*. Cambridge, Cambridge University Press.

Bourdieu, P. 1984. *Distinction: A Social Critique of the Judgment of Taste*. London, Routledge.

Bourdieu, P. 1990. *The Logic of Practice*. Cambridge, Polity.

Bourdieu, P. 1993a. *The Field of Cultural Production.* Cambridge, Polity.

Bourdieu, P. 1993b. *Sociology in Question.* London, Sage.

Bourdieu, P. 2000. *Pascalian Meditations.* Stanford, CA, Stanford University Press.

Bourdieu, P. and Passeron, J. 1977. *Reproduction in Education, Society and Culture.* London, Sage.

Bradley, H. 1996. *Fractured Identities: Changing Patterns of Inequality.* Cambridge, Polity.

Braverman, H. 1974. *Labour and Monopoly Capital.* New York, Monthly Review Press.

Bridge, G. 2001. Estate agents as interpreters of economic and cultural capital: the gentrification premium in the Sydney housing market, *International Journal of Urban and Regional Research,* 25(1), 87–101.

Bridge, G., Forrest, R. and Holland, E. 2004. *Neighbouring: A Review of the Evidence.* Bristol, Centre for Neighbourhood Research Paper 24.

Butler, T. 1997. *Gentrification and the Middle Classes.* Aldershot, Ashgate.

Butler, T. with Robson, G. 2003a. *London Calling: The Middle Classes and the Remaking of Inner London.* Oxford, Berg.

Butler, T. and Robson, G. 2003b. Negotiating their way in: the middle classes, gentrification and their deployment of capital in a globalizing metropolis, *Urban Studies,* 40(9), 1791–1809.

Byrne, D. 2003. Reciting the self: narrative representations of the self in qualitative interviews, *Feminist Theory,* 4(1), 29–49.

Cameron, S. 2006. From low demand to rising aspirations: housing market renewal within regional and neighbourhood regeneration policy, *Housing Studies,* 21(1), 3–16.

Castells, M. 1977. *The Urban Question: A Marxist Approach.* London, Matthew Arnold.

Castells, M. 1983. *The City and the Grassroots.* London, Edward Arnold.

Charlesworth, S. J. 2000. *A Phenomenology of Working-Class Experience.* Cambridge, Cambridge University Press.

Charlesworth, S. J. 2004. Northerners exposed: reflections on working-class space, being, and experience, *Space and Culture,* 7(3), 327–342.

Charlesworth, S. J. 2005. Understanding social suffering: a phenomenological investigation of the experience of inequality, *Journal of Community and Applied Social Psychology,* 15, 296–312.

Charlesworth, S. J. 2006. Heidegger and understanding the urban poor: chemical solutions to the question of being, *Practical Philosophy,* 9, 37–51.

Clapham, D. 2005. *The Meaning of Housing: A Pathways Approach.* Bristol, Policy Press.

Clarke, D. 2003. *The Consumer Society and the Postmodern City.* London, Routledge.

Clark, T. N. and Lipset, S. M. 1991. Are social classes dying? *International Sociology,* 6(4), 397–410.

Cohen, G. A. 1978. *Karl Marx's Theory of History: A Defence.* Princeton, NJ, Princeton University Press.

Cole, I. and Nevin, N. 2004. *The Road to Renewal.* York, York Publishing Services.

Cole, I., Hickman, P. and Reeve, K. 2004. *Interpreting Housing Market Change: The Case of Leeds.* Sheffield, Centre for Regional Economic and Social Research.

Cole, I., Goudie, R., Beattie, S,. Allen, C. and Hickman, P. 2005. *Understanding Perceptions in the Manchester Salford Housing Market Renewal Pathfinder: Research, Intelligence and Foresight Programme*. Sheffield, Centre for Regional Economic and Social Research.

Crompton, R. 1998. *Class and Stratification*, second edition. Cambridge, Polity.

Crooks, L. 2006. Non-statutory objection to the compulsory purchase orders 2006: written submission. Unpublished paper.

Dench, G., Gavron, K., and Young, M. 2006. *The New East End: Kinship, Race and Conflict*. London, Profile.

Devine, F. 1992. *Affluent Workers Revisited*. Edinburgh, Edinburgh University Press.

Dickens, P., Duncan, S., Goodwin, M. and Gray, F. 1985. *Housing States and Localities*. London, Methuen.

Donnison, D. 1967. *The Government of Housing*. London, Penguin.

Donnison, D. and Ungerson, C. 1982. *Housing Policy*. London, Penguin.

Dunleavy, P. 1981. *The Politics of Mass Housing in Britain 1945–1975: A Study of Corporate Power, and Professional Influence in the Welfare State*. Oxford, Clarendon Press.

Ecotec. 2005. *Understanding the Drivers of Housing Market Change in the Newheartlands Housing Market Renewal Area: A Review of the Evidence Base – Discussion Paper*. Birmingham, Ecotec.

Eley, G. and Nield, K. 2000. Scholarly controversy: farewell to the working class? *International Labour and Working-Class History*, 57, 1–30.

Elvin, D. and Litton, J. 2006. Opening submission on behalf of Liverpool City Council to Public Enquiry into the Compulsory Purchase of Houses in Newheartlands. Liverpool, July 2006.

Emms, P. 1990. *Social Housing: A European Dilemma?* Bristol, SAUS.

Erikson, R. and Goldthorpe, J. 1992. *The Constant Flux*. Oxford, Clarendon.

Esping-Andersen, G. 1993. *Changing Classes: Stratification and Mobility in Post-Industrial Societies*. London, Sage.

Evans, A. 1990. *Speculative House Building in the 1980s: Flexible Design and Flexible Production?* University of Sussex, mimeo.

Featherstone, M. 1991. *Consumer Culture and Postmodernism*. London, Sage.

Feinstein, S. 1994. *The City Builders: Property, Politics and Planning in London and New York*. London, Blackwell.

Finlay, B. 2002. Complaint vs. Liverpool City Council (Letter to District Auditor), 25 February.

Fisk, M. 1996. *Housing in the Rhondda 1800–1940*. Chesterfield, Merton Priory Press.

Ford, J. and Burrows, R. 1999. The costs of unsustainable home ownership in Britain, *Journal of Social Policy*, 28(2), 305–30.

Ford, J., Burrows, R. and Nettleton, S. 2001. *Home Ownership in a Risk Society: A Social Analysis of Mortgage Arrears and Possessions*. Bristol, Policy Press.

Forrest, R. and Kearns, A. 2001. Social cohesion, social capital and the neighbourhood, *Urban Studies*, 38(12), 2125–43.

Forrest, R. and Murie, A. 1980. Wealth, inheritance and housing policy, *Policy and Politics*, 8(1), 1–19.

Forrest, R. and Murie, A. 1994. Home ownership in recession, *Housing Studies*, 9(1), 55–74.

Foucault, M. 1977. *Discipline and Punish: The Birth of the Prison*. London, Penguin.

Foucault, M. 1994. *Power: The Essential Works 3*. London, Allen Lane.

Fraser, N. 1989. *Unruly Practices: Power, Discourse and Gender in Contemporary Social Theory*. Cambridge, Polity Press.

Fraser, N. 1995. From redistribution to recognition? Dilemmas of justice in a 'post-socialist' age, *New Left Review*, 212, 68–94.

Gershuny, J. 1994. Post-industrial career structures in Britain, in Esping-Andersen, G. (ed.) *Changing Classes*. London, Sage.

Gerth, H. H. and Mills, C. W. 1998 [1948]. *From Max Weber: Essays in Sociology*. London, Routledge.

Giddens, A. 1987. *Social Theory and Modern Sociology*. Cambridge, Polity.

Giddens, A. 1990. *The Consequences of Modernity*. Cambridge, Polity.

Giddens, A. 1991. *Modernity and Self-Identity: Self and Society in the Late Modern Age*. Cambridge, Polity.

Giddens, A. 1992. *The Transformation of Intimacy: Sexuality, Love and Eroticism in Modern Societies*. Cambridge, Polity.

Giddens, A. 1994. *Beyond Left and Right*. Cambridge, Polity.

Giordano, B. and Twomey, L. 2002. Economic transitions: restructuring local labour markets, in Peck, J. and Ward, K. (eds) *City of Revolution: Restructuring Manchester*. Manchester, Manchester University Press, pp. 50–75.

Glass, D. V. 1954. *Social Mobility in Britain*. London, Routledge and Kegan Paul.

Glass, R. 1964. Introduction: aspects of change, in Centre for Urban Studies (ed.) *London: Aspects of Change*. London, MacKibbon & Kee.

Goldthorpe, J. H. 1982. On the service class: its formation and future, in Giddens, A. and MacKenzie, G. (eds) *Social Class and the Division of Labour*. Basingstoke, Macmillan.

Goldthorpe, J. H. 1983. Women and class analysis: in defence of the conventional view, *Sociology*, 17(4), 465–78.

Goldthorpe, J. H. 1988. The intellectuals and the working class, in Rose, D. (ed) *Social Stratification and Economic Change*. London, Hutchinson.

Goldthorpe, J. H. 1998. Rational action theory for sociology, *British Journal of Sociology*, 49(2), 167–92.

Goldthorpe, J. H. and Lockwood, D. 1968. *The Affluent Worker: Industrial Attitudes and Behaviour*. Cambridge, Cambridge University Press.

Goldthorpe, J. H. and Lockwood, D. 1969. *The Affluent Worker in the Class Structure*. Cambridge, Cambridge University Press.

Goldthorpe, J. H. and Marshall, G. 1992. The promising future of class analysis, *Sociology*, 26, 381–400.

Goldthorpe, J. H., Lockwood, D., Bechhofer, F. and Platt, J. 1968. *The Affluent Worker: Industrial Attitudes and Behaviour*. Cambridge, Cambridge University Press.

Goldthorpe, J. H., Lockwood, D., Bechhofer, F. and Platt, J. 1969. *The Affluent Worker in the Class Structure*. Cambridge, Cambridge University Press.

Goldthorpe, J. H., with Llewellyn, C. and Payne, C. 1980. *Social Mobility and the Class Structure in Modern Britain*. Oxford, Clarendon.

Goldthorpe, J. H., with Llewellyn, C. and Payne, C. 1987. *Social Mobility and the Class Structure in Modern Britain*, second edition. Oxford, Clarendon.

Gorz, A. 1982. *Farewell to the Working Class*. London, Pluto.

Gould, A. 1993. *Capitalist Welfare Systems: A Comparison of Japan, Britain and Sweden*. London, Longman.

Gramsci, A. 1971. *Selections from the Prison Notebooks*. London, Lawrence and Wishart.

Green, C. 2006. *Proof of Evidence of Cath Green (Liverpool City Council)*. www.persona.uk.com/newheartlands/index.htm. Accessed 5 July 2007.

Gurney, C. 1996. Meanings of home and home ownership: myths, histories and experiences. Unpublished PhD thesis, School for Policy Studies, University of Bristol.

Halsey, A., Heath, A. and Ridge, J. 1980. *Origins and Destinations*. Oxford, Clarendon Press.

Hamnet, C. 1984. Gentrification and residential location theory: a review and assessment, in Herbert, D. and Johnston, R. (eds) *Geography and the Urban Environment: Progress in Research and Applications*. London, Wiley, pp. 283–319.

Hamnet, C. 1989. Consumption and class in contemporary Britain, in Hamnet, C., McDowell, L. and Sarre, P. (eds) *Restructuring Britain: The Changing Social Structure*. London, Sage.

Hamnet, C. 1999. *Winners and Losers: Home Ownership in Modern Britain*. London, Routledge.

Harloe, M. 1995. *The People's Home: Social Rented Housing in Europe and America*. Oxford, Blackwell.

Harrison, M. with Davis, C. 2002. *Housing, Social Policy and Difference*. Bristol, Policy Press.

Harvey, D. 1989. *The Condition of Post-Modernity*. Oxford, Blackwell.

Haylett, C. 2003. Culture, class and urban policy: reconsidering equality, *Antipode*, 35(1), 55–73.

Heath, A., Jowell, R. and Curtice, J. 1985. *How Britain Votes*. Oxford, Pergamon Press.

Heath, A., Jowell, R., Curtice, J. and Evans, G. 1989. *The Extension of Popular Capitalism*. Glasgow, Strathclyde Papers on Government and Politics 60.

Heath, A., Jowell, R., Curtice, J. and Evans, G. 1990. *The British Voter*. London, Pergamon.

Heath, A., Jowell, R., Curtice, J., Evans, G., Field, J. and Witherspoon, S. 1991. *Understanding Political Change: The British Voter 1964–1987*. Oxford, Pergamon Press.

Heidegger, M. 1962. *Being and Time*. Oxford, Blackwell.

Heidegger, M. 1998. *Pathmarks*. Cambridge, Cambridge University Press.

Henderson, J. and Karn, V. 1984. Race, class and the allocation of public housing in Britain, *Urban Studies*, 21(2), 115–28.

Henderson, J. and Karn, V. 1987. *Race, Class and State Housing: Inequality and the Allocation of Public Housing in Britain*. Aldershot, Gower.

Hickman, P., Robinson, D., Casey, R., Green, S. and Powell, R. 2007. *Understanding Housing Demand: Learning from Rising Markets in Yorkshire and the Humber*. Coventry, Chartered Institute of Housing.

Hill, J. 1986. *Sex, Class and Realism: British Cinema 1956–63*. London, British Film Institute.

Hoggart, R. 1956. *The Uses of Literacy*. Harmondsworth, Penguin.

Holton, R. J. and Turner, B. 1989. *Max Weber on Economy and Society*. London, Routledge.

Imrie, R. 1996. Transforming the social relations of research production, *Environment and Planning A*, 28, 1445–64.

Imrie, R. 2004. Urban geography, relevance and resistance to the 'policy turn', *Urban Geography*, 25(8), 697–708.

Jessop, R. 1990. Regulation theories in retrospect and prospect, *Economy and Society*, 19(2), 153–216.

Karn, V., Kemeny, J. and Williams, P. 1985. *Home Ownership in the Inner City*. Aldershot, Gower.

Kearns, A. 2004. *Social Capital, Regeneration and Urban Policy*. Bristol, Centre for Neighbourhood Research Paper 15.

Kemeny, J. 1992. *Housing and Social Theory*. London, Routledge.

Kemeny, J. 1995. *From Public Housing to the Social Market: Rental Policy in Comparative Perspective*. London, Routledge.

Kuhn, A. 1988. *Cinema, Censorship and Sexuality, 1909–1925*. London, Routledge and Kegan Paul.

Lash, S. and Urry, J. 1987. *The End of Organized Capitalism*. Cambridge, Polity.

Lash, S. and Urry, J. 1994. *Economies of Signs and Space*. London, Sage.

Lawler, S. 2005a. Disgusted subjects: the making of middle-class identities, *Sociological Review*, 53(3), 429–46.

Lawler, S. 2005b. Rules of engagement: habitus, class and resistance, in Adkins, L. and Skeggs, B. (eds) *Feminism after Bourdieu*. Oxford: Blackwell, 110–28.

Leather, P., Cole, I. and Ferrari, E. with Flint, J., Robinson, D., Simpson, C. and Hopley, M. 2007. *National Evaluation of the HMR Pathfinder Programme*. London, Department for Communities and Local Government.

Lee, P. and Nevin, B. 2002. *Renewing the Housing Market of Liverpool's Inner Core*. Birmingham, CURS.

Ley, D. 1996. *The New Middle Class and the Remaking of the Central City*. Oxford, Oxford University Press.

Ley, D. 2003. Artists, aestheticization and the field of gentrification, *Urban Studies*, 40(12), 2527–44.

Lipset, S. M. 1963. *Political Man*. New York, Doubleday.

Lipset, S. M. and Benedix, R. 1959. *Social Mobility in Industrial Society*. Berkeley, CA, University of California Press.

Lockwood, D. 1958. *The Blackcoated Worker*. London, Allen and Unwin.

Lockwood, D. 1966. Sources of variation in working-class images of society, *Sociological Review*, 14(3), 244–67.

Lockwood, D. 1996. Civic integration and class formation, *British Journal of Sociology*, 47(3), 531–50.

Lojkine, J. 1976. Contribution to a Marxist theory of capitalist urbanization, in Pickvance, C. (ed.) *Urban Sociology: Critical Essays*. London, Tavistock, 119–46.

McLay, F. (ed.) 1990. *Workers City – The Reckoning: Public Loss, Private Gain (Beyond the Culture City Rip-Off)*. Glasgow, Clydeside Press.

Marcus, L. 1994. *Auto/Biographical Discourses*. Manchester, Manchester University Press.

Marshall, T. H. 1967. *Social Policy*, second edition. London, Hutchinson.

Marx, K. 1954. *The Eighteenth Brumaire of Louis Bonaparte*. Moscow, Progress Publishers.

Merleau-Ponty, M. 1962. *Phenomenology of Perception*. London, Routledge and Kegan Paul.

Merleau-Ponty, M. 1964. *The Primacy of Perception*. Evanston, IL, Northwestern University Press.

Merret, S. 1979. *State Housing in Britain*. London, Routledge.

Mooney, G. 2004. Cultural policy as urban transformation: critical reflections on Glasgow, European City of Culture 1990, *Local Economy*, 19(4), 327–40.

Morris, J. and Winn, M. 1990. *Housing and Social Inequality*. London, Hilary Shipman.

Nead, N. 1988. *Myths of Sexuality: Representations of Women in Victorian Britain*. Oxford, Blackwell.

Nevin, B. 2006a. *Proof of Evidence of Brendan Nevin (Ecotec Research and Consulting Ltd)*. www.persona.uk.com/newheartlands/index.htm. Accessed 5 July 2007.

Nevin, B. 2006b. Rebuttal to the proof of evidence of Professor Chris Allen. Unpublished paper.

Nevin, B. and Lee, P. 2001. *Changing Demand: Making the Links between Housing and Planning across Merseyside*. Birmingham, CURS.

Nevin, B., Lee, P., Goodson, L., Murie, A. and Phillimore, J. 1999. *Changing Housing Markets and Urban Regeneration in the M62 Corridor*. Birmingham, CURS.

Nevin, B., Hall, S., Lee, P. and Srbljanin, A. 2001. *Stabilizing the Population of Liverpool: Employment Markets and Housing Choice*. Birmingham, CURS.

Newby, H. 1975. *The Deferential Worker*. London, Penguin.

Oliver, P. Davis, I. and Bentley, I. 1981. *Dunroamin: The Suburban Semi and its Enemies*. London, Barrie and Jenkins.

Ord, S. 2006. *Response/Rebuttal to Statement of Reasons of Liverpool City Council*. www.persona.uk.com/newheartlands/index.htm. Accessed 5 July 2007.

Pahl, R. 1975. *Whose City? And Further Essays on Urban Society*. Harmondsworth, Penguin.

Pahl, R. 1989. Is the emperor naked? Some questions on the adequacy of sociological theory in urban and regional research, *International Journal of Urban and Regional Research*, 13(4), 711–20.

Pakulski, J. and Walters, M. 1996. *The Death of Class*. London, Sage.

Poulantzas, N. 1973. On social classes, *New Left Review*, http://newleftreview.org/A1240. Accessed 8 March 2007.

Poulantzas, N. 1975. *Classes in Contemporary Capitalism*. London, Verso.

Power, A. 1987. *Property Before People: The Management of Twentieth Century Council Housing*. London, Allen and Unwin.

Power, A. 1993. *Hovels to High Rise: Social Housing in Europe since 1850*. London, Routledge.

Presthus, R. 1971. Interest groups and the Canadian Parliament: activities, interaction, legitimacy and influence, *Canadian Journal of Political Science*, 9(4), 444–60.

Reay, D. 1998. Rethinking social class: qualitative perspectives on class and gender, *Sociology*, 32(2), 259–75.

Reay, D. 2001a. Finding or losing yourself: working-class relationships to higher education, *Journal of Education Policy*, 16, 333–46.

Reay, D. 2001b. Making a difference? Institutional habituses and higher education choice, *Sociological Research Online*, 5, 4126–42.

Reay, D. 2004. Education and cultural capital: the implications of changing trends in education policies, *Cultural Trends*, 13(2), 73–86.

Reay, D., Davies, J., David, M. and Ball, S. J. 2001. Choice of degree or degrees of choice: class, 'race' and the higher education choice process, *Sociology*, 35(4), 855–74.

Rex, J. and Moore, R. 1967. *Race, Community and Conflict: A Study of Sparkbrook*. Oxford, Oxford University Press.

Rhoades, J. 2006. *Proof of Evidence of John Rhoades*. www.persona.uk.com/newheartlands/index.htm. Accessed 5 July 2007.

Robbins, B. 1986. *The Servant's Hand: English Fiction from Below*. Durham, NC, Duke University Press.

Roberts, P. and Sykes, H. (eds) 2000. *Urban Regeneration: A Handbook*. London, Sage.

Saunders, P. 1986. *Social Theory and the Urban Question*, second edition. London, Hutchinson.

Saunders, P. 1990. *A Nation of Home Owners*. London, Allen and Unwin.

Saunders, P. and Williams, P. 1988. The constitution of the home: towards a research agenda, *Housing Studies*, 3(2), 81–93.

Savage, M. 2000. *Class Analysis and Social Transformation*. Buckingham, Open University Press.

Savage, M. 2006. Working-class identities in the 1960s: revisiting the affluent worker study, *Sociology*, 39(5), 929–46.

Savage, M. and Edgerton, M. 1998. Social mobility, individual ability and the inheritance of class inequality, *Sociology*, 31(4), 645–72.

Savage, M., Barlow, J., Dickens, P. and Fielding, T. 1992. *Property, Bureaucracy and Culture: Middle-Class Formation in Contemporary Britain*. London, Routledge.

Savage, M., Bagnall, G. and Longhurst, B. 2000. Ordinary, ambivalent and defensive: class identities in the North West of England, *Sociology*, 35(4), 875–92.

Savage, M., Bagnall, G. and Longhurst, B. 2005. *Globalization and Belonging*. London, Sage.

Sayer, A. 2002. What are you worth? Why class is an embarrassing subject, *Sociological Research Online*, 7(3).

Sayer, A. 2005. Class, moral worth and recognition, *Sociology*, 39(5), 947–63.

Scott, J. 1996. *Stratification and Power: Structures of Class, Status and Command*. Cambridge, Polity.

Seager, A. 2007. First rung of property ladder reported missing, *The Guardian*, 11 June.

Sennett, R. and Cobb, J. 1971. *The Hidden Injuries of Class*. London, Fontana.

Sennett, R. and Cobb, J. 1993. *The Hidden Injuries of Class*, second edition. London, Fontana.

Silverstone, R. (ed.) 1997. *Visions of Suburbia*. London, Routledge.

Skeggs, B. 1997. B. *Formations of Class and Gender*. London, Sage.

Skeggs, B. 2004. *Class, Self, Culture*. London, Routledge.

Slater, T. 2006. The eviction of critical perspectives from gentrification research, *International Journal of Urban and Regional Research*, 30(4), 737–57.

Slater, T., Curran, W. and Lees, L. 2004. Gentrification research: new directions and critical scholarship, *Environment and Planning A*, 36, 1141–50.

Smelster, N. 1962. *Social Change in the Industrial Revolution*. Aldershot, Gregg.

Smith, N. 1979. Toward a theory of gentrification: a back to the city movement by capital not people, *Journal of the American Planning Association*, 45, 538–48.

Smith, N. 1989. Gentrification, the frontier, and restructuring of urban space, in Smith, N. and Williams, P. (eds) *Gentrification of the City*. Boston, MA, Allen and Unwin.

Smith, N. 1996. *The New Urban Frontier: Gentrification and the Revanchist City*. London, Routledge.

Smith, S., Munro, M. and Christie, H. 2006. Performing housing markets, *Urban Studies*, 43(1), 81–98.

Sprigings, N., Nevin, B. and Leather, P. 2006. Semi-detached housing market theory for sale: suit first time buyer or investor. Paper presented to the Housing Studies Association conference, 19–20 April.

SURF. 2002. *Hulme, Ten Years On*. Salford, SURF Centre.

Thompson, E. P. 1968 [1963]. *The Making of the English Working Class*. London, Penguin.

Thrift, N. and Williams, P. (eds) 1987. *Class and Space*. London, Routledge.

Townshend, T. 2006. From inner city to inner suburb? Addressing housing aspirations in low demand areas in Newcastle Gateshead, UK, *Housing Studies*, 21(4), 501–21.

Turner, B. S. 1996. *For Weber: Essays on the Sociology of Fate*. London, Sage.

Walter, T. 1994. *The Revival of Death*. London, Routledge.

Warde, A. 1994. Consumption, identity-formation and uncertainty, *Sociology*, 28, 877–98.

Warde, A., Martens, L. and Olsen, W. 1999. Consumption and the problem of variety: cultural omnivorousness, social distinction and eating out, *Sociology*, 33, 105–27.

Watson, W. B. and Barth, E. A. T. 1964. Questionable assumptions in the theory of social stratification, *Pacific Sociological Review*, 7(1), 10–16.

Watt, P. 2001. The dynamics of social class and housing: a study of local authority tenants in the London Borough of Camden. Unpublished PhD thesis, Kings College London.

Watt, P. 2005. Housing histories and fragmented middle-class careers: the case of marginal professionals in London council housing, *Housing Studies*, 20(3), 359–81.

Watt, P. 2006. Respectability, roughness and 'race': neighbourhood place images and the making of working-class social distinctions in London, *International Journal of Urban and Regional Research*, 30(4), 776–97.

Whyte, W. S. 1957. *The Organization Man*. New York, Touchstone.

Wilensky, H. 1975. *The Welfare State and Equality: Structural and Ideological Roots of Public Expenditure*. Berkeley, CA, University of California Press.

Wright, E. O. 1997. *Class Counts*. Cambridge, Cambridge University Press.

Wright, E. O. and Singlemann, J. 1982. Proletarianization in the changing American class structure 1960–1980, *American Journal of Sociology*, 88, 176–209.

Wynne, D. 1998. *Leisure, Lifestyle and the New Middle Class*. London, Routledge.

Young, M. and Wilmott, P. 1957. *Family and Kinship in East London*. Harmondsworth, Penguin.

Zukin, S. 1982. *Loft Living: Culture and Capital in Urban Change*. Baltimore, MD, Johns Hopkins University Press.

Zukin, S. 1998. Urban lifestyles: diversity and standardisation in spaces of consumption, *Urban Studies*, 35(5–6), 825–39.

Index